# Lecture Notes in Computer Science 12630

Abdelkader Hameurlain ·
A Min Tjoa · Richard Chbeir (Eds.)

# Transactions on Large-Scale Data- and Knowledge- Centered Systems XLVII

## Special Issue on Digital Ecosystems and Social Networks

 Springer

*Editors-in-Chief*
Abdelkader Hameurlain
IRIT, Paul Sabatier University
Toulouse, France

A Min Tjoa
IFS, Technical University of Vienna
Vienna, Austria

*Guest Editor*
Richard Chbeir (iD)
University of Pau and the Adour Region
Anglet, France

ISSN 0302-9743       ISSN 1611-3349   (electronic)
Lecture Notes in Computer Science
ISSN 1869-1994       ISSN 2510-4942   (electronic)
Transactions on Large-Scale Data- and Knowledge-Centered Systems
ISBN 978-3-662-62918-5       ISBN 978-3-662-62919-2   (eBook)
https://doi.org/10.1007/978-3-662-62919-2

# Preface

With the rapid advancements of Internet technologies, there is a shift in the focus of online applications towards more interaction and collaboration. Nowadays, there is a move from the Internet as a place of producers and consumers of content to a place of communities where everyone can publish information, interconnect, communicate, collaborate, and share. Moving from services provided by a single entity to more complex or integrated multi-stakeholder services requires new approaches for effective consideration of collaboration.

In this context, Digital Ecosystems have emerged to allow many digital entities/subsystems to interact by exchanging information in a wide variety of ways (Web, Cloud, etc.). They support in-between cooperation and promote collective knowledge sharing in order to provide mutual benefits, as a new way to handle collaboration in a distributed and heterogeneous environment. Interdependencies between entities can be based on automated, semiautomated, or manual relationships. The individual entities have their own purposes to achieve and could be managed locally. However, the efficiency of the whole Digital Ecosystem depends on the consistency of its use and a global, intelligent, balanced coordination of the various resources.

To model, develop, simulate, and validate such complex systems, several challenges remain. The aim of this special issue is to show several current studies addressing these challenges and evincing interesting research directions. The special issue is organized in self-contained papers to provide the greatest reading flexibility. It includes nine papers that have been selected after a very tight peer review, in which each paper has been reviewed by three reviewers. Several topics are addressed in the special issue, but mainly: **Social Big Data, Data Analysis, Cloud-based Feedback, Experience ecosystems, Pervasive Environments, and Smart Systems**. It is organized as follows.

The first paper is titled "Mapping Experience Ecosystems as Emergent Actor-Created Spaces" and is authored by *Andrea Resmini* and *Bertil Lindenfalk*. It introduces a conceptualization of experience ecosystems as semantic blended spaces instantiated by the activities carried out by independent actors moving freely and at will between different products, services, devices, people, and locations in pursuit of individual goals. This conceptualization is anchored to three distinct cultural and socio-technical shifts that characterize the current postdigital condition: the displacement of postmodernism as the cultural dominant; the embodiment of digitality and the emergence of a blended space of action; the occurrence of a postdigital society. It contributes to ongoing conversations on ecosystem-level and systemic design from the point of view of information architecture and user experience in five distinct ways: by centering the discourse on the actor-driven individual experience made possible by the postdigital condition; by framing the problem space from an embodied, spatial, and architectural perspective; by considering the environment systemically as a blend of digital and physical non-contiguous spaces; by recasting the object of design to be the semantic and spatial relationships that exist or could exist between the elements of the actor-centered eco-system; by introducing a mapping methodology that can be used to capture and spatially describe the relational complexity of said ecosystems for further intervention.

In the second paper of this special issue, *Kurosh Madani, Antonio M. Rinaldi*, and *Cristiano Russo* propose "A Semantic-Based Strategy to Model Multimedia Social Networks". Here, the authors explore the decisive role of the social facet of information in our quotidian life. An abstract representation and a proper management of Online Social Networks (OSNs) constitute a new challenge for communities of researchers. In addition, the need to extend OSNs to Multimedia Social Networks (MSNs) comes from the fact that the vast majority of data is unstructured and heterogeneous, making the reuse and integration of information effortful. In this paper, the authors propose a general high-level model to represent and manage MSNs. The proposed approach is based on property graphs represented by a hypergraph structure due to the intrinsically multidimensional nature of social networks and semantic relations to better represent the network's contents. Using the proposed graph structure singles out several levels of knowledge and helps in analysis of the relationships defined between nodes of the same type or different types. Moreover, the introduction of low-level multimodal features and a formalization of their semantic meanings give a more comprehensive view of the social network structure and content. The proposed data model could be useful for several applications. A case study is proposed in the cultural heritage domain.

In the third paper, titled "Social Big Data: Concepts and Theory", *Hiroshi Ishikawa* and *Yukio Yamamoto* explain the basic concepts of social big data and its integrated analysis. First, they explain the outline and examples of the real-world data, open data, and social data that compose social big data. They then describe interactions among the real-world data, open data, and social data. They also introduce basic concepts of an integrated analysis based on the "Ishikawa concept." Furthermore, after explaining the flow of integrated analysis in line with the basic concept, a data model approach for integrated analysis is introduced.

*Hiroshi Ishikawa* and *Yasushi Miyata* propose "Social Big Data: Case Studies" in the fourth paper. Based on the concepts and theory introduced in the previous paper "Social Big Data: Concepts and Theory", the authors concretely explain hypothesis generation and integrated analysis through several use cases.

In the fifth paper, "Data Analysis in Social Network: A Case Study" is proposed by *Mou De, Anirban Kundu,* and *Nivedita Ray De Sarkar*. Here, the authors propose a structural design of social networks to study the architecture of social networking sites and its working principles. Typical social networking sites have a three-tier architecture which induces higher searching time for user queries. The proposal presents a load-balancing module for protecting user enquiries before spreading them to the data server. In this paper, query optimization of user queries for faster results is discussed. Experimentation results exhibit possibilities of data (user queries) failure reduction due to external disturbances. The authors have analyzed large-scale data of a social network through a graph to reduce data loss and minimize network failure to maintain scale-free growth in the social network. Properties of the interface module and growth coefficient are analyzed to exhibit benefits of the proposed system architecture for balancing the load from the web server to the data server through the Hash table cache, Log table and index control module with scale-free query optimization.

"Smart Services Using Voice and Images" is proposed as the sixth paper by *Alexander I. Iliev* and *Peter L. Stanchev*. Here, the authors emphasize some of the most prominent advances in smart technologies that formulate the smart city ecosystem. They highlight the automation of numerous developments based on the extraction and analysis of digital media, using speech and images. At present, a multitude of practical systems is used for personalization and recommendation of different media. On the other hand, assorted types of services in different areas directly benefit from these advancements. Most of them were created with human-machine interaction methodology in mind, where people have to interact with the machines in various ways. In the past, this type of interaction has been completed through the use of conventional interfaces such as a mouse and a keyboard, where the user had to type a response manually, which was in turn recorded by the machine for subsequent analysis. Therefore, in order to simplify these types of interactions and lead to improvement of services, new methodologies must be studied, discovered, and developed so as to improve services such as recommendation and personalization services.

The seventh paper is dedicated to "Big Spatial and Spatio-Temporal Data Analytics Systems", authored by *Polychronis Velentzas, Antonio Corral,* and *Michael Vassilakopoulos*. It is true that we are living in the era of Big Data, and Spatial and Spatio-temporal Data are not an exception. Mobile apps, cars, GPS devices, ships, airplanes, medical devices, IoT devices, etc. are generating explosive amounts of data with spatial and temporal characteristics. Social networking systems also generate and store vast amounts of geo-located information, like geo-located tweets, or mobile users' captured locations. To manage this huge volume of spatial and spatio-temporal data, we need parallel and distributed frameworks. For this reason, modeling, storing, querying, and analyzing big spatial and spatio-temporal data in distributed environments is an active area for research with many interesting challenges. In recent years, a lot of spatial and spatio-temporal analytics systems have emerged. This paper provides a comparative overview of such systems based on a set of characteristics (data types, indexing, partitioning techniques, distributed processing, query language, visualization, and case-studies of applications). The authors present selected systems (the most promising and/or most popular ones), considering their acceptance in the research and advanced-applications communities. More specifically, they present two systems handling spatial data only (SpatialHaddop and GeoSpark) and two systems able to handle spatio-temporal data, too (ST-Hadoop and STARK) and compare their characteristics and capabilities. Moreover, they present in brief other recent/emerging spatial and spatio-temporal analytics systems with interesting characteristics. The paper closes with conclusions arising from investigation of the rather new, though quite large world of ecosystems supporting management of big spatial and spatio-temporal data.

The eighth paper addresses "Cloud Based e-Feedback Services Using Performance Analysis: A Linear Approach", authored by *Ayan Banerjee* and *Anirban Kundu*. Here, the authors propose an online feedback system having distinct layers to access frameworks through multiple entry points such as student module, administration module, and teacher module which can be operated from any geographically distributed locations. There is no need to install software-based applications and no need for extra hardware expenses to access the proposed cloud-based system, due to the usage of software-as-a-service and platform-as-a-service. Students provide specific information to the server-side for authenticity regarding entry to feedback question-naires. Administrative authorities analyze teacher performance based on students' feedback. A teacher observes individual performance from the server. Human effort and human activities have been reduced due to usage of paperless feedback. Teacher performance is measured using preparedness, class-performance, responsiveness, effectiveness, and overall grade. Different nodes are required in the proposed system for distributing and replicating server-side data storage. Time consumption and load dis-tribution of servers are analyzed based on the number of users and servers. Different nodes are accessed by multiple users working with different or the same modules of the system. An energy-efficient framework is incorporated into the proposed system to enhance system performance. The authors have incorporated different weighting factors in the energy efficient framework using distinct layers of the proposed system. Time complexity and space complexity are measured using proposed algorithms. A Web-based approach is required in the proposed system to reduce manpower con-sumption and workload. A comparative study between existing feedback systems and the proposed feedback system is established based on different characteristics.

The last paper of this special issue is titled "Semantic-Based Automatic Generation of Reconfigurable Distributed Mobile Applications in Pervasive Environments" and is written by *Abderrahim Lakehal, Adel Alti,* and *Philippe Roose*. It addresses a practical problem related to mobile applications available through interconnected smart con-nected objects. Several existing research works suffer from a lack of a distributed semantic-based agile strategy to improve accuracy and increase the system's efficiency. To address this problem, this paper comes up with a new flexible, modular, and hierarchical loosely coupled framework to efficiently generate context-aware applica-tions based on a user's location and his situation. The classification of the user's situations reveals new insight on identifying efficiently hierarchical composite situa-tions in order to meet the quality of the user's constraints. It ensures minimum exe-cution time for context-aware distributed mobile applications using a parallel and distributed strategy. Firstly, the framework filters the contextual user's constraints of different smart-domains into domain-specific user's context. Then, it detects parallel incoming events captured by sensors that are able to identify factorized composite situations. Based on these identifications, the authors automatically generate the application reconfiguration as a collection of adapted services that are deployed on available distributed devices. They compare the situation identification performance of the proposed reasoning approach to efficient map-reduce implementations for healthcare systems. Experimental results show the effectiveness, reusability, and scalability of the proposed approach.

We hope this special issue motivates researchers to take the next step beyond building models to implement, evaluate, compare, and extend proposed approaches. Many people worked long and hard to help this edition become a reality. We gratefully acknowledge and sincerely thank all the editorial board members and reviewers for their timely and insightful valuable comments and evaluations of the manuscripts that greatly improved the quality of the final versions. Of course, we offer thanks to all the authors for their contribution and cooperation. Finally, we express our thanks to the editors of TLDKS for their support and trust in us. Special thanks go to Gabriela

Wagner for her high availability and her valuable work in the realization of this TLDKS volume.

November 2020                                                    Richard Chbeir

# Organization

## SI Editorial Board

# Contents

# Mapping Experience Ecosystems as Emergent Actor-Created Spaces

Andrea Resmini[1,2]([email]) [iD] and Bertil Lindenfalk[1] [iD]

[1] Jönköping Academy for Improvement in Health and Welfare, School of Health and Welfare, Jönköping University, Jönköping, Sweden
andrea.resmini@hh.se, bertil.lindenfalk@ju.se
[2] Department of Intelligent Systems and Digital Design, School of Information Technology, Halmstad University, Halmstad, Sweden

**Abstract.** The paper introduces a conceptualization of experience ecosystems as semantic blended spaces instantiated by the activities carried out by independent actors moving freely and at will between different products, services, devices, people, and locations in pursuit of individual goals.

This conceptualization is anchored to three distinct cultural and socio-technical shifts that characterize the current postdigital condition: the displacement of postmodernism as the cultural dominant; the embodiment of digitality and the emergence of a blended space of action; the occurrence of a postdigital society.

It contributes to ongoing conversations on ecosystem-level and systemic design from the point of view of information architecture and user experience in five distinct ways: by centering the discourse on the actor-driven individual experience made possible by the postdigital condition; by framing the problem space from an embodied, spatial and architectural perspective; by considering the environment systemically as a blend of digital and physical non-contiguous spaces; by recasting the object of design to be the semantic and spatial relationships that exist or could exist between the elements of the actor-centered ecosystem; by introducing a mapping methodology that can be used to capture and spatially describe the relational complexity of said ecosystems for further intervention.

**Keywords:** Experience ecosystems · Systems thinking · Information architecture · Blended space · User experience design · Postdigital · Digimodernism · Embodiment · New media

## 1 Introduction

In 2004, before the iPhone, the mobile revolution, and the rise of social media, William J. Mitchell observed that "once there was a time and a place for everything; today, things are increasingly smeared across multiple sites and moments in complex and often indeterminate ways" (Mitchell 2004, p. 14). Mitchell was describing how, in the passage from the industrial age to the network age, "things" were losing their concrete anchoring

© Springer-Verlag GmbH Germany, part of Springer Nature 2021
A. Hameurlain et al. (Eds.): TLDKS XLVII, LNCS 12630, pp. 1–28, 2021.
https://doi.org/10.1007/978-3-662-62919-2_1

to one specific place and time. They were losing "thingness", becoming distributed, "smeared", and this "smearing" meant an increase in complexity and indeterminacy.

Some sixteen years later, ubiquitous data access, smartphones, tablets, sensors, ambient appliances, smart environments and wearables have made computing a dominant part of the cultural and social zeitgeist (Kirby 2009; Floridi 2014). Phenomena such as convergence (Jenkins 2008) and digital transformation (Skog 2019) have blurred the distinction between products and services (Norman 2009; Resmini and Rosati 2009) and between producers and consumers (Tapscott and Williams 2010); the rise of an online read/write culture (Lessig 2008, p. 28; Cramer 2015) and the generational shift (Prensky 2001; Swingle 2016) have challenged the centrality of authorship and ownership (Sterling 2005); linearity is losing its sway to the rhizome (Deleuze and Guattari 1987).

This has resulted in three distinct cultural and socio-technical shifts: i) the displacement of postmodernism as the cultural dominant (Kirby 2006); ii) the embodiment of digitality and the emergence of blended space (Benyon 2014); iii) the occurrence of a postdigital society (Pepperel and Punt 2000). When considered in their systemic relationships, these three will be collectively referenced throughout the paper as the "postdigital condition".

In design, the personal information revolution that started in the late 1980s has been variously interpreted, discussed, and acted upon. It has resulted, in the span of little more than thirty years, in entirely new mainstream artifacts such as video games, websites, mobile apps, and in new practices and specialized fields of study such as service design, information architecture, interaction design, and user experience design (Shostack 1982; Rosenfeld and Morville 1998; Cooper 2004; Garrett 2002). These practices, which will be collectively identified as "new media design" practices for the remainder of the paper, appear now to be at a point of inflection where the challenges introduced by a mature postdigital condition are not entirely understood nor properly addressed.

For example, Lacerda et al. (2018) observe that while information architecture has maintained a relatively stable epistemological purpose as "the structural design of information spaces that support an agent's production of meaning", it has nonetheless seen the intrinsic meaning of that purpose change as the postdigital condition has redefined what these information spaces are. These spaces are now "experienced differently, used differently", but the methods and tools employed by the practice have not entirely caught up with the changes and thus fail to capture critical systemic aspects now part of the design space. They coerce design practice into a reductionist way of thinking and conversely result in a reductionist way of doing.

We posit that to resolve this impasse it is necessary to acknowledge the systemic implications of Mitchell's 2004 intuition and thoroughly reconceptualize the object of design to consider the consequences of embodied digitality, post-postmodern, and postdigital culture.

We do this by methodologically anchoring our conversation to systems thinking and information architecture theory and by approaching the problem space from multiple points of view: a design process point of view, where we adopt for general reference a simplified version of a diverge/converge model (Gray et al. 2010); a philosophy of science point of view, where we adopt Van Gigch and Pipino's Meta-Modeling Method (1986) to frame the relationship between practice and research and to understand to what extent changes in the practice can be beneficial to design theory; and finally an object of design point of view, where we recast what it is that new media design practices actually design in accordance with the postdigital condition.

## 2  Reference Models

When discussing the design process, the paper assumes a generic lifecycle along the lines of the one described for "creative innovation" by Gray et al. (2010), in itself a simplification of the UK Design Council's own Double Diamond process (Design Council 2007). The Double Diamond diagram (Fig. 1) was developed as "a simple graphical way of describing the design process" and "it maps the divergent and convergent stages of the design process, showing the different modes of thinking that designers use" through four distinct formal phases called "Discover, Define, Develop and Deliver" (Design Council 2007).

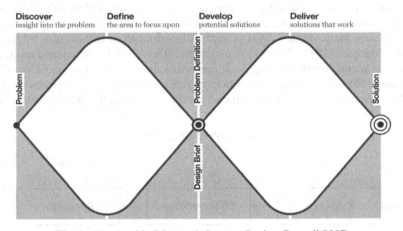

**Fig. 1.** The Double Diamond (Source: Design Council 2007)

Gray's "stubby pencil sharpened at both ends" (2010, p. 9) model shares both the idea of a rhythmic move from divergence to convergence and its visual representation with the Double Diamond. Drawing a parallel with playful behavior, Gray simplifies further the entire process (Fig. 2): at the beginning, the opening requires divergent thinking in order to "populate (the) world with as many and as diverse set of ideas" (Gray et al. 2010, p. 11). The opening is followed by an exploratory phase, where the conditions are created to "allow unexpected, surprising, and delightful things" to emerge. Finally, the process concludes with a closing, convergent phase where decisions are taken.

It is worth noting that Gray's is a fairly more open-ended process that is only concerned with the ideation phase and the creative process. In this sense, it does not need a conclusive "deliver" phase and could be argued to be a more extensive version of the first diamond in the Double Diamond model.

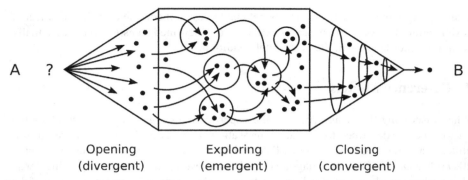

**Fig. 2.** 3-step creative process (Adapted from Gray, Brown, and Macalufo 2010) (Color figure online)

In approaching the meta-conversation involving the various fields and disciplines of design themselves, the relationship between practice and theory, and the role of this paper within those conversations, the primary point of reference is Van Gigch and Pipino's Meta-Modeling Methodology (M3) as applied to information architecture by Lacerda and Lima-Marques (2014). The M3 is a systemic framework to understand innovation processes as social constructs (Fig. 3). It comprises three levels of inquiry (Van Gigch and Pipino 1986): epistemology, the meta level, represents the conceptual framework of a scientific community and the locus of paradigm shifts; science, the object level, presents

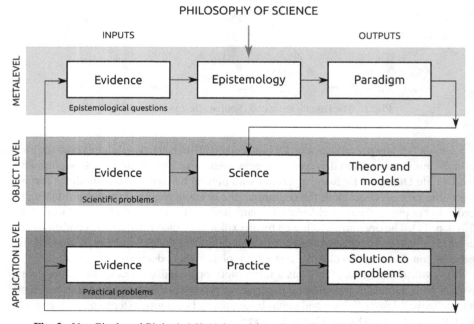

**Fig. 3.** Van Gigch and Pipino's M3 (Adapted from Lacerda and Lima-Marques 2014)

the theories and models that are used "to describe, explain and predict problems and their solutions" (Lacerda and Lima-Marques 2014); practice, the application level, is where practitioners work to solve everyday problems.

These three levels influence each other in a loop: epistemological questions fence the what and the how of scientific progress; scientific theories and methods are used by the practice to solve day-to-day issues. Day-to-day issues and solutions constitute "a source of evidence" that slowly trickles up to support or confute theories and methods and, ultimately, produce paradigm shifts.

## 3 The Space of Relationships

Mitchell points us to the dissolution of the solid materiality of individual artifacts as the process of digitization turns them into distributed, volatile, transient experiences. In Van Gigch and Pipino's M3, this is an epistemological observation. We maintain that the epistemological observations that characterize the postdigital condition necessarily also point to a reframe of our locus of attention at the object level, where new theories and methods should be coopted into the current body of knowledge, and at the application level, where the object of design should be conceptualized as the space of mutual relationships between artifacts.

Design scholar Gui Bonsiepe posited in the late 1960s that the most important element in an ontological view of design is the design of "interfaces", defined not as an "object" but as the "space where the interactions between the human body, the tools, and the goal is articulated" (Bonsiepe 1969, p. 10). In doing so, Bonsiepe frames design through a three-part schema: an agent who is ready to perform an action; the task the agent wants to accomplish; and the tool the agent needs to accomplish the task. Through their interplay, the interface "transforms mere physical existence (…) in opportunity" and the static, solid ontology traditionally associated with artifacts into a systemic set of interdependent relationships.

Interviewed in the mid 1970s, American architect and TED creator Richard Saul Wurman described how already in the early 1960s his lectures at the University of North Carolina focused on the importance of relationships. He would teach his students to "use the problem so they would think about designing the space between things rather than the things themselves", because "what's more important than the buildings is the space between the buildings" (My 2012).

In an influential marketing paper on "How to design a service" written in the early 1980s, Lynn Shostack described products, which are "tangible objects which exist in time and space", and services, that consist "solely of acts or process(es), and exist in time only", as ontologically different (1982). Shostack argued for a distinction to be made between "things" and "processes": "products are possessed" but "services cannot be possessed; they can only be experienced, created or participated in". She also pragmatically observed that the two terms bookend a continuum, a "comparative scale of dominance" that goes from pure product to pure service and which comprises middle-of-the-scale "hybrid entities (in which the) product and service elements are almost balanced". Shostack also introduced a rough conceptual hierarchy in that her model intrinsically considers products as being the end state or outcome of one or more services. In the context of new media design, Norman will explicitly address and nullify this hierarchy in the 2000s stating that for the user any "product is actually a service" (Norman 2009).

Shostack's 1982 conceptualization will lay the foundations of service design: the idea of designing "what is in between", the space of relationships, will instead become a mainstay of early information architecture in the 1990s (Rosenfeld and Morville 1998), carry over into the conversations on contemporary information architecture in the 2010s (Hinton 2008), and ultimately manifest itself in new media design practice and theory as a complete reconfiguration of the spatial and temporal categories used as differentiators by Shostack.

Spatially, new media design moves from artifacts such as chairs and lamps and telephones, whose solid materiality and spatial whereabouts can not be doubted, to intangibles such as software programs, websites or digital environments, whose "virtuality" or "digitality" is often juxtaposed to some other form of "reality" (Maldonado 1992). Space "becomes a media type" that can be "instantly transmitted, stored, (...) and interacted with" primarily through immersion and navigation (Manovich 2000, p. 251–252).

Temporally, attention shifts from static, finished objects, whose durability by and large depends only on the normal tear and wear of physical interactions, to ever changing, transient, volatile structures whose continued existence is inextricably linked to socio-technical processes of engagement and co-production (Resmini and Rosati 2011, p. 53; Lucas et al. 2012; Benyon 2014).

This spatial and temporal reconfiguration has been variously acknowledged in specialist theories of design (Garrett 2002; Kolko 2011; Sangiorgi and Prendiville 2017): however, in the practice, the framing of the problem space is ultimately left to the design practitioner to articulate and explore, and this is usually done through consolidated design approaches, tools and methods that comply with current management and organizational practices (Davies and Saunders 1988).

## 4  Design Practice and Complexity

In different ways, new media design practices such as user experience design and service design aim to improve service encounters for the customer by focusing on their entire journey (Polaine et al. 2013, p. 34). They thus overcome, at least conceptually, some of the problems deriving from the linearization and compartmentalization of traditional product design. Still, the myth that a designer can design a perfectly bounded, finished artifact and simply drop it in place within a dynamic environment holds fast, at least in the practice (Lindenfalk and Resmini 2016). This can be ascribed to reasons both organizational and methodological: on one side, organizations have cultural, practical, and economic incentives to frame and manage a service as an intangible product that can be quantified and properly commercialized; on the other, many of the tools and methods used in the practice have been repurposed from preexisting, product-oriented sources and carry with them an artifact-bound point of view.

For example, customer journeys and service blueprints are two common deliverables used during the design or redesign process to communicate the design practitioner's understanding of people in their role as customers or potential customers and their experience of a company's process or processes (Stickdorn and Schneider 2010; Polaine et al. 2013, p. 91; Gibbons 2018). Both tools allow to articulate and then synthetically communicate aspects of what has been learned from the exploratory phases in a collaborative, empathetic format (Blomkvist and Segelström 2014). Both also predate digital (Whittle and Foster 1989; Shostack 1984).

Service blueprints and customer journeys offer a rather comprehensive over-view of the service process as they center on the customer's point of view and do not focus exclusively on the organizational perspective. However, the organization remains the entity originating and dictating the boundaries of the problem space for its "customers": additional third-party factors and relationships that are relevant to these "customers" but not to the organization do not usually fall within their scope. When such insights are gained during research, they are either downplayed, discarded, or moved to different sets of deliverables, for example to a competitive analysis report, because the primary task these tools perform is to describe the client-product-customer relationship through a linear, synthetic timeline of its pivotal moments. Unfortunate side-effects of such synthesis are a loss in complexity, an overreliance on known knowns, and an underestimation of unknown unknowns.

An example of such a case is discussed in literature by Culén and Gasparini (2014, p. 91), who describe the redesign of the services of an academic library using a customer journey approach. The case is primarily of interest for how it entirely neglects, or better chooses not to explore the role of the library within the specific context in which it exists, considering it instead as a "finished", perfectly bounded artifact and discarding "the spaces between the objects". The primary insight offered by the case is that library staff and management were very much focused on their physical assets while their largest group of patrons, the students, were instead mainly considering the library's digital touchpoints. While the authors clearly state that "libraries are practically forced to rethink their role in academic life, their use of technology and willingness to innovate", the description of the various workshops conducted in the course of the project illustrates how any effort to challenge the unspoken assumption of what a library supposedly "is" did not result in divergent openings but rather in quiet dismissals. As these efforts did not comply with the well-defined organizational and spatial boundaries put in place by the "client", the library, their role was minimized and underplayed. When students described how their journeys started almost always online, the librarians immediately refocused the conversation on the library building (Culén and Gasparini 2014, p. 92), greatly diminishing the impact and design value of the students' assertions in the process. The design problem was framed around the role of the library as part of the university brick-and-mortar infrastructure rather than around its role in the lives of students.

We do not believe this can be simply characterized as the result of research inadequacies or of a design failure: it is rather the necessary outcome of the limitations that tools such as customer journeys introduce. Very often, as in the example just discussed, the complexity deriving from the interplay of the many heterogeneous socio-technical parts involved in the process is reduced to figuring out optimal linear flows for a number of well-identified activities across a number of touchpoints under the direct control of the organization driving the design efforts. Customer journeys are the typical tools, albeit not the only ones, through which such simplification happens.

There are obvious and very visible benefits in focusing on a number of unambiguous, identifiable interactions along clearly established touchpoints: control is the most immediate one; transforming a complex experience into a simpler, more manageable linear narrative is another. Unfortunately, such abrupt simplifications artificially constrain or do away with the consequences of Mitchell's "smearing" and thus increase the possibility of unwanted reductionism and introduce risky trade-offs. In this light, it is possible to read Wurman's and Bonsiepe's ontological reassessments of the object of design, a space of relationships rather than an artifact, as opening the way to a different, more systemic approach.

While the very ideas of compounding multiple points of view into a unified vision and of moving at varying levels of granularity are widely acknowledged and long-standing characteristics of architectural processes (Borden et al. 2014), a systemic approach to human-centered design has consolidated only recently (Jones 2014; Hill 2014). This "systemic design", defined as a design approach that "outlines and plans the flow of matter running from one system to the others, pursuing a metabolization processes which should reduce the ecological footprint and generate profitable economic flows" and that "optimizes all the actors and parts of an ecosystem allowing for their coherent and mutual evolution" (Bistagnino and Campagnaro 2014) represents as of today a big design, top-down approach tackling large-scale initiatives, and one that has yet to achieve widespread adoption in the new media design communities of practice. In this paper we propose a different, bottom-up systemic approach that:

- directly addresses the application level in the M3 by building on past and current attention given to the "spaces between things" in some of the new media practices;
- introduces a perspective shift in new media design practices from a reductionist approach to a systemic approach to respond to current challenges brought on by the postdigital condition;
- leverages current information architecture and user experience ways-of-doing to facilitate the transition from holistic to systemic (Armson 2011);
- makes the digital/physical space of relationships freely instantiated by systems of actors the object of design.

## 5   Reductionist, Holistic, and Systemic

While "holistic" and "systemic" are often used interchangeably in both academic discourses on design and the practice, systems thinking literature considers them different concepts. Figure 4 illustrates the relationship between reductionist thinking, sociotechnical thinking, holistic thinking, and systems thinking as described in Armson (2011). Left to right, the horizontal axis sees an increase in complexity, from reductionism to holism; bottom to top, the vertical axis sees an increase in the number of perspectives that can be simultaneously held as truthful.

Reductionist thinking considers the system a summation of its parts: understanding the individual components in isolation also leads to an understanding of the functioning of the system. Scientific/mechanistic thinking (bottom left) is a single perspective reductionist approach. It is best exemplified by traditional Western science and education models. Reductionist thinking adopting multiple perspectives is what Armson calls

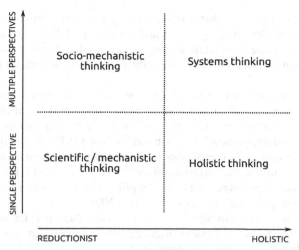

**Fig. 4.** Systemic v holistic thinking (Adapted from Armson 2011)

"socio-mechanistic" thinking (top left). Examples are "many forms of social science" in which "different interpretations, coming from different perspectives, co-exist but in a reductionist form" (Armson 2011, p. 50).

Holistic thinking (bottom right) sacrifices attention to detail to favor the investigation of the whole over its parts. Holism still favors one single perspective, that of the whole, and hence "retain(s) the mechanistic qualities of single-perspective thinking" (Armson 2011, p. 50). Much of the theory and practice of current new media design that adopts holistic approaches, including much of the practice of experience and service design, falls into this category.

Systems thinking (top right) considers multiple viewpoints at once: it acknowledges that complex processes, such as those related for example to the design inquiry, cannot be centered around one single optimal approach, whatever that approach might be. These processes require instead conscious movement between multiple and possibly contrasting perspectives at different levels of granularity for the inquirer to attain a more complete understanding of what is being investigated.

Systemic approaches recognize that complex issues configure "messes" (Gharajedaghi 2011) or "wicked problems" (Rittel and Webber 1973, p. 160) and that even reaching an agreement on what the problem is in itself, what its parts are and where its boundaries lie, is more often than not a controversial process that requires negotiation. In approaching messes, exclusive use of any individual approach can lead to an impoverished understanding (Armson 2011, p. 32) and invariably result in a reductionist take on the problems at hand.

# 6   Transition to Systemic

New media design practices as they are currently framed are not set up for an easy transition towards systemic ways of doing. They are constrained by organizational structures, legacy methods, and processes that reinforce linearity and reductionism, as in the case of the library project described by Cúlen and Gasparini. Holistic approaches as well fall victim to these same constraints and reproduce product logic in their addressing the object of design as finite, finished, and artificially constrained within organizational boundaries.

Additionally, the language in which the conversation is carried out is steeped in product thinking even when discussing experiences or services (Lindenfalk and Resmini 2016), defined as encompassing "all aspects of the end-user's interaction with the company, its services, and its products" (Norman and Nielsen nd). Focus remains centered on how "a company intentionally uses services (…) to engage individual customers" to provide them with a complete, organization-driven "memorable event" (Pine and Gilmore 1998, p. 98) and hence postulates the exact coupling of one "service provider's explicit action(s)" with "the customer's choices" (Koivisto 2009).

Mapping this situation onto Van Gigch and Pipino's M3 provides us with a better understanding of the nature and extent of the current misalignment and of the specific challenges that differently impact the three levels.

At the metalevel, that of epistemology, new media design appears to be at odds with moving past a postmodern sensibility especially in relation to the deeper consequences of mass co-creation. While distributed authorship and ownership have been internalized, albeit in different forms and at different levels of maturity (Manzini 2015; Spool 2015), letting go of the superstructures of corporate stewardship that result in inward-focused, artificially bound, and facilitated problem framing is proving to be harder.

At the object level, that of science, the conversation around how to consolidate, integrate and expand the current body of knowledge is stunted and fragmentary. New media design is currently perceived to be primarily a practice-driven craft, with academic discourse falling behind (Resmini 2013; Reeves and Ljungblad 2018) and failing to fill the expectation gap existing between the developments in the job market and formal professional and academic education (Maccarone and Doody 2016). Theories and methods remain anchored to product logic and do not address the volatile, network-like architectures that characterize the postdigital condition.

At the application level, that of the practice, even as the object of design is increasingly shaped by the postdigital condition, in itself inherently embodied and systemic, the tools and processes remain reductionist in nature, enforce a problematic separation between the digital and physical elements that support an experience, and are artificially constrained by the linearity of traditional management processes.

Because of the practice-driven nature of new media design, we maintain that efforts should be directed at realigning the M3 loop starting at the application level. We thus:

- propose that the postdigital object of design is not a tangible, finished, individual artifact, but rather the volatile actor-instantiated spaces of relationships between artifacts;
- observe that such a shift in the object of design implies a shift in design methods and processes to account for the multiplication of perspectives and variations of granularity (Benyon 2014) that are brought in by the systemic interplay of a multiplicity of actors;
- characterize postdigital new media design as the design of the relationships between the elements of an actor-centered ecosystem, defined as the blended, digital/physical

environment in which human experience unfolds and occurs (Benyon and Resmini 2017);

- posit that postdigital new media design practice is systemic, architectural, and spatial in nature and that it primarily concerns itself with the structural and relational design of leverage points to influence behavior within said ecosystem.

We explicitly anchor this reframe and its implications for new media design practice and theory to the ongoing shift towards digimodernist forms of co-production and consumption (Kirby 2009), embodied forms of computing (Dourish 2001), and a postdigital culture (Pepperel and Punt 2000).

## 7   Digimodernism, Embodiment, and a Postdigital Culture

While there is general agreement in cultural studies that the displacement of postmodernism started in the 1990s, what it is that is taking its place is matter of ample debate and has been variously defined as post-post, trans-, or meta-modernism (Vermeulen and van den Akker 2010). We adopt here the perspective of digimodernism as introduced by Kirby (2009) as it specifically pays attention to the changes induced by digital transformation and to the social aspects of production and consumption processes. Kirby considers the "effects of computing on society and culture" as the primary catalyst for change: he frames postmodernism as both a rejection and a continuation of modernism and of its "fetishing" the author, and identifies the main differentiation between postmodernism and digimodernism in how the latter centers on the recipient to such a degree that they become indistinguishable from the author (Kirby 2006).

Kirby argues that digital has redefined the nature of authorship, readership, and textuality, and the relationships between these. Using reality TV shows as a template, he argues that digimodernism is a culture without an "audience" and built instead on "participants". Such participation is immediate, necessary, "raw, uncut, visceral", and thus profoundly different from the detachment, irony, and intellectual pastiche valued by postmodernism (Hutcheon 1988). It is in this sense that Kirby frames postmodernism as inextricably tied to old media: books, films, the television screen, all fundamentally built on some form of top-down control on a finished, complete product usually readily identifiable with a support medium.

Digimodernism on the other hand is a bottom-up new media phenomenon (Manovich 2001), predicated on disintermediation and remediation, perfectly exemplified by artifacts such as AirBnB, Facebook, or online open world video games such as Minecraft that "cannot (exist) and do not exist unless the individual intervenes physically in them" (Kirby 2006) and that are in a constant state of flow, unfinished, evanescent, transient, and factually co-produced or co-created by an anonymous mass (Kirby 2009, pp. 59–60).

Postdigital (or post-digital) is a term initially used in art-related discourses to refer to a renewed interest in the human side of human-computer interactions and to the possibility of exploring the consequences of digital culture. "The tendrils of digital technology have in some way touched everyone (and) the revolutionary period of the digital information age has surely passed" (Cascone 2000): digital has been "trivialized", as Negroponte predicted in a vastly influential article written for Wired in 1998. On one hand this means it should be possible to observe and examine "digital" critically; on the other, since digital has permeated every aspect of society, it marks the emergence of a novel hybrid landscape in which digimodernism acts as the primary cultural aesthetics (Jenkins 2011).

The identification of postdigital from parts of the literature with a specific "contemporary disenchantment with digital information systems and media gadgets, or (with) a period in which our fascination with these systems and gadgets has become historical" (Cramer 2015) is here treated as consequential to digital having indeed become "like air and drinking water" (Negroponte 1998). Rather than diminishing its cultural significance, this becoming just another part of the day-to-day fabric signals an increase in its importance, as technology for the sake of technology becomes a secondary concern and allows digital to turn into fertile "commercial and cultural compost for new ideas" (Negroponte 1998). In such a context, arguing for "digital solutions" is not only once again a one-perspective, reductionist approach, but an argument as out of its time as one in support of "electrical solutions" would be.

Navigating a postdigital world requires "avoid(ing) binarism, determinism, and reductionism" if we want to "explain (the) complex phenomena" that have been set in motion and the continuity between them (Pepperel and Punt 2000, p. 2). It is in this sense that "post-digital is not anti-digital" but rather "extends digital into the beyond. The web becomes not a destination in itself but a route map to somewhere real" (Jenkins 2011). This commingling of digital and physical is thoroughly changing our understanding of the relationship between the two and has important consequences in terms of the role of embodiment and of the design attention it receives.

Human-computer interaction literature has explored at length the interplay between our embodiment and our interactions with digital (Weiser 1991; Dourish 2001). More recently, architectural research (Mallgrave 2013; Williams Goldenhagen 2017) and neuroscientific research have illuminated an even more relevant role that embodiment plays in the way we interact with digitally-mediated information and information spaces, pointing to spatial constructs as the fundamental building blocks of human cognition and to all sense-making as being fundamentally embodied (Benn et al. 2015; Constantinescu et al. 2016; Bellmund et al. 2018).

However, the level of abstraction at which systemic research has been conducted has often meant that the role of embodiment within the ecosystem representing the space of relationships between artifacts, locations, objects, and people has found little consideration so far. With a few notable but relatively inconsequential exceptions (Horan 2000; Institute for the Future 2009), architectural research and information systems research have been respectively focusing on embodiment in the physical world (Norberg-Schulz 1971) and on the meaning of embodiment for our conceptualization of digital spaces, and have rarely crossed paths. Benyon's concept of blended space (2014) allows to bridge the gap.

Imaz and Benyon (2007) initially applied Fauconnier and Turner's conceptual blending theory (2002) to the study of human-computer interaction and software engineering. Benyon then formalized blended space as a space "where a physical space is deliberately integrated in a close-knit way with a digital space" (2014, p. 79), creating a new type of space with its own emergent structure, a different set of affordances, and a novel user experience predicated on a different sense of presence. Benyon's blended space is user-centered and characterized by its ontology, topology, agency, and volatility. A multiplayer video game called "Johann Sebastian Joust", designed by Danish independent studio Die Gute Fabrik, can be used to better explain how the concept of blended space can help frame embodiment in digital/physical spaces and the design of postdigital experiences.

"Johann Sebastian Joust" (Fig. 5) is a variation on the theme of a musical chairs game. As the game website describes it, it "is a no-graphics, digitally-enabled playground game designed for motion controllers. The goal is to be the last player remaining. When the music (…) plays in slow-motion, the controllers are very sensitive to movement. When the music speeds up, the threshold becomes less strict, giving the players a small window to dash at their opponents. If your controller is ever moved beyond the allowable threshold, you're out!" (Die Gute Fabrik 2014).

**Fig. 5.** A game of Johann Sebastian Joust (Source: Die Gute Fabrik presskit. Photo: B. Knep-per)

"Johann Sebastian Joust" is most certainly a video game and a new media artifact: it is written as software and requires a Playstation game console to run. On the other hand, the game cannot be played against the system and requires multiple human players; it also requires an abundance of physical space for players to move around, an uncommon trait for a video game; the kinetic Move controllers physically manifest the game's logic in analog space via sound and light; players play without the aid of screens and do not need any of the hand-eye coordination normally required by traditional video games; rounds are won and lost based on player-to-player interactions that include pushing, shoving, and grabbing one's opponents in the physical world.

In terms of Benyon's blended space, "Johann Sebastian Joust"'s ontology contains the Playstation game console, the game itself, the players, the Move controllers, their relationships in space and "what functions and facilities they have" (Benyon 2014, p. 80). Players and controllers are both "nodes" in the physical space of the game, and "information artifacts" in the digital space of the game; its topology reflects their mutual spatial relationships and remains relatively dense as the players cannot move too far away from each other; its volatility is spatially constrained by topology but varies greatly through time as the players react to the music and the controllers react to the action; its agency blends "the artificial agents" represented by the game's own logic and by the controllers with the players' decision and "opportunities for action" in physical space.

## 8   Experience Ecosystems

If embodiment in blended space is one of the key aspects of postdigital new media, Kirby's anonymous mass co-production is another essential component, one that characterizes any contemporary information-enabled product or service. Co-production may happen voluntarily, as with most social media or with algorithm-driven services such as Spotify or Netflix, or involuntarily, through the tracking, analysis, and clustering of one's activities across physical and digital space by means of smartphones, sensors, or credit cards.

In a postdigital landscape, any product or service, or parts of it, can be repurposed by actors to become part of a different experience, as relationships between artifacts are followed, exploited, or dismissed arbitrarily depending on the idiosyncratic needs and objectives of actors. Since the "creative organization of information creates new information" (Wurman 1989, p. 3), this constant process of remediation and reorganization of information configures an ecosystem-level co-creation activity that stems from individual experiences.

While service marketing literature has introduced the concept of service ecosystem (Vargo and Akaka 2012), which consists of the combined resources of several service systems that come together through the combined actions of actors (Vargo and Lusch 2011; Akaka and Vargo 2015), the conceptualization of ecosystems we propose here is more appropriately framed as experience-centered. It follows seminal work by Resmini and Rosati on pervasive information architectures (2011), Resmini and Lacerda's formalization of cross-channel ecosystems (2016), Benyon's conceptualization of blended spaces (2014), and Resmini and Benyon's subsequent joint developments (2017).

Resmini and Lacerda build on previous work on crossmedia (Jenkins 2008), bridge experiences (Grossman 2006), and information architecture (Resmini and Rosati 2011) to outline a generative, bottom-up approach to design, structured around a systemic view that ties together actors, activities, touchpoints, the seams between touchpoints, and individual goals into transient, personal, information-based ecosystems (Resmini and Lacerda 2016).

An ecosystem configures the place in which experiences unfold (Benyon and Resmini 2017) and is instantiated by the "actor-driven choice, use, and coupling of touchpoints, either belonging to the same or to different systems, within the context of the strategic goals and desired future states actors intend to explicitly or implicitly achieve" (Resmini and Lacerda 2016). In this sense, Resmini and Lacerda describe a radically user-centered design approach: an ecosystem is an emergent structure instantiated by the activities carried out by independent actors moving freely and at will and who connect different products, services, devices, people, and locations in pursuit of individual goals. Such products, services, devices, people and locations configure a varying set of physical, digital or biological touchpoints, making the resulting ecosystem a semantic structure that straddles multiple non-contiguous digital and physical spaces of relationships and a blended space of action as described by Benyon (2014). We call this volatile postdigital construct an experience ecosystem.

An experience ecosystem is not a finite artifact, product or service, resulting from an organizational process and one that can be fully or wholly designed: it is rather a space of opportunity entirely structured by actors in which designers can operate at multiple levels of granularity and from multiple perspectives, brokering between the different instances presented by the space of relationships that identifies the ecosystem itself, the actors, and the designers' own vision. As a result, design interventions are not concerned with the (re)design "of" an ecosystem but rather with influence and design "within" an ecosystem to increase its resilience and adaptability, so that social or business opportunities can be maximized and individual or organizational issues minimized. This usually happens in the form of a recast of one or more specific touchpoints and their seams (Benyon and Resmini 2017).

An ecosystem approach has been successfully adopted for the design of such diverse systems as the environment of a national art gallery (Resmini 2013), the customer experience for outdoor recreation gear and sporting goods retailers (Tate 2011), and ambient assisted living solutions for the elderly (Lindenfalk and Resmini 2019).

## 9 Design Process for Experience Ecosystems

The design process for experience ecosystems concerns itself primarily with the global structure and dynamics of the ecosystem itself as defined by the contrasting goals, views, and desires of the actors in play. In this sense, it is an information architecture approach to "dissolving the second-order machine" responsible for "generating undesirable patterns of behavior" that maintain and recreate the current homeostasis (Gharajedaghi 2011, p. 150). Change in the behavioral patterns existing within an ecosystem is enacted by introducing "a set of alternatives" that can challenge "underlying assumptions" (Gharajedaghi 2011, p. 65).

This happens through two interrelated processes of discovery and improvement, loosely mapped over the diverge/explore and explore/converge moments of Gray's model (Fig. 2). These first identify "what is relevant and supportive to (…) a desirable future", and then diagnose "what turns out to be part of the 'mess' and therefore obstructive to (…) renewal and progress": "we want to keep the first and dispose of the second" (Gharajedaghi 2011, p. 150). It must be stressed that "dispose" here does not necessarily mean physically or conceptually eliminate what appear to be harmful processes or artifacts from the ecosystem, but rather act on the information architecture so that actors have ways to exit stressful or unuseful information loops, create new virtuous ones, and break out of counterproductive system archetypes (Stroh 2015, p. 67).

In its early stages, the process is formally structured around a series of mapping activities. Mapping is based on data describing the actors' behavior within the (current) state of relationships acquired through user research and consists of two distinct phases: the mapping of individual paths, and the mapping of the ecosystem itself (Lindenfalk and Resmini 2019). Two versions of the ecosystem are produced during this latter phase: one documenting the organizational view and the designers' observations, called the prescriptive version; one resulting from the actors' data, called the emergent version, documenting the ecosystem resulting from the actors' actions. This is done to establish the distance between projected use, deriving from the organization's views and desires, and real use.

The methods used to gather data for these two types of maps are usually, but not necessarily, different: prescriptive maps are often derived from existing documentation, briefs, and project meetings; emergent maps are derived from ethnographic research, interviews, or questionnaires that are meant to capture the personal narratives that will be subsequently streamlined into individual paths.

This is a straightforward process: touchpoints are identified within the narratives in conjunction with a task and arranged in a temporal sequence expressed topologically. For example, an actor describes "going to the movies" according to the following narrative: "I saw the trailer for a new movie on YouTube yesterday so I checked if the local cinema was screening it. They did, so I called a friend to see if she wanted to come see it with me and then I booked the tickets online. I had dinner home, took a bus, and we met in the lobby fifteen minutes before the 9 pm show. We both liked it". An analysis of the narrative identifies "trailer", "YouTube", "website", "cinema", "friend", "tickets" as the initial individual touchpoints, related to tasks such as "knowing about the movie", "checking availability", "asking for company", "buying tickets".

A simple syntax is then used to represent these touchpoints as elements in an individual path in a standardized, spatially-oriented way (Fig. 6). Touchpoints are represented by colored hexagonal tiles, and seams are represented by gray hexagonal tiles between them. Seams identify steps in the path: an actor that moves from a touchpoint "a" to a touchpoint "b" through a seam moves one step. Arrows are employed to provide a general indication of directionality from start point to end point. With every single step, an actor has the option to move to another touchpoint within the ecosystem which is either at their immediate disposal, in their proximity, or not in their proximity.

Immediately available touchpoints are "personal", color-coded green, and syntactically occupy the straight-on position (Fig. 6). Touchpoints in the actor's proximity are "local", color-coded yellow, and take one of the two right-handed positions: right-forward identifies a stronger local touchpoint, right-backward a weaker one, "based on the degree of effort their usage requires", with "stronger touch-points requir(ing) less effort (and) weaker touchpoints requir(ing) more effort" (Lindenfalk and Resmini 2019).

Touchpoints not in the actor's proximity are "remote", color-coded red, and take one of the two left-handed positions: left-forward identifies a stronger remote touchpoint, left-backward a weaker one, following the conventions laid out for local touchpoints. Seams are always laid out between touchpoints in the straighton, forward position: this allows to keep the touchpoints themselves consistently oriented all along the time arrow of the narrative path. In Fig. 6, the remote touchpoint in step 2 is a weaker

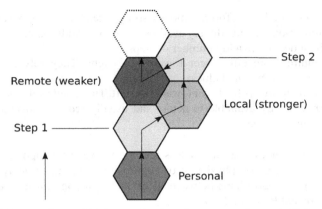

**Fig. 6.** Spatial syntax for positioning touchpoints along a narrative path (Color figure online)

remote touchpoint (left-backward, red) following a stronger local touchpoint in step 1 (right-forward, yellow).

Seams represent the information flows that allow actors to move from one touchpoint to the next. In the case of a local touchpoint, that might be information they themselves already possess, such as "prior knowledge of how to book tickets online" in the movie example given above, or "something they carry on their person, such as a smartphone" (Lindenfalk and Resmini 2019). In the case of local touchpoints, it might be "a real-time display that can be checked for information" or "a bystander who can be asked". In the case of remote touch-points, usually implying delay, movement, or both, it might be "a rarely used or previously unknown online source" or "a public office when the actor is home".

As paths traverse the blended space of the ecosystem, proximity between two touch-points can be either physical or semantic. If necessary and if data is available to support an increase in detail, the level of granularity can be dynamically adjusted to zoom in (or in case zoom out) at specific steps along a path: a "mobile phone" could satisfyingly represent a meaningful touchpoint as much as "mobile phone", a specific "app installed on the same phone", and a specific "task performed via the app" could represent the same as three consecutive touchpoints, depending on context and design needs. The final result of this phase is a variable number of path diagrams illustrating how individual actors scope out the ecosystem by simply traversing it.

It is important to observe that paths represents the actors' own sense-making rationalization of their actions and remain a linear narrative: they do not represent in any way the full extent of the relationships existing within the ecosystem and they do not individually represent the ecosystem itself.

On the other hand, the topological syntax used to describe paths heuristically illustrates how any given step in the narrative "relates to the principle of least effort for acquiring information" (Bates 2002), so that paths effectively provide an initial visual appreciation of "how easy or strenuous it is for specific actors to attain a certain desired future state" (Lindefalk and Resmini 2019). Considering the right-left spatial continuum resulting from the application of the syntax, the diagrams immediately show that:

- paths that require the least effort are mostly straight sequences. They rely primarily on personal touchpoints, immediately available to actors. Additionally, these paths do not usually include an unwieldy number of steps;
- paths that require more effort veer towards the right. They rely more on local touchpoints and environmental clues;
- paths that require the most effort veer towards the left. These paths rely more on remote touchpoints not readily available to actors and usually require movement between locations or temporal delays.

In general, all experiences that have actors moving between touchpoints that are far apart from each other, either physically or cognitively, will suffer delays, introduce additional touchpoints and seams between them, and as a consequence require more effort (Lindenfalk and Resmini 2019).

In the second phase, existing spatial relationships between touchpoints identified in the individual narratives represented in the path diagrams are merged into one or more synthetic maps of the ecosystem. Colored hexagon tiles are used for touchpoints and gray hexagon tiles are used for seams. Touchpoints which appear in any of the path diagrams belong to the experience ecosystem and are mapped as clusters of tiles "whose number equals the number of times overall in which that specific touchpoint has been a part of an actor's path" (Lindenfalk and Resmini 2019). Seams connect touchpoints which have been mentioned as connecting at least once by any one actor.

The synthetic maps of the ecosystems discount any type of directionality and only account for touchpoints and seams and their mutual relationships of physical or conceptual proximity: "any two touchpoints which are more than one seam away from each other, or which are separated by empty slots, do not share a relationship" (Lindenfalk and Resmini 2019) and did not see actors move between them. In this sense, the ecosystem maps are more akin to cartography maps describing a territory than to the diagrammatic "journeys" new media design has been traditionally using.

Additional useful pieces of information can be added to the map by means of color, for example highlighting channels ("all digital touchpoints" or "all touch-points which belong to production processes regardless of organizational boundaries"), or shapes, for example signaling through increasingly thicker borders how many times a certain seam has been traversed. This sub-phase is usually repeated at least twice: once to produce the map describing the prescriptive view, usually amounting to the organizational conceptualization of what the experience ecosystem is; and once to produce the emergent map of the ecosystem as it comes into being from the individual actions of actors trying to achieve a future state.

The prescriptive map and the emergent map can be immediately compared to visually measure the distance between the organizational view and the actual ecosystem in which the actors' experience takes place: for example, how the degree of integration of touchpoints (Chalmers 1999), their relative weight, their semantic distance vary between the two maps; how information flows or does not flow between specific touchpoints and what effects point-to-point recasts such as opening new seams, eliminating or introducing additional touchpoints would have on the ecosystem; identify factual fallacies in the predicted interplay of the diverse constitutive elements or structural weaknesses that globally affect the ecosystem.

These observations are usually formalized through any number of deliverables that "tell the story" (Gharajedaghi 2011) and identify leverage points to be recast to better suit the goals of some or all of the different actors at play. The practical, exploratory nature of the mapping phases themselves is also an important part of this "telling the story": the intimate understanding of the complex space of relationships constituting the ecosystem that derives from the necessity to make its architecture explicit, so that it can be observed and discussed, is a most important design outcome.

These mapping activities are intended to gradually shift attention away from the linearity of individual narratives to the systemic space of relationships of the ecosystem, represented by means of reciprocal spatial relationships of proximity or separation that avoid any enforcement of directionality. Their primary outcome is to provide designers with a way to discuss interventions that take into account the second-order structure of the ecosystem so that:

- relationships are made explicit and the risk of unintended consequences reduced;
- leverage points that can influence systemic change are identified;
- unwanted behaviors are addressed by their root causes and not symptomatically;
- virtuous behaviors are supported;
- the resilience of the ecosystem itself is increased.

In line with Armson's systemic approach, the exploratory and convergent activities that follow usually see the adoption of multiple different perspectives working at different levels of granularity, with individual interventions being implemented according to the specific tools and methods of existing new media practices. For example, a change in a mobile interface might require user interface and interaction design expertise.

This design process thoroughly differs from that of user experience design (Garrett 2002; Unger and Chandler 2012). It also differs from how the design of services is practiced by Culén and Gasparini (2014) or as it is described by Polaine (Polaine et al. 2013, p. 22) in both its object and its conceptual foundation. In Polaine's example the customer is hampered by "the division of the (organization's) silos (that) makes sense to the business units, but makes no sense to the customer, who sees the entire offering (of the organization) as one experience." The ecosystem approach outlined here posits that the customer is first and foremost an actor whose behavior is inextricably intertwined with the current layout of the ecosystem and with its information flows, and that their experience is in no way limited to what is offered or supported solely by any single actor or organization.

The process described here (Fig. 7) can be represented as a variation of the Double Diamond model in which the two diamonds (here hexagons) explicitly work at two different levels of granularity: the first one considering the ecosystem view and the second one working at the specific practice level required to "develop" and "deliver" the leverage point recasts that have been "discovered" and "defined" through the mapping activities.

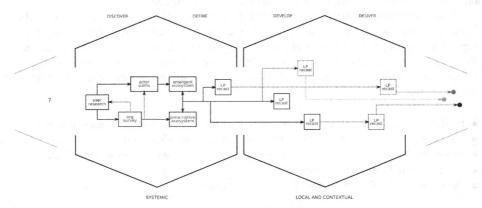

**Fig. 7.** Design process model for experience ecosystems

An individual, organizational, or social pain acts as a catalyst for the process (represented by the question mark symbol as in Gray's model). Organization is here to be intended in a broader sense and to include also public bodies or non-profit operations. User research is performed and both influences and is influenced by a parallel data collection activity conducted on the organization, its goals, its structure, and its outlook (org survey in Fig. 7). These two activities produce respectively the actor path diagrams and the prescriptive ecosystem map, with the org survey having possible bearing also on the actor paths. For example, in some further specification of the actor groups being considered.

The actor paths, obtained through the mapping activities described in the previous section (mapping phase 1), are used to produce the emergent ecosystem map (mapping phase 2). The two maps are compared, discussed, and used to identify leverage points for recast (LP recast in Fig. 7). LP recasts are defined towards the end of the systemic stage and developed and delivered as part of the local and contextual stage. Methods, tools, and perspectives change in scope, disciplinary context, and granularity between the two stages.

### 9.1 "Better Courses"

Figures 8 and 9 show respectively two individual actor paths and the emergent ecosystem map part of a course project run with students from the Master in Informatics at Jönköping University (JU) in 2014–15. The project was concerned with "improving courses" and originated with school management informally asking staff to identify ways to "make courses better". It was run as a series of collaborative workshops that started by asking students to first define what "better" meant in the context, and then consequently identify who were the primary actors. Agreement was quickly reached that "better" should be taken to mean as "improving the students' own overall experience of courses", since they were the primary recipients, and that very little was known about this. With students becoming the primary actor group instantiating the course ecosystem, staff and management were cast as the organizational counterpart.

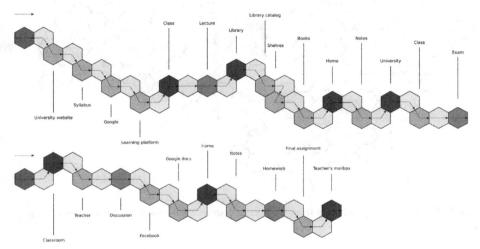

**Fig. 8.** Two individual path diagrams from the "better courses" ecosystem mapping project

Data for the prescriptive ecosystem map was then gathered from briefs and documents and by examining the course infrastructure in place at the time, while a total of fifty students were asked to describe what was their goal when attending a course, how they went through a course, and what activities that implied, to provide standing ground for the emergent ecosystem map. Data was collected over a period of one week by means of an open-format local online survey that allowed the students to narrate their "course experience" using as many steps and touchpoints they needed, and through four subsequent individual semi-structured interviews with selected students belonging to the same sample group.

The students who responded to the anonymous questionnaire were 54% male and 36% female and their median age was 26: "knowing more about the subject" (92%), "passing the course" (36%), and "no specific goal" (6%) were the three primary non-exclusive goals declared in the questionnaire. The minimum number of steps in any individual path was four (and five touchpoints) and the maximum was fifteen (and seventeen touchpoints), with an average of eleven steps (and fourteen touchpoints). An initial insight derived from mapping phase 1 was that a consistent number of students began their courses way before classes started, either by "investigating the topic", by "find(ing) more info from a google search or specific site", by "looking at the syllabus (online)", but they did not engage teaching or administrative staff beforehand.

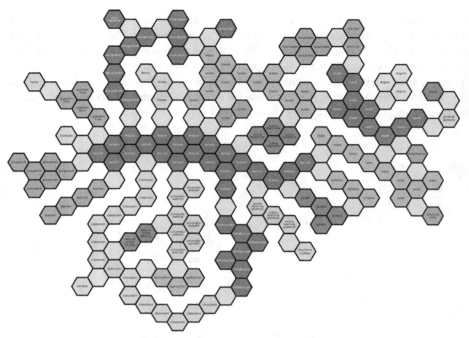

**Fig. 9.** Emergent ecosystem map from the "better courses" ecosystem mapping project (simplified)

The two sample paths in Fig. 8 exemplify these different behaviors: the top diagram sees the student engaging with a number of different online touchpoints, explicitly identified in the narrative, with the goal of "finding out" about the course; the bottom one abruptly begins with the student attending class.

Both paths veer to the right of the directional arrows (the bottom here as the two figures are turned ninety degrees clockwise), due to a prevalence of mostly stronger local digital touchpoints (university website, online syllabus, library catalog). Third-party, non-university platforms such as Facebook and Google Docs appear as intermediate steps between the content of lectures and homework leading to final assignments. Remote touchpoints indicating physical movement between locations such as the student's home and campus, where classrooms, the library, and the teacher's physical mailbox are located, are also named.

The emergent ecosystem map in Fig. 9 is a scaled down version of the final one realized during mapping phase 2 for the project: it only accounts for twenty-two out of fifty actor paths. The clusters of similarly colored tiles represent touch-points, for example "Groupwork", with the number of tiles equaling the number of times that specific touchpoint was instantiated as part of any of the twenty-two actor paths. In the case of "Groupwork", six times (Fig. 9).

The gray tiles represent the seams between two touchpoints. If any two touch-points have no seam between them, or are separated by empty slots or by more than one single seam tile, no actor reported moving between them and no relationship was identified:

the significance of this absence, whether positive, negative, or neutral, and whether it warrants or requires any type of design intervention, entirely depends on the context of the experience ecosystem being described.

As this is a compound view, the presence of a seam between two touchpoints means that at least one actor took that specific step, and that some piece of information allowing passage (personal, local, or remote, and contextually defined) was available, even if temporarily, within the ecosystem.

A first observation is that this ecosystem configures a blended space of action that is semantically contiguous but spread out both temporally and spatially. Its touchpoints include a number of different physical locations (campus, classrooms, library, homes), a number of digital environments (the online courseware platform, Facebook, Google Docs, the online library, online book stores, the university website, and more), a few actors (teachers, classmates), and course-related formal events (final assignment, group-work, lectures, exam). A few of these touchpoints were both significant sizewise and presented a high degree of integration: lectures (22, 16), books (13, 9), classrooms (15, 5), and exam (10, 6).

These are some of the additional observations that were offered during discussion of the map and that were later summarized in a list of possible leverage points that could be recast to "improve courses":

- "Lectures" were clearly a central moment for students. The fact that they had a seam from and towards "Teacher" and "Classroom" indicated a certain relevance of the physical nature of "being in class";
- no seam between "Teacher" and "Exam", even though teachers were and are directly responsible for the content of exams and for grading them;
- no seam between "Exam" and "Groupwork", even though project work accounted for 45% of the final credits in the course;
- no seam between "Syllabus" and "Books". Syllabi at JU contain course bibliography and teachers constantly point to them when asked about what needs to be read for a course. The map suggested this was not an effective strategy;
- Facebook was only mentioned once and was not particularly central to any experience. The data is from 2014–2015: anecdotal observations suggest its weight and degree of integration would be different if data were to be collected now;
- the introductory lecture ("Introduction") had some weight (7) but very little integration (3). Despite the rather central role given to it by staff and administration, students mostly only used it to receive information about how to access the online courseware platform.

It is important to stress that these observations were contextual to this specific inquiry and that Fig. 9 does not describe a generic "course" ecosystem that can be used to represent any "course" anywhere: this is a very specific ecosystem whose spatio-temporal dimension is an integral part of its ontology (what elements it contains), of its topology (how do these elements relate), of its volatility (when did these elements relate), and of its agency (what did these elements afford). Hence, its resulting map is more akin to a map of the world from a specific time than to a diagram. It is also both the outcome of a systemic design process and the originating moment for interventions that will vary greatly in scope and perspective.

## 10  Conclusions and Further Research

Even when adopting holistic perspectives, new media design practices still suffer organizational and methodological constraints that reproduce long-standing assumptions, inevitably pushing the design process towards what is ontologically a product-oriented approach. This results in unwanted reductionism and shallow symptom-level solutions.

We present here an expanded conceptualization of experience ecosystems as semantic blended spaces instantiated by the activities carried out by independent actors moving freely and at will between different products, services, devices, people, and locations in pursuit of individual goals. This conceptualization expands on work by Lindenfalk and Resmini (2019) and is based on extant previous work in the fields of information architecture and user experience design (Resmini and Rosati 2011; Resmini and Lacerda 2016; Benyon and Resmini 2017). We introduce a mapping methodology that can be used to capture and spatially describe the relational complexity of said ecosystems.

The conceptualization is anchored in the acknowledgment of three distinct cultural and socio-technical shifts that characterize the postdigital condition: i) the displacement of postmodernism as the cultural dominant (Kirby 2006); ii) the embodiment of digitality and the emergence of blended space (Benyon 2014); iii) the occurrence of a postdigital society (Pepperel and Punt 2000). It introduces a meta-level shift rooted in Van Gigch and Pipino's M3 for scientific and innovation processes that reformulates the problem space from being an organization-space problem (as the library is in Culén and Gasparini's case) to being a user- or actor-space problem (as the courses were in the JU course project example). In doing so, we:

- move the conversation to a bottom-up, actor-centered systemic way of doing that is rooted in systems thinking and in architectural rather than design conceptualizations;
- consider the environment actors move in systemically, as a blend of digital and physical, and one that is directly experienced and primarily understood through embodiment and the spatial relationships existing between elements;
- suggest that instead of focusing on what individual touchpoints in a specific sequence a generic "consumer" interacts with, a systemic approach has as it object of design the ecosystem itself, the semantic and spatial relationships of its components, their interplay, and the resulting mess.

By altering the way the problem space is framed, the conceptualization of experience ecosystems and the mapping methodology presented here provide new media design practices a non-reductionist approach to respond to the changed socio-technical and cultural landscape, thus providing increased value to both individual actors and organizations, and to strategically make long-term human-centered change a design priority by primarily:

- helping realign the practice, science and epistemology of new media design in response to the changes brought on by the postdigital condition;

- producing a view of the ecosystem that is not organizationally bound, thus removing some of the constraints that compel design practitioners to respond to systemic issues with organizational quick-fixes;
- providing a practice-friendly tool that acknowledges complexity and contributes to practice-based understanding of the object of design as a space of relationships by explicitly structuring it spatially and systemically.

The ecosystem maps resulting from the application of the methodology do not offer the narrative directionality of widely used tools such as customer journeys, but rather make use of spatial primitives such as proximity or separation in a way similar to world maps to provide the point of view of actors going through an experience by mapping the actors themselves, the tasks, touchpoints and seams within the ecosystem they instantiate through their actions while pursuing a desired future state.

# References

Akaka, M.A., Vargo, S.L.: Extending the context of service: from encounters to ecosystems. J. Serv. Market. **29**(6/7), 453–462 (2015)

Armson, R.: Growing Wings on the Way: Systems Thinking for Messy Situations. Triarchy Press Limited, Axminster (2011)

Bates, M.: Toward an integrated model of information seeking and searching. New Rev. Inf. Behav. Res. **3**(1), 1–15 (2002)

Bellmund, J.L.S., Gärdenfors, P., Moser, E.I., Doeller, C.F.: Navigating cognition: spatial codes for human thinking. Science **362**(6415) (2018)

Benn, Y., et al.: Navigating through digital folders uses the same brain structures as real world navigation. Sci. Rep. **5**(1), 1–8 (2015)

Benyon, D.R.: Spaces of interaction, places for experience. Morgan and Claypool, Milton Keynes (2014)

Benyon, D., Resmini, A.: User experience in cross-channel ecosystems. In: Proceedings of the British HCI Conference 2017. Sunderland (2017)

Bistagnino, L., Campagnaro, C.: Systemic design. In: Michalos, A.C. (ed.) Encyclopedia of Quality of Life and Well-Being Research. Springer, Dordrecht (2014)

Blomkvist, J., Segelström, F.: Benefits of external representations in service design: a distributed cognition perspective. Des. J. **17**(3), 331–346 (2014)

Bonsiepe, G.: Do Material ao Digital. Edgard Blucher, São Paulo (1969)

Borden, I., Fraser, M., Penner, B.: Forty Ways To Think About Architecture - Architectural History and Theory Today. Wiley, Hoboken (2014)

Cascone, K.: The aesthetics of failure: 'post-digital' tendencies in contemporary computer music. Comput. Music J. **24**(4), 12–18 (2000)

Chalmers, M.: Informatics, architecture and language. In: Munro, A., Höök, K., Benyon, D. (eds.) Social Navigation in Information Space. Springer, New York (1999)

Constantinescu, A.O., OReilly, J.X., Behrens, T.E.J.: Organizing conceptual knowledge in humans with a gridlike code. Science **352**(6292), 1464–1468 (2016)

Cooper, A.: The Inmates are Running the Asylum. SAMS Publishing, Carmel (2004)

Cramer, F.: What is post-digital? In: Berry, D.M., Dieter, M. (eds.) Postdigital Aesthetics: Art, Computation, and Design. Palgrave McMillian, Basingstoke (2015)

Culén, A.L., Gasparini, A.A.: Find a book! Unpacking customer journeys an academic library. In: Proceedings of ACHI 14, The Seventh International Conference on Advances in Computer-Human Interactions. Barcelona, Spain, pp. 89–95 (2014)

Davies, R.M.G., Saunders, R.G.: Applying systems theory to project management problems. Int. J. Project Manage. **6**(1), 19–26 (1988)

Deleuze, G., Guattari, F.: A Thousand Plateaus. University of Minnesota Press, Minneapolis (1987)

Design Council. A Study of the Design Process (2007). https://www.designcouncil.org.uk/sites/default/files/asset/document/ElevenLessons_Design_Council%20(2).pdf

Die Gute Fabrik Johann Sebastian Joust website. http://www.jsjoust.com/presskit/. Accessed 13 Apr 2020

Dourish, P.: Where the Action Is: The Foundations of Embodied Interaction. The MIT Press, Cambridge (2001)

Fauconnier, G., Turner, M.: The Way We Think: Conceptual Blending and the Mind's Hidden Complexities. Basic Books, New York (2002)

Floridi, L.: The Fourth Revolution. Oxford University Press, Oxford (2014)

Garrett, J.J.: The Elements of User Experience. New Riders, Indianapolis (2002)

Gharajedaghi, J.: Systems Thinking: Managing Chaos and Complexity: A Platform for Designing Business Architecture. Morgan Kaufmann, Burlington (2011)

Gibbons, S.: Journey Mapping 101. Norman Nielsen Group. https://www.nngroup.com/articles/journey-mapping-101/. Accessed 13 Apr 2020

Gray, D., Brown, S., Macalufo, J.: Gamestorming: A Playbook for Innovators, Rulebreakers, and Changemakers. O'Reilly, Sebastopol (2010)

Grossman, J.: Designing for Bridge Experiences. UXMatters. http://www.uxmatters.com/mt/archives/2006/06/designing-for-bridge-experiences.php. Accessed 13 Apr 2020

Hill, D.: Dark Matter and Trojan Horses: A Strategic Design Vocabulary. Strelka Press, Moscow (2014)

Hinton, A.: Linkosophy. https://andrewhinton.com/2008/04/15/linkosophy/. Accessed 13 Apr 2020

Horan, T.A.: Digital Places: Building Our City of Bits. Urban Land Institute (2000)

Hutcheon, L.: A Poetics of Postmodernism-History, Theory. Fiction. Routledge, New York (1988)

Imaz, M., Benyon, D.: Designing with Blends–Conceptual Foundations of Human-Computer Interaction and Software Engineering. The MIT Press, Cambridge (2007)

Institute for the Future. Blended Reality (2009). https://www.iftf.org/uploads/media/SR-122~2.PDF

Jenkins, H.: Convergence Culture. New York University Press, New York (2008)

Jenkins, S.: Welcome to the post-digital world: an exhilarating return to civility – via Facebook and Lady Gaga. The Guardian. https://www.theguardian.com/commentisfree/2011/dec/01/post-digital-world-web. Accessed 13 Apr 2020

Jones, P.H.: Systemic design principles for complex social systems. In: Metcalf, G.S. (ed.) Social Systems and Design. TSS, vol. 1, pp. 91–128. Springer, Tokyo (2014). https://doi.org/10.1007/978-4-431-54478-4_4

Kirby, A.: Digimodernism. Bloomsbury, London (2009)

Kirby, A.: The death of postmodernism and beyond. Philos. Now. **58**(1), 34–37 (2006)

Koivisto, M.: Frameworks for structuring services and customer experiences. In: Miettinen, S., Koivisto, M. (eds.) Designing Services with Innovative Methods. University of Art and Design Helsinki, Helsinki (2009)

Kolko, J.: Thoughts on Interaction Design. Morgan Kaufmann, Burlington (2011)

Lacerda, F., Lima-Marques, M.: Information architecture as a discipline: a methodological approach. In: Resmini, A. (ed.) Reframing Information Architecture. Human-Computer Interaction Series. Springer, New York (2014)

Lacerda, F., Lima-Marques, M., Resmini, A.: An information architecture framework for the Internet of Things. Philos. Technol. 1–18 (2018)

Lessig, L.: Remix: Making Art and Commerce Thrive in the Hybrid Economy. Bloomsbury Academic, London (2008)

Lindenfalk, B., Resmini, A.: Blended spaces, cross-channel ecosystems, and the myth that is services. In: Proceedings of ServDes 2016. Copenhagen. Aalborg University Copenhagen (2016)

Lindenfalk, B., Resmini, A.: Mapping an ambient assisted living service as a seamful cross-channel ecosystem. In: Pfannstiel, M., Rasche, M. (eds.) Service Design and Service Thinking in Healthcare and Hospital Management: Theory, Concepts, Practice, pp. 289–314. Springer, New York (2019)

Lucas, P., Ballay, J., McManus, M.: Trillions: Thriving in the Emerging Information Ecology. Wiley, Hoboken (2012)

Maccarone, D., Doody, S.: The UX of Learning UX is Broken. Medium. https://medium.com/@danmaccarone/the-ux-of-learning-ux-is-broken-f972b27d3273. Accessed 13 Apr 2020

Maldonado, T.: Reale e virtuale. Feltrinelli, Milano (1992)

Mallgrave, H.F.: Architecture and Embodiment. Routledge, Abingdon-on-Thames (2013)

Manovich, L.: The Language of New Media. The MIT Press, Cambridge (2001)

Manzini, E.: Design, When Everybody Designs. The MIT Press, Cambridge (2015)

Mitchell, W.J.: Me++: The Cyborg Self and the Networked City. The MIT Press, Cambridge (2004)

My (2012) Lifeboat #5: Richard Saul Wurman. In: My (1976). What Do We Use As a Lifeboat When the Ship Goes Down? Harper & Row. (Out of print). Reprinted in the Journal of Information Architecture. 3(2). http://journalofia.org/volume3/issue2/02-my/

Negroponte, N.: Beyond Digital. Wired. Issue 6(12) (2012). http://www.wired.com/wired/archive/6.12/negroponte.html

Norberg-Schulz, C.: Existence, Space and Architecture. Studio Vista, London (1971)

Norman, D.: Systems Thinking: A Product Is More Than the Product. Interactions (2009). http://www.jnd.org/dn.mss/systems_thinking_a_product_is_more_than_the_product.html

Norman, D., Nielsen, J.: (nd) The Definition of User Experience. Norman Nielsen Group. https://www.nngroup.com/articles/definition-user-experience/. Accessed 13 Apr 2020

Pepperel, R., Punt, M.: The Postdigital Membrane-Imagination, technology, and desire. Intellect Books, Bristol (2000)

Pine, B.J., Gilmore, J.H.: Welcome to the experience economy. Harvard Bus. Rev. July-August, 97–105. Reprint 98407 (1998)

Polaine, A., Løvlie, L., Reason, B.: Service Design–From Insight to Implementation. Rosenfeld Media, New York (2013)

Prensky, M.: Digital natives, digital immigrants. On the Horizon. 9(5). MCB University Press (2001)

Reeves, S., Ljungblad, S.: Proceedings of the Nottingham Symposium on Connecting HCI and UX (2018). https://doi:org/10.17639/8vez-c741. http://www.cs.nott.ac.uk/~pszsr/files/hci-ux-symposium-report.pdf

Resmini, A.: Les architectures d'information. Études de communication. 41(1), 31–56 (2013)

Resmini, A., Lacerda, F.: The architecture of cross-channel ecosystems-from convergence to experience. In: Proceedings of ACM MEDES 16-The 8th International Conference on Management of Digital Ecosystems (2016)

Resmini, A., Rosati, L.: Information architecture for ubiquitous ecologies. In: Proceedings of MEDES 09–The International Conference on Management of Emergent Digital Ecosystems. ACM (2009)

Resmini, A., Rosati, L.: Pervasive Information Architecture-Designing Cross-channel User Experiences. Morgan Kaufmann, Burlington (2011)

Rittel, H.W.J., Webber, M.: Dilemmas in a General Theory of Planning. Policy Sci. 4(2), 155–169 (1973)

Rosenfeld, L., Morville, P.: Information Architecture for the World Wide Web, 1st edn. O'Reilly, Sebastopol (1998)

Sangiorgi, D., Prendiville, A. (eds.): Designing for Service: Key Issues and New Directions. Bloomsbury Academic, London (2017)

Shostack, G.L.: How to design a service. Eur. J. Market. **16**(1), 49–63 (1982)

Shostack, G.L.: Designing services that deliver. Harvard Bus. Rev. January 1984

Skog, D.: The Dynamics of Digital Transformation: The Role of Digital Innovation. Ecosystems and Logics in Fundamental Organizational Change. Umeå University Press, Umeå (2019)

Spool, J.M.: Designing without a Designer. UIE. https://articles.uie.com/designing_without_a_designer/. Accessed 13 Apr 2020

Sterling, B.: Shaping Things. The MIT Press, Cambridge (2005)

Stickdorn, M., Schneider, J.: This is Service Design Thinking: Basics, Tools, Cases. BIS Publishers (2010)

Stroh, D.P.: Systems Thinking for Social Change. Chelsea Green Publishing, White River Junction (2015)

Swingle, M.K.: i-Minds. New Society Publishers, Gabriola Island (2016)

Tapscott, D., Williams, A.D.: Wikinomics: How Mass Collaboration Changes Everything. Portfolio, New York (2010)

Tate, T.: The Rise of Cross-channel UX Design. UX Matters. http://www.uxmatters.com/mt/archives/2011/10/the-rise-of-cross-channel-ux-design.php. Accessed 13 Apr 2020

Unger, R., Chandler, C.: A Project Guide to UX Design. New Riders, Berkeley (2012)

Van Gigch, J.P., Pipino, L.L.: In search of a paradigm for the discipline of information systems. Future Comput. Syst. **1**(1), 71–97 (1986)

Vargo, S.L., Akaka, M.A.: Value cocreation and service systems (re)formation: a service ecosystems view. Serv. Sci. **4**(3), 207–217 (2012)

Vargo, S.L., Lusch, R.F.: It's all B2B … and beyond: toward a systems perspective of the market. Ind. Market. Manage. **40**(2), 181–187 (2011)

Vermeulen, T., van den Akker, R.: Notes on metamodernism. J. Aesthetics Culture **2**(1), 5677 (2010)

Weiser, M.: The computer for the 21st century. Sci. Am. September issue. 94–104 (1991)

Wetter-Edman, K., Sangiorgi, D., Edvardsson, B., Holmlid, S., Grönroos, C., Mattelmäki, T.: Design for value co-creation: exploring synergies between design for service and service logic. Serv. Sci. **6**(2), 106–121 (2014)

Whittle, S., Foster, M.: Customer profiling: getting into your customer's shoes. Manage. Decis. **27**(6), 27–30 (1989)

Williams Goldenhagen, S.: Welcome to Your World: How the Built Environment Shapes Our Lives. HarperCollins, New York (2017)

Wurman, R.S.: Hats. Design Quarterly. No. 145. The MIT Press (1989)

# A Semantic-Based Strategy to Model Multimedia Social Networks

Kurosh Madani[1], Antonio M. Rinaldi[2,3]([✉]), and Cristiano Russo[1]

[1] LISSI Laboratory, Université Paris-Est, 3956 Champs-sur-Marne, EA, France
madani@u-pec.fr, cristiano.russo@univ-paris-est.fr
[2] Department of Electrical Engineering and Information Technologies,
University of Naples Federico II, Naples, Italy
antoniomaria.rinaldi@unina.it
[3] IKNOS-LAB Intelligent and Knowledge Systems-LUPT, Naples, Italy

**Abstract.** The social facet of information has a deciding role in our quotidian life. An abstract representation and a proper management of Online Social Networks (OSNs) constitute a new challenge for communities of researchers. In addition, the need of extending OSNs to Multimedia Social Networks (MSNs)come from the fact that the vast majority of data is unstructured and heterogeneous, making the reuse and integration of information effortful. In this chapter we propose a general high-level model to represent and manage MSNs. Our approach is based on property graph represented by a hypergraph structure due to the intrinsic multidimensional nature of social networks and semantic relations to better represent the networks contents. Using the proposed graph structure is helpful to single out several levels of knowledge analysing the relationships defined between nodes of the same or different type. Moreover, the introduction of low-level multimodal features and a formalization of their semantic meanings give a more comprehensive view of the social network structure and content. Using this approach we call the represented network Multimedia Semantic Social Networks ($MS^2N$). The proposed data model could be useful for several applications and we propose a case study on cultural heritage domain.

**Keywords:** Semantic Multimedia Bigdata · Social networks · GraphDB

## 1 Introduction

The social parts of web advancements and the emerge of numerous online networks and interpersonal organizations need of novel formal information structure to speak to this sort of data and the counters among substance. Also, the utilization of cell phones permits the making of a gigantic measure of information regarding volume, speed and assortment and [19] such universality change the Internet into an innovation channel for the conveyance of gigantic number of multimodal contents. To give an idea, data generation has been estimated at

© Springer-Verlag GmbH Germany, part of Springer Nature 2021
A. Hameurlain et al. (Eds.): TLDKS XLVII, LNCS 12630, pp. 29–50, 2021.
https://doi.org/10.1007/978-3-662-62919-2_2

2.5 Exabytes(1Exabyte=1.000.000Tb) of data per day [44]. Indeed, the advancement of mobile technologies and the improvement of Internet transfer speed abilities drove the change from basic text interchanges to a more rich and interactive media experience enabling clients to share sight and sound information, for example, video, pictures and content. Then again, the growing number of individuals utilizing Online Social Networks(OSNs) make new scenarios appear, where data must be gathered in an increasingly effective manner and molded into information. The new difficulties are for the most part focussed on issues, for example, information preparing, information stockpiling, information portrayal, and how information can be utilized for example mining, analysing user behaviours, among others. The combination of multimedia data and social networks has resulted in Multimedia Social Networks (MSNs) that support new ways of user-to-user and user-to-content interaction. In this context, user-shared multimedia objects are playing an increasingly central role, becoming an interesting trend in the literature. The term Multimedia Social Network (MSN) has been increasingly used over the last years together with Social Multimedia Network or Social Media Network to indicate information networks that leverage multimedia data in a social environment for different purposes [33, 40, 47, 66]. This kind of structure provides new perspective from which the multimedia context can be understood, but all these approaches focus only on single problems addressing specific aspects like the popularity and the status of given users [4], moral ethics [9], users' privacy protection [22]. The methodologies introduced so far are basically application-oriented and can deal only with data from a limited number of MSNs.

OSNs show a very rich structure. They don't have so many connections between content objects, while showing a significant number of connections among clients and content or between clients, if we confine ourselves to these sort of nodes. In this unique situation, we have at any rate, yet conceivably increasingly, two dimensions of connection among the elements included which permit to extricate learning from the system.

In this viewpoint, a standout amongst the most significant perspective to consider is the heterogeneity originating from MSNs.

Actually, the huge amounts of information delivered on a daily basis are for the most part unstructured and don't pursue any plans or norms which could be useful for structure general and dynamic models. In the most recent years numerous endeavours were made after this bearing and the outcome was a renewed enthusiasm for semantic-web related advancements and dialects.

These questions are stressed in the context of Semantic Web [6], because multimedia contents need to be semantically annotated in order to be discovered and exploited by services, agents and applications. However, bridging the gap between the concepts behind MSNs entities and the available low-level multimedia descriptors is an open problem and some approaches have been proposed to smooth it [56].

Despite the noteworthy advances made on automatic segmentation or structuring of multimedia content and the recognition of low-level features, the creation of multimedia content descriptions is yet risky both for the unpredictability of information and the subjectivity of portrayals created by human operators.

Ontology-oriented solutions have been widely used in order to reduce or possibly delete conceptual or terminological messes. Some approaches use linguistic matching to integrate in a unified and global common view the concepts related to entities coming from two or more different ontologies [13, 14, 16, 43, 55]. On the other hand, graph-based models have been exploited in order to define comprehensive models able to integrate networks that combine the information on users belonging to one or more social communities, with all the multimedia contents that can be generated and used within the related environments [17, 52–54]. Starting from all these considerations, we can argue that MSNs applications stress all the dimensions that typically characterize the 5Vs Big Data model:

- the *volume* of produced data is huge
- the speed(*velocity*) at which data is produced is dramatic
- many types of structured and unstructured data come from MSNs (*variety*)
- we cannot trust all data from MSNs (*veracity*)
- data can generate huge competitive advantages (*value*)

If we combine the issues related to MSN and Bigdata we have to define a data model with generic features to be used with different types of social networks and heterogeneous data and, at the same time, a scalable framework based on it that is able to manage large volume of information.

The model we propose presents novel functionalities based on the hypergraph structure. From a theoretical perspective it is a semantically-labelled graph, whose properties are appropriately weighted so as to express the quality of relations among the model elements. In particular, we are interested in representing in a formal way the knowledge in a MSN using multimedia *"signs"* defined as "something that stands for something, to someone in some capacity" [24]. Generally speaking, all of the ways in which information can be communicated as a message by any sentient, reasoning mind to another.

In our vision, we want to represent a Multimedia Semantic Social Networks ($MS^2N$). As a matter of fact, our approach allow to integrate heterogeneous information coming from OSNs, or related to multimedia sharing systems, like multimedia contents and relationships typical of such environments. The whole, efficiently managed with a unique semantic and social model.

This chapter is structured as follows. Section 2 provides a detailed overview of related works presented in literature; in Sect. 3 we describe the proposed model and its properties, with some using examples. Section 4 shows a real applicative case study in the cultural heritage domain. Eventually, Sect. 5 presents a discussion of our approach, the effectiveness of our novel model in different domains and illustrates the future work and possible improvements.

## 2   Related Work

These days, multimedia social networks, along with a standout amongst the most explored research topics. In late years, several models, methodologies and systems have been proposed using ontologies or graph-based models. There is not a clear distinction between these two kind of approaches because they could be see as two sides of the same coin but we prefer discuss them in separate a fashion in order to better present the literature and the difference with our framework. The methodologies dependent on ontologies give well-organized data to improve the exactness in information portrayal, mining and retrieval processes. Moreover, Semantic web technologies additionally encourage the integration of heterogeneous information sources and formats therefore, well-structured formalism are crucial to provide advanced methodology for several aspects in the context of data and application management.

One of the first proposed system [58] uses ontologies for images semantic annotation. The system has some tools to annotate photos and search for specific images. An approach to build a multimedia ontology using MPEG-7 descriptors has been proposed in [32]. In [36], the authors present a knowledge infrastructure for multimedia analysis, which is composed by a visual description ontology and a multimedia structure ontology, while [31] shows how the definition of a top-level and extensible ontology is an essential step for knowledge engineering tasks proposing the independence of ontology from any domain-specific metadata vocabulary. In [2], the author developed a core multimedia ontology based on a re-engineering of MPEG-7, and using DOLCE as foundational ontology. An approach for multimedia ontology modeling is presented in [39], in which the authors combine semantic hierarchy of multimedia content and MPEG-7 standard to create a multimedia ontology proposing a support to spatial-temporal relation of multimedia data. An ontology mediated multimedia information retrieval system is described in [60], where a combination of logic-based strategies and multimedia feature-based similarity are used. An end-to-end adaptive framework based on an ontological model has been presented in [59]. The framework aims at enhancing the management, retrieval and visualization of multimedia information resources based on semantic techniques. The relevant data are retrieved using metadata formats such as MPEG-7, RDF and OWL taking advantage of the semiautomatic annotations created by the system. The framework implements also a P2P method to share data and metadata with other systems.

A framework for the semantic retrieval of multimedia contents based on domain ontologies, user preferences and context analysis is presented in [37]. Wang et al. [64] investigate on the selection of semantic concepts for lifelogging which includes reasoning on semantic networks using a density-based approach. In [49,62], the state-of-the-art techniques in semantic multimedia retrieval are highlighted and discussed addressing the performances of multimedia retrieval systems based on combination of techniques, such as low-level multimedia feature extraction and common semantic representation schemes. A study about several multimedia retrieval techniques based on ontologies in the semantic web is discussed in [35] where the authors perform a comparison of the used techniques to put in evidence the advantages of text, image, video and audio based retrieval systems. Many approaches are based on deep neural networks for image detection [23,26,61]. Image similarity search is witnessed in [42] and [3] where the authors present a system intended for scalable web datasets.

These works don't address as a whole the problem of using multimedia from a complete ontological point of view and the knowledge represented by this kind of systems is usually only organized around metadata or low-level features without a comprehensive knowledge model. In addition, very few studies have been made in using multimedia ontologies along with social components.

The use of ontologies taking into account multimedia components is still limited and often they are too much oriented to information related with low-level descriptors, losing in generality. Furthermore, they don't consider at all the social component.

One of the first attempt to include this aspect in semantic networks is presented in [45] by means of the widely known "folksonomies" to derive better semantic schemes in particular types of social contexts.

Several complex models for social information networks, embedding multimedia data, have been introduced and it is possible to classify them on the base of four main categories. The first category includes all models that consider social networks as a graph composed by heterogeneous vertices, such as users, tags, multimedia objects and so on. In [50], the authors propose an algorithm that combines both context and content network information for multimedia annotation purposes. Jin et al. [34] use network and content-based information to propose a new image similarity concept. The second type of approaches is based on bipartite graphs. Zhu et al. [67] propose a user-content bipartite graph model to compute the influence diffusion in a social network, while Gao et al. [27] exploit a bipartite graph - composed by users' group and objects - in order to address a consensus maximization problem. The third category uses tripartite graphs. In [41], a strategy that exploits users, tags and resources for clustering goals is proposed. A similar approach is then proposed by Qi et al. [51], they leverage a tripartite graph in order to cluster multimedia objects. In [21], the authors propose a different approach that allows to model the interaction existing between user, query and videos in order to define a personalized video recommendation. Eventually, the last group contains the approaches based on hypergraph theory. In [10] the authors propose an approach based on hypergraph network in order to develop a music recommendation exploiting both social and acoustic based information. In [1], authors propose a tensor decomposition approach for communities learning in 3-uniform hypergraph. Finally, a news recommendation system via hypergraph learning is described in [38].

Regarding to the classifications of these works, only few of them have models for social networks, and a small number of them consider multimedia objects as a structured data type. They rather focus on specific aspects and applications related to MSNs, like for example user behavior analysis in online social networks in [47], overlapping community detection in [65], information propagation over the network, development of a trust model for multimedia social networks [66] or measuring influence in online social network [67].

In our model we propose a clear distinction between the basic components of an MSN and how these components are related among them. Moreover, the use of a semantic ontology based model allows the representation of all possible relations to express the meanings of "signs" used to represent MSN knowledge. Other innovations of the proposed approach are the following:

- it is independent from specific application fields;
- it provides linguistic, syntactic and semantic relationships, to give a well defined meaning to generic relationships typical of the most common social networks; these relationships are provided from the upper ontology model as it will be described in Sect. 3.
- it adds weights to the relations to better represent and quantify the relationship strength among entities and allow the design of applications that use measures on them, such as recommendation systems, ranking metrics, social networking analysis, collaboration systems.

Moreover, we implement our model using a graph based NoSQL technology and we also provide a real use case.

## 3  The Proposed Model

In this section we will depict our model for multimedia social networks defining involved entities, relations and semantics. In our vision, an MSN can be seen as a graph, made of hubs and connections between them. The hubs, or nodes, are categorized according three different types, as introduced in the following:

- *Users (U)*: this kind of node represents, persons, institutions, companies, organizations , bots, and other entities that are part of a social network. Information about user profile, preferences and other features of these entities are also are also considered in our model as attributes.
- *Concepts (C)*: as the name suggests, anything having a specific meaning in real life. It is represented using signs.
- *Multimedia (M)*: all kind of resources collected from an MSN, like images, videos, files, posts, etc. fall into this category. From a general point of view, it is any kind of sign used to represent a concept

On the other hand, starting from the graphs theory, relationships can be classified dividing them into categories based on their domain and co-domain, i.e. the types of nodes involved in the relation.

We define the following general categories for relationships:

- *User to User*: these relationships represent all the interactions between users, like friendship, following, co-working, similar to, etc.
- *User to Multimedia*: it represents the interaction that a user has with multimedia objects, as posting, like, comment, etc.
- *Multimedia to User*: the inverse of the previous category.
- *Multimedia to Multimedia*: with this type we this category we define all the relationships between multimedia objects. For example, a possible kind of relationship is to link an audio track to an image, a caption to a video, etc.
- *Multimedia to Concept*: a multimedia object could represent one or more concepts. We call this relationship *hasConcept*.
- *Concept to Multimedia*: the inverse of the previous category. The name of this relationship is *hasMM*.

- *Concept to concept*: all the possible relationships between concepts from a linguistic a semantic point of view as hyperonymy, hyponymy, meronymy, holonymy, etc.

These relations follow a taxonomy which identifies their nature. We have three main categories, namely *semantic-linguistic*, *social* and *similarity*.

Table 1 shows a schematic description of relationship and macro-categories previously defined and in Fig. 1 the proposed model has been drawn.

**Table 1.** Taxonomy of relationships

|  | Semantic-Linguistic | Social | Similarity |
|---|---|---|---|
| User to User |  | ✓ | ✓ |
| User to Multimedia |  | ✓ |  |
| Multimedia to Multimedia |  |  | ✓ |
| Multimedia to Concept | ✓ |  |  |
| Multimedia to User |  | ✓ |  |
| Concept to Multimedia | ✓ |  |  |
| Concept to Concept | ✓ | ✓ |  |
| Concept to Multimedia | ✓ |  |  |

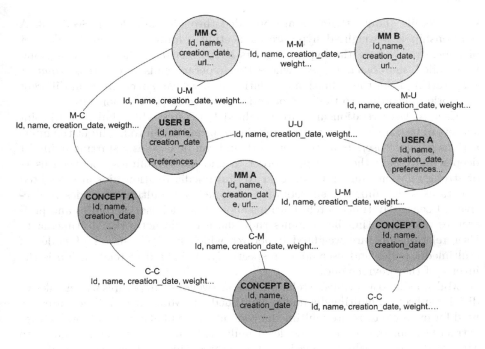

**Fig. 1.** $MS^2N$ Model

## 3.1 Model Description

The proposed model is based on the graph theory. We provide in the following a context for it giving definitions of Multimedia Social Network and relationships according to our vision previously described; then we present some metrics useful to recognize network topology and structure. Last considerations are left for showing some practical examples which help a detailed understanding on the possible uses and capabilities of our model. A Multimedia Social Network, or MSN, is a graph represented by a triple of vertices (nodes), edges (arcs) linking two or more nodes in the network and weights defined on each arc in the network. Weights values are normalized in the range $[0, 1]$ and represents the strength of the considered link. Both nodes and arcs have their own sets of properties which characterize them. These properties are represented by attributes. For each kind of node or arc, there is a number of mandatory attributes, while others can be optionally defined for a specific application. All nodes and arcs have attributes with regards to of their type. A subset of attributes is listed in the following:

- *id*: this attribute gives an unique identification to a node or an arc in the network, i.e. two nodes or two arcs cannot have the same id.
- *name*: it is a representative term for a node
- *description*: it is a text field used to describe a node.
- *date_of_creation*: this attribute stores the time in which an entity in the network was created.

Other details about attributes are provided through examples in Sect. 3.3. A relationship is a weighted hyperarc connecting a finite set of nodes. The set of nodes from where the hyperarc starts is the *owner* of the relationship and it is called *source set*, the set where the hyperarc ends is called *destination set*. Starting from the definition of relationship, we can specialize it in different categories, according to the type of nodes involved in the relationship.

User to User relationships are weighted hyperarcs which link two disjoint subsets of user nodes. User to User relationships are useful to highlight the interactions between users in a social network and can be used as a starting point for deeper analysis of the network in order to find hidden affinities between users or strong relations among them. User to Multimedia relationships are weighted hyperarcs which link two subsets of user nodes and multimedia nodes respectively. User to Multimedia relationships allow to model user' activities and preferences about multimedia contents they share in the network. Multimedia to User relationships are weighted hyperarcs which link two subset of nodes of multimedia nodes and user nodes respectively. This kind of relationship is the inverse of the previous one.

Multimedia to Multimedia relationships are weighted hyperarcs which link two disjoint subsets of multimedia nodes. Multimedia to Multimedia relationships are used for example to relate multimedia contents by exploiting metadata, features extracted from the contents, low-level multimedia descriptors, etc. Concept to Multimedia relationships are weighted hyperarcs which link two subsets of concept nodes and multimedia nodes respectively. This relationship, named *hasMM*, is used to define a link between the Concept and Multimedia nodes. Multimedia to Concept relationships are weighted hyperarcs which link two subsets of multimedia nodes and concept nodes respectively. With this relationship we are able to associate a multimedia "sign" to a set of concepts. As previously described, we use the *hasConcept* property defined in the top level ontological model.

In the model each multimedia is related to the concept it represents by the *hasConcept*, whereas a concept is related to multimedia that represent it using *hasMM*. Concept to Concept relationships are weighted hyperarcs which link two disjoint subsets of concept nodes. This kind of link is used to exploit the semantic and linguistic properties between Concept nodes. The use of general top level ontological model for Multimedia and Concepts [56] allows us to exploit all the potentials of ontologies, highlighting the importance of a strong formalization and organization of data. Linguistic, syntactic and semantic relationships are inherited from the upper-level ontology model above discussed. In this way we can extend the model and improve the representation of our MSN. In fact, an ontology containing details of Audio-Visual Features, Words and their related properties, like for example'entailment','cause' or'verbGroup', could be linked to the top-level ontological model made of Concepts and Multimedia Objects.

## 3.2 Metrics

Several studies in the field of social network analysis have highlighted the importance of understanding the network topology and the relative importance of nodes in a network [28, 29]. In fact, the use of a quantitative analysis could be useful to rank nodes and find social network structures. The proposed model can be exploited to retrieve information about the network structure, the degree of interaction between two or more users, their distances or to extract a ranking score about topics by means of metrics defined for a MSN. The *density* of a specific social network is the result of the division between the number of all the connections between the nodes and the number of potential connections within the same set of nodes [5]. Dense networks are typical of small, stable communities, not connected to external contacts and with a high level of social compactness. On the other hand, loose social networks are organized into larger and more unstable communities that have many external contacts and show a lack of social cohesion [63]. *Member closeness centrality* is the measure of the proximity of a single user to all the other users in the network. A user with high closeness centrality is a central member, and therefore has frequent interactions with other members of the network. A central member of a community tends to be under pressure to maintain the rules of that network, while a peripheral member of the network (i.e. with a low closeness centrality score) is not exposed to this pressure [46]. *Multiplexity* is the number of separate social connections between any two users. It has been defined as the "interaction of exchanges within and across relationships" [7]. We explicit point out that using our formalization a number of additional metrics could be defined in different applicative contexts. A single interaction between individuals, such as a shared workplace, is an uniplex relationship. An interaction between individuals is multiplex when those individuals interact in multiple social contexts [5]. For instance, *John* is the boss of *Bob*, and they have no relationship outside work, so their relationship is uniplex. However, while *Albert* is both *Bob*'s co-worker and friend, so the relationship between *Bob* and *Albert* is multiplex, since they interact with each other in more than a single social context.

### 3.3    Examples

We are now in the position of describe a subset of possible social community relations that can be defined with our model. We introduce some real examples to investigate some domains of interest and their range of validity.

**User to User Relationships** In order to characterize the interaction between users in a MSN, several types of relationships can be defined among them.

*Example 1.* Co-worker relationship
A *co-worker* relationship is a user to user relationship, useful for modelling the professional level of interaction between two users of a social community. Typical real examples of this relationship can be found in *LinkedIn*.

Figure 2a, shows an example of co-worker relationship. One possible exploit could be the discovering of common professional interests between two or more individuals which do not know each other but have common colleagues as in the case of *User A* and *User C*.

*Example 2.* Following relationship
A *following* relationship is a user to user relationship, useful for modelling the interest of a user w.r.t other user's activities in a social community. Typical real examples of this relationship can be found in *Twitter*.

The following relationship can also be considered as a strong and reliable indicator of users having great popularity and influence among the community.

*Example 3.* Friendship relationship
A *friendship* relationship is a user to user relationship, useful for modelling a strong interaction between two users in a social community. Typical real examples of this relationship can be found in *Facebook* and *Google+*.

Figure 2b, shows an example of friendship relationship. One possible exploit could be the discovering of new friends starting from common friends as in the case of *User B* and *User C*, having *User A* as a common friend. It is worthy to note that the verse of the link is used to define who sent the friendship request and who received it.

*Example 4.* Acquaintance relationship
An *acquaintance* relationship is a user to user relationship, useful for modeling a weak interaction between two users in a social community.

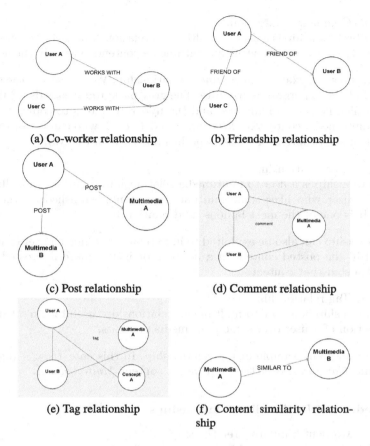

(a) Co-worker relationship      (b) Friendship relationship

(c) Post relationship      (d) Comment relationship

(e) Tag relationship      (f) Content similarity relationship

**Fig. 2.** M$S^2$N relationships

For instance, two or more users in a multimedia social network exchanging occasional messages or cooperating for solving tasks can be considered as acquaintances. It is important to note that this relation is totally independent from the friendship relation, since two user can be acquaintances, being or not friends at the same time. More interesting, also the contrary can be true, i.e. two user can be friends without knowing each other.

## User to Multimedia Relationships

*Example 5.* Post relationship
A *post* relationship is a user to multimedia relationship, useful for modeling the action of a user publishing some multimedia contents on his/her wall.

Figure 2c, shows an example of post relationship. One possible exploit could be that the discovering of new friends that posted similar multimedia contents or finding similar contents shared in the MSN that could be interesting for a user.

*Example 6.* Comment relationship
A *comment* relationship is a user to multimedia relationship, useful for modelling the action of a user in commenting on multimedia contents posted in the network.

Figure 2d, shows an example of comment relationship. We can see all the expressive power of the hypergraph structure. The gray background stands for the new space in which nodes are immersed and the hyperarc allows to connect *User A* with the multimedia content *Multimedia A* and *User B*, who can be for example the owner of such content or a user who has posted it in the MSN.

*Example 7.* Like relationship
A *like* relationship is a user to multimedia relationship, useful for modelling the action of a user who likes some multimedia contents published on the social network. It is one of the most famous used relationships.

This relationship can also be exploited to investigate how much a user is actually interested in the posted content in a network or if it is more interested in the user that posted that content.

*Example 8.* Tag relationship
A *tag* relationship is a user to multimedia relationship, useful for modeling the tagging action of a user over some multimedia contents.

Figure 2e shows an example of tag relationship. In this case *User A* tags both *User B* and *Concept A* over the multimedia content *Multimedia A*.

## Multimedia to Multimedia Relationships

*Example 9.* Content Similarity relationship
A *Content similarity* relationship is a multimedia to multimedia relationship, useful for modeling the similarity between multimedia contents in the MSN.

Figure 2f, shows an example of content similarity relationship. The similarity could be expressed for example by means of low-level multimedia features, tags present on the content or whatever is considered valid measure for a similarity assessment.

*Example 10.* Synonymy relationship
A *synonymy* relationship is a multimedia to multimedia relationship, linking two multimedia objects representing the same concept.

It is useful to note that the synonymy relationship is not a relationship between concepts, but it is a relationship between different "sign" representing the same concept. Hence, we have defined here this kind of link as an extension of the commonly known synonymy relationship to multimedia objects.

**Multimedia to Concept and Concept to Multimedia Relationships**

*Example 11.* HasConcept relationship

A *hasConcept* relationship is a multimedia to concept relationship. It links the multimedia object with one or more Concept, adding semantic and linguistic capabilities to the analysis that can be performed on the meaning of the multimedia represent.

*Example 12.* HasMM relationship

A *hasMM* relationship is a concept to multimedia relationship. It links the Concept with one or more Multimedia Objects, adding multimedia information to specific concepts.

**Concept to Concept Relationships.** In our framework we use a semantic approach to represent relations between concepts in the MSN. Some examples of the possible semantic relations are:

*Example 13.* Hyponymy relationship

A *hyponymy* relationship is a concept to concept relationship, useful for describing a Concept more specific with respect to another Concept. For example the Concept *snake* is a hyponym of the Concept *animal*

*Example 14.* Hypernymy relationship

A *hyPeronymy* relationship is a concept to concept relationship, inverse of hyponymy relationship.

*Example 15.* Meronymy relationship

A *meronnymy* relationship is a concept to concept relationship, useful for describing a concept that is part of another concept, like for example a *page* is meronym of a *book*.

*Example 16.* Holonymy relationship

A *holonymy* relationship is a concept to concept relationship, inverse of meronym relationship.

## 4 Case Study

In this Section we will show how our model can be used in a real scenario introducing a possible application related to cultural heritage. In our scenario the network is composed of tourists which are interested in visiting cultural heritage sites around the world, like museums or, more generally, cities. Each user has some preferences about places, and can interact with other users sharing his/her opinions. Users may post multimedia contents(e.g. text, photos, videos) of places they are visiting or they would like to visit.

In addition the presence of geospatial and temporal information extends the number of functionalities for the application also allowing spatial queries.

With respect to our model, the entities involved in our scenario are defined on the basic nodes previously defined, as:

- *Tourists* ⇒ Users: every person interested in cultural heritage, being either a tourist or a visitor looking for Places.
- *Places* ⇒ Concepts: a place is a generic term, used in this context to identify each entity containing cultural heritage, i.e. cities and attractions to explore like museums, collections, events, etc.
- *Text, photos, videos* ⇒ Multimedia Objects: every content shared by social network users related to places, photos and videos of paintings, landscapes, etc.

We create a dataset for our application using the graph database *Neo4J* by means of *Cypher* queries. Figure 3 shows an excerpt of the used dataset. Graph visualization is a challenging task in data representation and analysis [11,12,15,18] and in our case we use *ScreenCast*, the native Neo4J browser to show and highlighting some capabilities of the proposed model. In the picture there are 14 nodes and 17 relationships between them covering most of the features of the model above discussed. For example we have that the user "Albert" is friend of "Bob", who likes the place "Naples", while two similar images (multimedia nodes) of skylines in place "Dubai" and place "New York" are linked by the content similarity relationship.

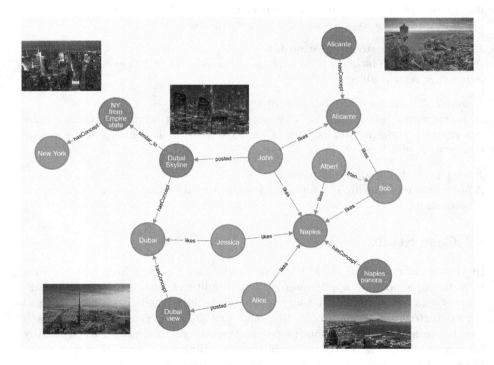

**Fig. 3.** Excerpt database for tourists recommendation

Low-level multimedia features represent the information extracted from an image in terms of numerical values, also often referred as descriptor.

For our purpose, we decided to store global descriptor *Pyramid of Histograms of Orientation Gradients(PHOG)*, and the *Joint Composite Descriptor(JCD)* due to their performances [57]:

- PHOG: The basic idea [8] is to represent an image by its local shape and the spatial layout. This descriptor consists in a histogram of orientation gradients over each image subregion at each resolution level. The distance between two PHOG image descriptors reflects the property of images to contain similar shapes in the correspondent spatial layout.
- JCD: It is a combination of two *MPEG-7* [20,48] descriptors, CEDD and FCTH. Based on the fact that the color information given by the two descriptors comes from the same fuzzy system, it is assumed that joining the descriptors would result in the combining of texture areas carried by each descriptor. JCD is composed of seven texture areas, with each of those made up of 24 subregions that correspond to color areas (the 24-bins histogram of FCTH and CEDD).
- Auto color correlogram: This color feature has been presented in [30]. The main characteristics of the Auto Color Correlogram feature are: spatial correlation of colors; possibility to be used to describe global distribution of local color spatial correlation; low computational effort; small size of the feature.
- Edge histogram descriptor: This feature [25] represents the spatial distribution of five types of edges, that is four directional edges and one non-directional edge. According to the MPEG-7 standard, the image retrieval performance is significantly improved combining the edge descriptor with other descriptors such as the color histogram feature. This descriptor is scale invariant and supports rotation invariant and rotation sensitive matching operations.

These multimedia descriptors are used as a weighted similarity metric for evaluating the content similarity score between images. The feature descriptors above discussed belong to the category of global features, i.e. the numerical vectors extracted take into account the whole content of an image. Such descriptors suffer from some problems in similarity matching because of their nature, for example different condition in lights or the type of picture could affect the final result. The use of different kind of features, such as local features (SIFT, SURF) or deep features would likely give much better results in term of image similarity matching. In our approach, we decided to use the global features for two important reasons to take into account when considering multimedia social networks. The first one is the size of the feature to be stored. The global features considered are much more compact and hence require less space in the knowledge graph when they have to be stored. In a social network scenario considering millions images this is a crucial issue that need to be addressed. The second reason is the computational efficiency, since the matching results can be obtained faster with global features with respect to others.

## 4.1  Functionalities

In the following we will show some of functionalities that can be implemented
in our scenario using the proposed model. The application might be seen as a
recommendation system

**Trending Places.** The first and more intuitive operation is to find trending
places i.e. the most visited and liked by users. In order to achieve this task,
we need to query our database searching for places, for example, with higher
number of likes relationships.

Figure 4 shows the results obtained for a simple *Cypher* query.

```
MATCH p=()-[r:likes]->(c:Concept)
RETURN c
```

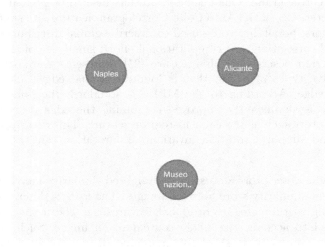

**Fig. 4.** Query result for trending places

Adding some complexity to the query it could be also possible to rank places or
select only those above a certain threshold and so on.

**Friend Suggestion.** A tourist can discover new friends by means of classical
ways used in social networks like for example common friends, neighbours, or
common interests with other users for similar places or multimedia contents.

This information can be obtained as the result of the following query:

```
MATCH (m:Multimedia),(m2:Multimedia)
WHERE m.feature=m2.feature
WITH m,m2
MATCH p=(u:User)-[r:posted]->(m),(m2)
RETURN u
```

It highlights the possible relationship of friendship that can be established between users *Alice* and *John* since they posted two similar images of paintings *Flagellazione di Cristo* and *La Zingarella*, which are both exposed at *Museo Nazionale di Capodimonte*.

**Place Suggestion.** A tourist can find new places in which him/her that could be interested. A place can be considered interesting for a user if it is close or similar to places he/she visited, if it is related to multimedia objects similar to multimedia objects he/she liked, posted, etc. or if it is a place related with friends' activities.

In this case we use the relation of similarity defined between multimedia objects posted by the user, that is the painting *Flagellazione di Cristo* exposed at *Museo Nazionale di Capodimonte* and the painting Martirio di Sant'Orsola exposed at Palazzo Zevallos, hence possibly being an interesting place to visit for user *John*. The following query characterize the depicted scenario.

```
MATCH p=(u:User)-[r:posted]->
(m:Multimedia)
WITH p
MATCH (m)-[r2:similar_to]->
(m2:Multimedia)
WITH m2
MATCH (m2)-[r3:hasConcept]->(c:Concept)
RETURN c
```

The previous examples have been used to better explain our model and its efficiency in representing real applicative scenario.

## 5   Conclusion and Future Work

The consistent generation of computerized data originating from various ICT sources gives us tons of data, from which we could extricate valuable and helpful information. This issue turns out to be more featured presenting mixed media information deriving from social networks. In this setting the use of formal model to represent and oversee data is a silver bullet task to implement intelligent information systems. The aim of our work has been to provide a novel model to represent in a formal and complete way the structure and knowledge of a generalized multimedia social networks. In this chapter we have portrayed the issue of data heterogeneity and the effect of the multimedia social networks have had in most recent couple of years. In this scenario, we propose a formal model combining top-level ontology models and property graph represented by a hypergraph structure to take into account both semantic, multimedia and social aspects. We demonstrate a genuine application to show that our model appropriately handles the heterogeneous data that can be recovered from existing social networks in a complex scenario as digital cultural heritage. Nonetheless, given its highly abstract definition, our model is suitable as well for a number of different applications by reification of the Concept nodes, as we have shown in our case study. Possible ideas for other applications could be derived for user signaling in emergency contexts, reviews of specific items, etc. The future works will aim to extend the current model providing new capabilities, such as the inclusion of sounds and voices as audio features. Moreover, we plan to extend the similarity search between videos, which are common contents in online social networks. There are other research lines to be examined as the implementation of a system based on our model in different applications areas with a specific interest on spatio-temporal data, the definition of strategies for heterogeneous knowledge sources using our model and, the implementation of a very large knowledge base to support intelligent information systems. In addition, we are also interested in finding more efficient techniques to visualize and analyse data stored in very large knowledge bases and to define strategies and perform experiments for the evaluation of our model and approaches.

# References

1. Anandkumar, A., Sedghi, H.: Learning mixed membership community models in social tagging networks through tensor methods. arXiv preprint arXiv:1503.04567 (2015)
2. Arndt, R., Troncy, R., Staab, S., Hardman, L.: COMM: a core ontology for multimedia annotation. In: Staab, S., Studer, R. (eds.) Handbook on Ontologies. IHIS, pp. 403–421. Springer, Heidelberg (2009). https://doi.org/10.1007/978-3-540-92673-3_18
3. Batko, M., et al.: Building a web-scale image similarity search system. Multimed. Tools Appl. **47**(3), 599–629 (2010)
4. Benevenuto, F., Rodrigues, T., Cha, M., Almeida, V.: Characterizing user behavior in online social networks. In: Proceedings of the 9th ACM SIGCOMM Conference on Internet Measurement Conference. pp. 49–62. ACM (2009)
5. Bergs, A.: Social networks and historical sociolinguistics: studies in morphosyntactic variation in the Paston letters (1421–1503), vol. 51. Walter de Gruyter (2005)
6. Berners-Lee, T., Hendler, J., Lassila, O., et al.: The semantic web. Sci. Am. **284**(5), 28–37 (2001)
7. Bliemel, M.J., McCarthy, I.P., Maine, E.: An integrated approach to studying multiplexity in entrepreneurial networks. Entrepreneurship Res. J. **4**(4), 367–402 (2014)
8. Bosch, A., Zisserman, A., Munoz, X.: Representing shape with a spatial pyramid kernel. In: Proceedings of the 6th ACM International Conference on Image and Video Retrieval. pp. 401–408. ACM (2007)

9. Brass, D.J., Butterfield, K.D., Skaggs, B.C.: Relationships and unethical behavior: a social network perspective. Acad. Manage. Rev. **23**(1), 14–31 (1998)
10. Bu, J., Tan, S., Chen, C., Wang, C., Wu, H., Zhang, L., He, X.: Music recommendation by unified hypergraph: combining social media information and music content. In: Proceedings of the 18th ACM International Conference on Multimedia. pp. 391–400. ACM (2010)
11. Caldarola, E., Picariello, A., Rinaldi, A.: Experiences in wordnet visualization with labeled graph databases. Commun. Comput. Inf. Sci. **631**, 80–99 (2016)
12. Caldarola, E., Rinaldi, A.: Big data visualization tools: a survey: the new paradigms, methodologies and tools for large data sets visualization. In: DATA 2017 - Proceedings of the 6th International Conference on Data Science, Technology and Applications. pp. 296–305 (2017)
13. Caldarola, E., Rinaldi, A.: A multi-strategy approach for ontology reuse through matching and integration techniques. Adv. Intell. Syst. Comput. **561**, 63–90 (2018)
14. Caldarola, E.G., Picariello, A., Rinaldi, A.M.: An approach to ontology integration for ontology reuse in knowledge based digital ecosystems. In: Proceedings of the 7th International Conference on Management of Computational and Collective Intelligence in Digital EcoSystems. pp. 1–8. ACM (2015)
15. Caldarola, E.G., Picariello, A., Rinaldi, A.M.: Big graph-based data visualization experiences: The wordnet case study. In: 2015 7th International Joint Conference on Knowledge Discovery, Knowledge Engineering and Knowledge Management (IC3K), vol. 1, pp. 104–115. IEEE (2015)
16. Caldarola, E.G., Rinaldi, A.M.: An approach to ontology integration for ontology reuse. In: 2016 IEEE 17th International Conference on Information Reuse and Integration (IRI), pp. 384–393. IEEE (2016)
17. Caldarola, E.G., Rinaldi, A.M.: Modelling multimedia social networks using semantically labelled graphs. In: 2017 IEEE International Conference on Information Reuse and Integration (IRI) pp. 493–500 (2017)
18. Caldarola, E.G., Rinaldi, A.M.: Improving the visualization of wordnet large lexical database through semantic tag clouds. In: 2016 IEEE International Congress on Big Data (BigData Congress), pp. 34–41. IEEE (2016)
19. Caldarola, E.G., Rinaldi, A.M.: Big data: A survey-the new paradigms, methodologies and tools. In: DATA. pp. 362–370 (2015)
20. Chang, S.F., Sikora, T., Purl, A.: Overview of the mpeg-7 standard. IEEE Trans. Circuits Syst. Video Technol. **11**(6), 688–695 (2001)
21. Chen, B., Wang, J., Huang, Q., Mei, T.: Personalized video recommendation through tripartite graph propagation. In: Proceedings of the 20th ACM International Conference on Multimedia. pp. 1133–1136. ACM (2012)
22. Cheng, Y., Park, J., Sandhu, R.: Preserving user privacy from third-party applications in online social networks. In: Proceedings of the 22nd International Conference on World Wide Web. pp. 723–728. WWW 2013 Companion, ACM, New York, USA (2013). https://doi.org/10.1145/2487788.2488032
23. Cireşan, D.C., Giusti, A., Gambardella, L.M., Schmidhuber, J.: Mitosis detection in breast cancer histology images with deep neural networks. In: Mori, K., Sakuma, I., Sato, Y., Barillot, C., Navab, N. (eds.) MICCAI 2013. LNCS, vol. 8150, pp. 411–418. Springer, Heidelberg (2013). https://doi.org/10.1007/978-3-642-40763-5_51
24. Danesi, M., Perron, P.: Analyzing Cultures. Indiana University Press, Bloomington, Indiana, USA (1999)
25. Deselaers, T., Keysers, D., Ney, H.: Features for image retrieval: an experimental comparison. Inf. Retrieval **11**(2), 77–107 (2008)

26. Erhan, D., Szegedy, C., Toshev, A., Anguelov, D.: Scalable object detection using deep neural networks. In: Proceedings of the IEEE Conference on Computer Vision and Pattern Recognition. pp. 2147–2154 (2014)

27. Gao, J., Liang, F., Fan, W., Sun, Y., Han, J.: A graph-based consensus maximization approach for combining multiple supervised and unsupervised models. IEEE Trans. Knowl. Data Eng. **25**(1), 15–28 (2013). https://doi.org/10.1109/TKDE.2011.206

28. Ghali, N., Panda, M., Hassanien, A.E., Abraham, A., Snasel, V.: Social networks analysis: tools, measures and visualization, pp. 3–23. Springer, London (2012) https://doi.org/10.1007/978-1-4471-4054-2_1

29. Ghosh, R., Lerman, K.: Parameterized centrality metric for network analysis. Phys. Rev. E **83**(6), 066118 (2011)

30. Huang, J., Kumar, S.R., Mitra, M., Zhu, W.J., Zabih, R.: Image indexing using color correlograms. In: Proceedings., 1997 IEEE Computer Society Conference on Computer Vision and Pattern Recognition, pp. 762–768. IEEE (1997)

31. Hunter, J.: Enhancing the semantic interoperability of multimedia through a core ontology. IEEE Trans. Circuits Syst. Video Technol. **13**(1), 49–58 (2003). https://doi.org/10.1109/TCSVT.2002.808088

32. Hunter, J.: Adding multimedia to the semantic web: Building an mpeg-7 ontology. In: Proceedings of the First International Conference on Semantic Web Working. pp. 261–283. CEUR-WS. org (2001)

33. Ji, X., Wang, Q., Chen, B.W., Rho, S., Kuo, C.J., Dai, Q.: Online distribution and interaction of video data in social multimedia network. Multimed. Tools Appl. **75**(20), 12941–12954 (2016)

34. Jin, X., Luo, J., Yu, J., Wang, G., Joshi, D., Han, J.: Reinforced similarity integration in image-rich information networks. IEEE Trans. Knowl. Data Eng. **25**(2), 448–460 (2013)

35. Kannan, P., Bala, P.S., Aghila, G.: A comparative study of multimedia retrieval using ontology for semantic web. In: IEEE-International Conference On Advances In Engineering, Science And Management (ICAESM -2012). pp. 400–405 (2012)

36. Kompatsiaris, I., Avrithis, Y., Hobson, P., Strintzis, M.G.: Integrating knowledge, semantics and content for user-centred intelligent media services: The acemedia project. In: Proceedings of Workshop on Image Analysis for Multimedia Interactive Services (WIAMIS 2004. pp. 21–23 (2004)

37. Lee, M., Kim, M., Yeom, J., Lee, K., Suh, Y., Kim, H., Cho, J.: Ontological knowledge base-driven framework for semantic multimedia contents retrieval. In: 2012 14th International Conference on Advanced Communication Technology (ICACT). pp. 1304–1309 (Feb 2012)

38. Li, L., Li, T.: News recommendation via hypergraph learning: encapsulation of user behavior and news content. In: Proceedings of the sixth ACM International Conference on Web Search and Data Mining. pp. 305–314. ACM (2013)

39. Li, Q., Lu, Z., Yu, Y., Liang, L.: Multimedia ontology modeling: An approach based on mpeg-7. In: 2011 3rd International Conference on Advanced Computer Control. pp. 351–356 (2011). https://doi.org/10.1109/ICACC.2011.6016430

40. Liu, D., Ye, G., Chen, C.T., Yan, S., Chang, S.F.: Hybrid social media network. In: Proceedings of the 20th ACM International Conference on Multimedia. pp. 659–668. ACM (2012)

41. Lu, C., Hu, X., Park, J.R.: Exploiting the social tagging network for web clustering. IEEE Trans. Syst. Man, and Cybernetics-Part A: Systems and Humans **41**(5), 840–852 (2011)

42. Lv, Q., Charikar, M., Li, K.: Image similarity search with compact data structures. In: Proceedings of the Thirteenth ACM International Conference on Information and Knowledge Management. pp. 208–217 (2004)
43. Madani, K., Russo, C., Rinaldi, A.: Merging large ontologies using bigdata graphdb. In: Proceedings - 2019 IEEE International Conference on Big Data, Big Data 2019. pp. 2383–2392 (2019)
44. McAfee, A., Brynjolfsson, E., Davenport, T.H., Patil, D., Barton, D.: Big data: the management revolution. Harvard Business Rev. **90**(10), 60–68 (2012)
45. Mika, P.: Ontologies are us: A unified model of social networks and semantics. 5, 5–15 (2007)
46. Milroy, L., Milroy, J.: Social network and social class: toward an integrated sociolinguistic model. Lang. Soc. **21**(1), 1–26 (1992)
47. O'Donovan, F.T., Fournelle, C., Gaffigan, S., Brdiczka, O., Shen, J., Liu, J., Moore, K.E.: Characterizing user behavior and information propagation on a social multimedia network. In: Multimedia and Expo Workshops (ICMEW), 2013 IEEE International Conference on. pp. 1–6. IEEE (2013)
48. Ohm, J.-R.: The mpeg-7 visual description framework — concepts, accuracy, and applications. In: Skarbek, W. (ed.) CAIP 2001. LNCS, vol. 2124, pp. 2–10. Springer, Heidelberg (2001). https://doi.org/10.1007/3-540-44692-3_2
49. Pino, C., Di Salvo, R.: A survey of semantic multimedia retrieval systems. In: Proceedings of the 13th WSEAS International Conference on Mathematical and Computational Methods in Science and Engineering. pp. 353–358. MACMESE 2011, World Scientific and Engineering Academy and Society (WSEAS), Stevens Point, Wisconsin, USA (2011)
50. Qi, G.J., Aggarwal, C., Tian, Q., Ji, H., Huang, T.: Exploring context and content links in social media: a latent space method. IEEE Trans. Pattern Anal. Mach. Intell. **34**(5), 850–862 (2012)
51. Qi, G.J., Aggarwal, C.C., Huang, T.S.: On clustering heterogeneous social media objects with outlier links. In: Proceedings of the Fifth ACM International Conference on Web Search and Data Mining. pp. 553–562. ACM (2012)
52. Rinaldi, A., Russo, C.: A matching framework for multimedia data integration using semantics and ontologies. In: Proceedings - 12th IEEE International Conference on Semantic Computing, ICSC 2018. vol. 2018-January, pp. 363–368 (2018)
53. Rinaldi, A., Russo, C.: A semantic-based model to represent multimedia big data. In: MEDES 2018–10th International Conference on Management of Digital EcoSystems. pp. 31–38 (2018)
54. Rinaldi, A., Russo, C.: User-centered information retrieval using semantic multimedia big data. In: Proceedings - 2018 IEEE International Conference on Big Data, Big Data 2018. pp. 2304–2313 (2019)
55. Rinaldi, A., Russo, C., Madani, K.: A semantic matching strategy for very large knowledge bases integration. Int. J. Inf. Technol. Web. Eng. **15**(2), 1–29 (2020)
56. Rinaldi, A.M.: A multimedia ontology model based on linguistic properties and audio-visual features. Inf. Sci. **277**, 234–246 (2014)
57. Rinaldi, A.M.: Using multimedia ontologies for automatic image annotation and classification. In: 2014 IEEE International Congress on Big Data (BigData Congress), pp. 242–249. IEEE (2014)
58. Schreiber, A.T., Dubbeldam, B., Wielemaker, J., Wielinga, B.: Ontology-based photo annotation. IEEE Intell. Syst. **16**(3), 66–74 (2001)

59. Sokhn, M., Mugellini, E., Khaled, O.A., Serhrouchni, A.: End-to-end adaptive framework for multimedia information retrieval. In: Masip-Bruin, X., Verchere, D., Tsaoussidis, V., Yannuzzi, M. (eds.) WWIC 2011. LNCS, vol. 6649, pp. 197–206. Springer, Heidelberg (2011). https://doi.org/10.1007/978-3-642-21560-5_17
60. Straccia, U.: An ontology mediated multimedia information retrieval system. In: 2010 40th IEEE International Symposium on Multiple-Valued Logic (ISMVL), pp. 319–324. IEEE (2010)
61. Szegedy, C., Toshev, A., Erhan, D.: Deep neural networks for object detection. In: Advances in Neural Information Processing Systems. pp. 2553–2561 (2013)
62. Tousch, A.M., Herbin, S., Audibert, J.Y.: Semantic hierarchies for image annotation: A survey. Pattern Recogn. **45**(1), 333–345 (2012). https://doi.org/10.1016/j. patcog.2011.05.017,
63. Trudgill, P.: Investigations in sociohistorical linguistics: Stories of colonisation and contact. Cambridge University Press (2010)
64. Wang, P., Smeaton, A.F.: Semantics-based selection of everyday concepts in visual lifelogging. Int. J. Multimed. Inf. Retri. **1**(2), 87–101 2012). https://doi.org/10. 1007/s13735-012-0010-8
65. Xie, J., Kelley, S., Szymanski, B.K.: Overlapping community detection in networks: The state-of-the-art and comparative study. ACM Comput. Surv. **45**(4), 1–35 (2013). https://doi.org/10.1145/2501654.2501657
66. Zhang, Z., Wang, K.: A trust model for multimedia social networks. Soc. Netw. Anal. Mining **3**(4), 969–979 (2013)
67. Zhu, Z., Su, J., Kong, L.: Measuring influence in online social network based on the user-content bipartite graph. Comput. Hum. Behav. **52**, 184–189 (2015)

# Social Big Data: Concepts and Theory

Hiroshi Ishikawa[1]([⊠]) and Yukio Yamamoto[2]

[1] Tokyo Metropolitan University, Tokyo, Japan
`ishikawa-hiroshi@tmu.ac.jp`
[2] Japan Aerospace Exploration Agency (JAXA), Kanagawa, Japan
`yamamoto.yukio@jaxa.jp`

**Abstract.** This paper explains the basic concepts of social big data and its integrated analysis. First, we will explain the outline and examples of the real-world data, open data, and social data that compose social big data. After we will describe interactions among the real-world data, open data, and social data, we will introduce basic concepts of an integrated analysis based on "Ishikawa concept." Furthermore, after explaining the flow of integrated analysis in line with the basic concept, a data model approach for integrated analysis will be introduced. Based on that, integrated hypotheses and integrated analysis will be specifically explained in another paper "Social Big Data: Case Studies" in this issue through several use cases.

**Keywords:** Big data · Social data · Open data · Hypothesis generation · Difference · Ishikawa concept

## 1 Big Data

### 1.1 Features of Big Data

We describe the features of the big data (Ishikawa 2015). In general, big data can be described by the following four words starting with V:

- (Volume) The total amount of generated data is large.
- (Velocity) The speed of generated data is fast.
- (Variety) There are many types of generated data.
- (Vagueness) There are ambiguities in generated data,

It will not be necessary to explain the first three Vs. Therefore, we will make comments on the fourth V here. For example, if there are multiple data, there occurs vagueness related to data such as missing data and inconsistencies between related data. Thus, big data inherently contain vagueness with respect to accuracy. Decreasing such vagueness increases Veracity of big data. Further, with regarding the use of the generated data, at present there is vagueness with respect to the description of big data applications. This vagueness causes another vague concern of the users as to how their data are handled.

A. Hameurlain et al. (Eds.): TLDKS XLVII, LNCS 12630, pp. 51–79, 2021.
https://doi.org/10.1007/978-3-662-62919-2_3

The latter type of vagueness is described in detail in Sect. 2.5 of this paper. Finally, integrated analysis of social big data can provide new Value which separate analyses cannot.

Big data are classified into real-world data, open data, and social data. Let's look at each in detail along with specific examples in the following.

**Fig. 1.** Hayabusa page in Jaxa's DARTS site.

## 1.2  Real-World Data

Real-world data include a variety of data that are generated by the actions and activities of human beings in the physical real-world.

The sizes of the measuring devices, such as a pulse meters, accelerometers, and gyro sensors, have been reduced in recent years. Therefore, through a wearable device such as a smart watch, data on the activities of human beings such as heart rates and the number of steps can be easily recorded.

With the miniaturization of the devices of GPS (Global Positioning System), position information is added to various data generated by humans.

Similarly, log data accumulated when humans interact with machines, systems, and media are considered to be a kind of real-world data.

The sources of real-world data are not limited to the human activities. The states of motor vehicles used in our daily life, equipment and machinery at production sites, and spacecrafts in the universe are measured by various sensors and become a kind of real-world data as a result. In general, the device having a sensor connected to a network such as the Internet is called IoT (Internet of Things) (IEEE IoT 2019) device.

Data generated by mechanical or visual observation of natural phenomena such as rainfalls and flowering of cherry blossoms are also a kind of real-world data.

Real-world data include specifically the amount of activity data (derived from wearable devices), vehicle driving data (probe data), transportation IC card data, log data of viewing various media, sensor data (data derived from IoT devices), meteorological data, and scientific data (Jaxa lunar and planetary data) (Yamamoto 2009, 2020).

Figure 1 shows the page about data of "Hayabusa" in Jaxa's DARTS (Data ARchives and Transmission System)  site (JAXA DARTS 2019).

Figure 2 shows an example of usage of the vehicle driving data.

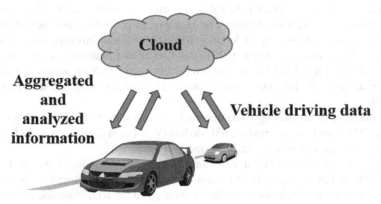

**Fig. 2.**  System for vehicle driving data.

## 1.3 Open Data

**Definition of Open Data.** Next, we will explain open data. Public organizations such as national governments, local governments, and research institutions collect, organize, and publish data for all the people to be able to access. Such data are called open data.

First, open data are conventionally published in the HTML (HyperText Markup Language) format or PDF (Portable Document Format) format assuming it is sufficient for only human beings to see open data, Recently, however, open data are classified based on their available formats as follows (Ministry of Internal Affairs and Communications 2019):

1. Machine-processable data format: data formats under proprietary licenses, such as XLS, DOC.
2. Easy-to-reuse data format: open data formats such as CSV, XML.
3. Data format that allows external linkage and search: LOD (linked open data and RDF (Resource Description Framework) (W3C Linked Data 2019).

Here as open data, the format 1 is at the most rudimentary level while the format 3 is at the most sophisticated level. The format 2 inherits the features of the format 1 while the format 3 inherits the features of the format 2.

The open data provided by organizations such as national and local governments contain statistical information such as population dynamics and disaster prevention information such as evacuation facilities that the organizations have collected.

Articles as academic resources, especially those published in open access journals, are a kind of open data in the sense that anyone can access them. Studies aimed at discovering academic trends using such open access journals are also being conducted (Ishikawa et al. 2016).

Open data and real-world data are not necessarily exclusive to each other. Open data are also present in the real-world data. For example, as phenological observations provided by the Japan Meteorological Agency (Ministry of Land, Infrastructure, Transport and Tourism Meteorological Agency 2019) and lunar and planetary science data provided by JAXA through DARTS, data which are obtained by observation and published together with location and time information are also a kind of open data (Yamamoto et al. 2020).

In addition, data created by everyone such as map data (OpenStreetMap) (OpenStreetMap 2019) and encyclopedia (Wikipedia) (Wikipedia 2019) are included in the open data in the sense that they can be accessed by everyone.

Figure 3 shows an example of RDF data published in the site of the W3C (W3C SPARQL 2019). For example, book1 (subject) has "SPARQL Tutorial" (object) as its title (predicate). Figure 4 shows examples of queries on the RDF data and its execution results by using the language called SPARQL.

**Open Data Example.** Two examples of open data are introduced below.

*OSM.* OpenStreetMap (OSM) (OpenStreetMap 2019) [Wikipedia OpenStreetMap 2019] is a joint project aimed at creating an editable world map. Triggered by restriction in the use and availability of map information in many countries of the world as well as

```
@prefix dc: <http://purl.org/dc/elements/1.1/> .
@prefix : <http://example.org/book/> .
@prefix ns: <http://example.org/ns#> .

:book1 dc:title "SPARQL Tutorial" .
:book1 ns:price 42 .
:book2 dc:title "The Semantic Web" .
:book2 ns:price 23 .
```

**Fig. 3.** Example of RDF data.

```
PREFIX dc: <http://purl.org/dc/elements/1.1/>
SELECT ?title
WHERE { ?x dc:title ?title
        FILTER regex(?title, "^SPARQL")
      }
```

| title |
|-------|
| "SPARQL Tutorial" |

**(a) Compare character string**

```
PREFIX dc: <http://purl.org/dc/elements/1.1/>
PREFIX ns: <http://example.org/ns#>
SELECT ?title ?price
WHERE { ?x ns:price ?price .
        FILTER (?price < 30.5) ?x dc:title ?title .
      }
```

| title | price |
|-------|-------|
| "The Semantic Web" | 23 |

**(a) Compare numerical values**

**Fig. 4.** Example of queries and results in SPARQL.

appearance of inexpensive GPS devices, OSM is born and developed. OSM is one of the prominent examples of geographic information systems created on a volunteer basis.

Inspired by the facts that Wikipedia (2019) has been successful and commercial maps have been dominant in the countries including the United Kingdom, OSM was created by Steve Coast in 2004. OSM has grown up in the project which can collect data through the use of manual survey, GPS devices, aerial photography, and other free information sources with more than two million registered users. Data thus crowdsourced are available through a license of ODbL (Open Database License) (ODbL 2019).

For example, OSM contains the following data:

- POI (Point of Interest): Natural objects (e.g., mountains, rivers), facilities (e.g., aquariums, art museums), stores (e.g., restaurants, hamburgers), shrines and temples.
- Road information: roads, bridges, and tunnels.

Figure 5 is a map around Shinjuku Gyoen National Park created by the OSM project.

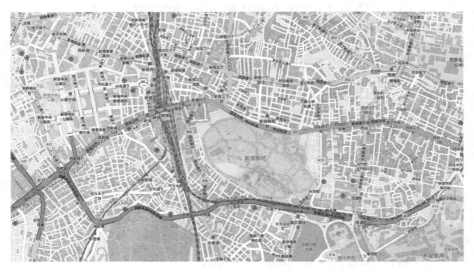

**Fig. 5.** Example of OSM map.

*DBpedia.* DBpedia (2019) (Wikipedia DBpedia 2019) is a project that aims to extract structured content from the information that has been created by the Wikipedia project. The information thus structured is also available on the World Wide Web (WWW). A semantic query based on attributes and relationships of data in the Wikipedia articles allows the users an inquiry aware of the structures of the data. In other words, Wikipedia's content can be searched using SPARQL in DBpedia.

Tim Berners-Lee, inventor of the WWW (Wikipedia Tim Berners-Lee 2019), has said that DBpedia is one of the most prominent efforts to LOD.

## 1.4  Social Data

**Social Media.** Social data are basically data available from social media in the cyber world on top of the Internet, which enable the members to mutually exchange information among them. Here social media are social network services (SNS) in the broad sense. In particular, this book focuses on social data as social big data.

Generally, a social media site consists of an information system as its platform and its users on the Web. The system enables the user to perform direct interactions with it. The user is identified by the system along with other users as well. Two or more users constitute explicit or implicit communities, that is, social networks in the narrow sense. The user in social media is generally called an actor in the context of social network analysis. By participating in the social network as well as directly interacting with the system, the user can enjoy services provided by the social media site.

More specifically, social media can be roughly classified into the following categories based on the contents of mainly used services and media.

- *Blogging*: Services in this category enable the user to publish explanations, sentiments, evaluations, actions, and ideas about certain topics including personal or social events in a text in the style of a diary. For example, Ameba Blog (Ameblo 2019) is popular in Japan.
- *Micro blogging*: The user describes a certain topic more frequently in shorter texts in micro blogging. For example, a tweet, an article of Twitter ( 2019), consists of at most 140 characters.
- *SNS (Social Network Service)*: Services in this category literally support creating social networks among users. For example, Facebook (2019) is very popular worldwide.
- *Sharing service*: Services in this category enable the user to share movies, audios, photographs, and bookmarks. For example, YouTube (2019), Flickr (2019), Instagram (2019), Spotify (2019), Deezer (2019), and Delicious (2019) are included.
- *Instant messaging service*: In the service of this category, using the text among users, it is possible to perform a chat and a conference. For example, WhatsApp (2019), Line (2019), and WeChat (2019) are included.
- *Video communication*: The users can hold a meeting and chat with other users using live videos as services in this category. For example, skype (2019) and RingCentral (2019) are available.
- *Social search*: Services in this category enable the user to reflect the likings and opinions of current search results in the subsequent searches. Other services allow not only experts but also users to directly reply to queries. For example, ChaCha (Wikipedia ChaCha 2019), Mahalo (Wikipedia Mahalo2019) were used. Unfortunately, however, all of these are currently closed.
- *Social news*: Through services in this category the user can contribute news as a primary source and can also re-post and evaluate favorite news items which have already been posted. For example, Slashdot (2019) and Digg (2019) are popular.
- Review Service: The user in this service can share the evaluation of the spot (Point of Interest) such as restaurant with respect to dishes and services. For example, Yelp (2019) and TripAdvisor (2019) are popular.
- *Social gaming*: Services in this category enable the user to play games with other users connected by SNS. For example, FarmVille (2019) and Minecraft (2019) are included.

- *Crowd sourcing*: Through services in this category, the users can outsource a part or all of their work to outside users who are capable of doing the work. For example, Mechanical Turk (2019) and micro Worker (Micro Workers 2019) are used.
- *Collaboration*: Services in this category support cooperative work among users and they enable the users to publish a result of the cooperative work. For example, G suite (2019) and Office 365 (Office 2019) are included.

Social data can be often collected through the API (Application Program Interface) provided by the media site in the media, As details will be described later in this paper, social data with position information as well as time information are focused on because such data allow the match of different data sources such as Twitter and Flickr and the acquisition of reliable data.

Note that a certain kind of time information has basically been attached to social data. It can be said that social data with the time information and position information are a kind of real-world data which were created by the actions of human beings. If the open API are provided by the social media, such social data can be regarded as a kind of open data.

**Social Data Example.** Twitter and Flicker are described as social media mainly used in this study.

*Twitter.*

(1)  Category and founding

Twitter (2019) (Wikipedia Twitter 2019) is one of the platform services for micro blogging founded by Jack Dorsey in 2005.

Twitter started from the ideas about development of media which are highly live and suitable for communication among friends. It is said that it has attracted attention partly because its users have increased so rapidly. For example, in Japan, when the animation movie "Castle in the Sky" by Hayao Miyazaki was broadcast as a TV program in 2011, there were 25,088 tweets in one second, which made it the center of attention.

Figure 6 illustrates a portion of the tweets obtained as a result of the search from Twitter specifying the hash tag #shibuyacrossing showing Shibuya Crossing popular among foreigners.

(2)  Numbers

- Active users: 300 M (M: Million)
- The number of tweets per day: 500 M

(3)  Data structures

   (Related to users)

- Account
- Profile

   (Related to contents)

- Tweet

   (Related to relationships)

- Links to Web sites, video, and photo
- The follower-followee relationship between users
- Memory of searches
- List of users
- Bookmark of tweets

(4)  Main interactions

- Creation and deletion of an account.
- Creation and change of a profile.
- Contribution of a tweet: Tweets contributed by a user who are followed by another user appear in the timeline of the follower.
- Deletion of a tweet.
- Search of tweets: Tweets can be searched with search terms or usernames.
- Retweet: If a tweet is retweeted by a user, the tweet will appear in the timeline of the follower. In other words, if the user follows another user and the latter user retweets a certain tweet, then the tweet will appear in the timeline of the former user.
- Reply: If a user replies to a message by user who contributed the tweet, then the message will appear in the timeline of another user who follows both of them.
- Sending a direct message: The user directly sends a message to its follower.
- Addition of location information to tweets.
- Inclusion of hash tags in a tweet: Tweets are searched with the character string starting with "#" as one of search terms. Hash tags often indicate certain topics or constitute coherent communities.
- Embedding URL of a Web page in a tweet.
- Embedding of a video as a link to it in a tweet.
- Upload and sharing of a photo.

(5)  Comparison with similar media

Twitter is text-oriented like general blogging platforms such as WordPress (2019) and Blogger (2019). Of course, tweets can also include links to other media as described

**Fig. 6.** Example of Twitter articles.

above. On the other hand, the number of characters of tweets is less than that of general blog articles and tweets are more frequently posted. Incidentally, WordPress is not only a platform of blogging, but it also enables easy construction of applications upon LAMP (Linux Apache MySQL PHP) stacks, therefore it is widely used as CMS (Content Management System) for enterprises.

(6)  API

Twitter provides REST (Representational State Transfer) and streaming as its Web service API. REST enables to obtain data in JSON (JavaScript Object Notation) format accessing the service by specifying a URI and parameters according to the HTTP protocol. Streaming enables to get JSON format data from the Twitter stream being posted.

*Flickr*

(1)  Category and foundation

Flickr (2019) (Wikipedia Flickr 2019) is a photo sharing service launched by Ludicorp, a company founded by Stewart Butterfield and Caterina Fake in 2004. Flickr focused on a chat service with real-time photo exchange in its early stages. However, the photo sharing service became more popular and the chat service, which was originally the main purpose, disappeared, partly because it had some problems.

Figure 7 illustrates a portion of the images obtained as a result of the search from Flickr specifying the hash tag #shibuyacrossing as in Twitter.

**Fig. 7.**  Example of Flicker photos.

(2)  Numbers

- Registered users: 90 M
- The number of photos: 10 B

(3)  *Data structures*

(Related to user)

- Account
- Profile

(Related to contents)

- Photo

- Set collection of photos
- Favorite photo
- Note
- Tag
- Exif (Exchangeable image file format) (Related to relationships)
- Group
- Contact
- Bookmark of an album (a photo)

(4)  *Main interactions*

- Creation and deletion of an account.
- Creation and change of a profile.
- Upload of a photo.
- Packing photos into a set collection.
- Appending notes to a photo.
- Arranging a photo on a map.
- Addition of a photo to a group.
- Making relationships between friends or families from contact.
- Search by explanation and tag.

(5). Comparisons with similar media

Although Google Photo (Google Photo 2019) and Photobucket (Photobucket 2019) are also popular like Flickr in the category of photo sharing services, here we will take up Pinterest (2019) and Instagram (2019) as new players which have unique features. Pinterest provides lightweight services on the user side compared with Flickr. That is, in Pinterest, the users can not only upload original photos like Flickr but can also stick their favorite photos on their own bulletin boards by pins, which they have searched and found on Pinterest as well as on the Web. On the other hand, Instagram offers the users many filters by which they can edit photos easily. In June 2012, an announcement was made that Facebook acquired Instagram.

(6)  API

Flickr offers REST, XML-RPC (XML-Remote Procedure Call), and SOAP (originally, Simple Object Access Protocol) as Web service API.

## 2  Social Big Data

In this study, real-world data, open data, and social data described so far are collectively called social big data. However, social big data is not only pointing to data. We will explain this in more detail in the following.

## 2.1  Interaction Between Social Big Data

Every moment in our around, real-world data, open data, and social data are produced in diverse kinds and large amounts as social big data.

However, a meaning is essentially implicit with real-world data in particular. In other words, it is not possible to extract a clear meaning from the real-world data alone. In order to know the meaning of the real-world data, it is necessary to correspond the features of the real-world data to the meaning outside the features such as different data which contain an explicit meaning or knowledge and intuition, which are not represented as data.

Meanwhile social data, whether texts (e.g., Twitter) or images (e.g., Flicker), often have an explicit meaning. In Twitter, the interests, opinions, and thoughts are directly expressed as words. In Flickr, the interest itself is reflected in the photographs.

Therefore, if relationships between different data sources are discovered, it will be possible to match or synchronize the relevant data contained in separate data sources by using the relationships as a clue. However, let us keep in mind that it is not always possible to find such a relationship.

## 2.2  Universal Key

Data attributes available for generally comparing similar data are referred to as the universal keys in this study. In general, it is not easy to find such a universal key among multiple given data. However, the position and time in the real world are candidate universal keys to combine different data sources. In other words, it is possible to synchronize or combine different data by using the same position or region and the same time point or interval.

By synchronizing different data by using the universal key, which have both the same location and time, or either of them, it is possible to extract the explicit meaning from the data. This type of analysis is called synchronous analysis. In other words, by the synchronous analysis of real-world data and social data, a latent or implicit meaning existent in the real-world data can be supplemented with an explicit meaning existent in the synchronized portion of social data.

Furthermore, if different data have semantic information such as texts, tags not in the real world but in the semantic space (e.g., vector space model) created by the words or concepts contained in the data (Ishikawa 2015), when the similarity of data (e.g., feature vectors) is large or when the distance, the opposite concept, is small, such a measure as a certain kind of universal key enables synchronization of different data sources. For example, it is conceivable to use the similarity between the tags attached to Twitter articles and those attached to Flicker images.

Recently, there is a web service (for example, Google Cloud Vision API (Google Cloud Vision API 2019)) that generates a tag indicating a category of an object included in the image content itself. By using such a service, regardless of the difference of the media such as image and text, it is possible to synchronize analysis between different data sources in the unified semantic space.

In addition, even if multiple data sources cannot be synchronized, selection of data from one data source can be effectively performed by using attribute or feature values of results obtained by analysis of data from another data source, which can be regarded as a kind of synchronization.

### 2.3 Ishikawa Concept

By performing analysis of different data (social big data) by synchronizing them with their position and time, detection of relationships such as correlations in the broad sense and generation of hypotheses are possible. Based on the result, it is possible to build a variety of applications such as problem-solving, recommendation, cause investigation, and near-future prediction.

The basic concept of such an analysis technique is referred to as *Ishikawa concept* (Olshannikova et al. 2017). Real-world data, open data, and social data and the analysis approach for them based on *Ishikawa concept* are collectively referred to as social big data in this study.

Based on this concept, this study explains how to describe actual applications in a high-level fashion through examples.

Figure 8 illustrates Ishikawa concept.

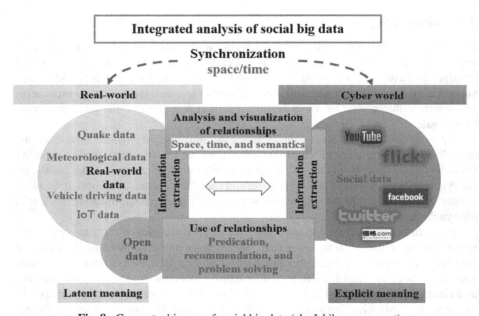

**Fig. 8.** Conceptual image of social big data (aka Ishikawa concept).

Here, a little attention is made as to data sources to be combined by this method.

This approach includes synchronously analyzing social data and open data as different data sources.

As a special case of the synchronous analysis, it is possible to obtain new knowledge from synchronous analysis of different social data by utilizing differences in their characteristics.

Furthermore, let's consider an extreme case. That is, even data in a single data source, if attached with time and location, are more associated with the events and spots which can be identified with respect to time and location than data without such information. In other words, analysis based on data with position and time information is more likely to be realistic or hands-on analysis. For example, in social data a talk about a place in Japan (for example, Harajuku of Tokyo) done in cities outside Japan (for example, Paris of France) before visiting the place is less relevant to the place than a talk about the place done when visiting the place actually because the content of social data is generally based on experiences.

If time series data have an exact location, they are a target of analysis by our method. Past data and moving average of past data can be regarded as different data similar to the original data.

Data and transformation of the original data such as rotation can be considered to be different data as well.

Data observed by different means for the same object (the same time and space) can be regarded as different data.

## 2.4   General Flow of Using Social Big Data

First, we describe the basic flow of using social big data by taking social data as follows:

1. Collection of social data and database storage
   Acquire data using the search and streaming API provided by the social media site and store the data in a collection database.
2. Search database
   Search the collection database by specifying the conditions according to the purpose.
3. Data preprocessing
   Preprocess the retrieved data as needed. For example, aggregation, transformation, and cleaning are included by preprocessing.
4. (Optional) Storage in analysis database
   Store the preprocessed data in the analysis database. Usually a database different from the collection database are used for analysis.
5. Hypothesis generation and verification
   Apply the algorithms of data mining and machine learning to preprocessed data and generate a hypothesis or verify an already generated hypothesis (Ishikawa 2015). For example, clustering, classification, and regression are included by the algorithms.
6. Visualization and knowledge of hypotheses
   Visualize a generated hypothesis or a verified result using visualization techniques such as maps, graphs (networks) and various charts.

Based on this processing flow, synchronous analysis can be divided as follows.

- (Parallel analysis) Perform the processes from 1 to 6 for both of different data in parallel. Then perform the processes 5 and 6 to further analyze by synchronizing results obtained for each data source.

- (Serial analysis) Perform the processes from 1 to 6 for one data. Perform the process 1 for another data. Based on the result obtained for the first data, perform the processes from 2 to 6 for another data.

Real-world data and open data are also collected and stored in the database as they occur or as needed.

If a hypothesis is created, data necessary to verify it are selected from the database and the necessary processing is performed to conduct an experiment.

On social media sites, when various events (e.g., posting and check-in) occur in the real world, data on such events are stored in a database in the sites or clouds before 1. Then, they are displayed on the timeline of the users and can be accessed through provided API. Of course, data accessed by the users outside the sites are part of the stored data.

Figure 9 shows parallel analysis and serial analysis.

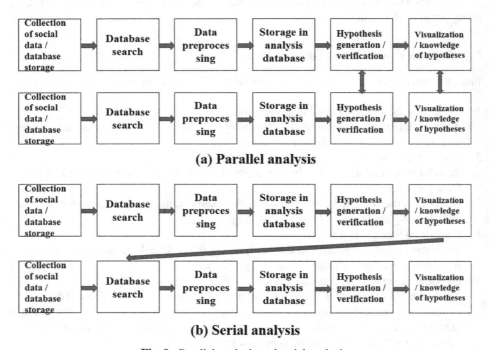

**Fig. 9.** Parallel analysis and serial analysis.

## 2.5   Fourth V of Social Big Data

**Issues.**   Vague concerns related to big data as the fourth V of big data features will be explained in more detail.

One means for solving the user's anxiety or vague concern is to fulfill accountability on applications. In order to fulfill accountability regarding analysis, it is sufficient to explain the analysis procedure to the user. For that purpose, words or methods for that explanation are required first of all.

A naive explanation method is to present the program itself used for analysis. It is theoretically possible if the reader has knowledge of the programming language. However, the size of the entire program is usually quite large. So even if there is such knowledge, the time it takes to understand the program is very huge. There is also a problem with the intellectual property rights of the program. Therefore, this is not a very realistic method.

As another method, it is conceivable to explain the program by natural language. However, if you dare to explain the program as it is in natural language, it is very hard to explain the application so that it can be understood by users who are experts in the field but not analytical experts, because the abstraction level of the program is low. Then this does not suit the purpose, either.

Therefore, a method that is higher in abstraction level than a program and is independent of individual programming languages (e.g. Python, Java) is required. In other words, it is necessary to be able to describe the procedure as meaning of the program.

**Data Model Approach.**  A data model approach to solution of ambiguity in explanation is considered to be effective here. The data model (Ishikawa et al. 2018) basically consists of the following components: Data structure and data manipulation. In other words, the data model consists of the basic data structures and operations on them. In general, the conditions (data constraints) to be satisfied on data or between data are added to the constituent elements of the data model, but here in this paper we will focus on the data structures and data operations only.

The need for a data model approach can be summarized as follows in terms of the digital ecosystem, hypothesis, and reproducibility.

*Different Digital Ecosystem.*  According to our observation of social big data applications, such applications often consist of data management of social big data and data mining against them. Data management and data mining are separately developed digital ecosystems (MEDES 2019) (hereinafter simply referred to as ecosystem). In general, the ecosystem is an interdependent system consisting of multiple vendors and users through products and services. Many of social big data applications are hybrid applications consisting of data management, data mining, and machine learning, which have been separately developed as different ecosystems.

(a)  *Data management ecosystem.* The data model for the relational database, which is widely used, consist of the set of tuples (i.e., relations) and the operations on them (relational algebra or SQL realizing the algebra). However, as an exception, *groupby* function of SQL (grouping and aggregate functions) is beyond the concept of sets and is rather based on the partition concept. That is, a set of tuples to be searched is exclusively grouped into a subset of tuples whose key of the grouping has the same value, and an aggregate function is applied to each set. In other words, only the aggregate function is based on the mathematical concept of a collection of sets (i.e., a family to be more correct (Smith et al. 2014)). In short, traditional data management is based on sets with family as an exception.

(b) *Data mining, machine learning, and artificial intelligence ecosystem.* In data mining (Ishikawa 2015), both clustering and classification (classes, i.e., categories) take a set as the input data structure and gives a collection (family) of partitions as the output data structure. That is, in clustering (exclusive clustering), each cluster corresponds to one partition of an input set. In classification, each class corresponds to one partition of the input set. In association rule mining, the input and output data structures are both elements of the power set of the original set (i.e., subsets).

In short, the data model for explaining the social big data applications needs to be able to explain the hybrid ecosystem of data management and data mining (machine learning or artificial intelligence) together. Therefore, a data structure as a concept of integrating these two is required.

*Diversity of Hypothesis.* On the other hand, the hypothesis itself can have two different views as follows.

- Declarative hypothesis: A declarative hypothesis corresponds to one in traditional data analysis. The main task for this kind of hypothesis is verification of the hypothesis
- Procedural hypotheses: A procedural hypotheses is generated by performing procedures or programs as a result. Of course, even in this case, verification of the generated hypothesis is necessary.

Especially in the latter kind of hypothesis, the procedure for generating the hypothesis itself will play a more important role.

*Reproducibility as Science.* Generally speaking, the reliability of a scientific article is primarily based on preparing data by a procedure written in the article and executing another procedure described in the article against that data. It depends on being able to obtain the same result as the described result (reproducibility).

In other words, computer science or information science is also science in a broad sense, and reproducible explanation about a procedure or program is also indispensable for the reliability of applications of computer science (Peng 2011).

In short, to describe procedures in social big data applications, it is necessary to define data structures and data operations on them as an integrated data model with higher abstraction than programming languages.

Then, according to this data model approach, we will study methodologies to generate a hypothesis by using multiple data sources in the integrate fashion and develop enabling technologies to realize the methodologies as follows.

**Family of Sets is Basic Data Structures.** Here, we will summarize the data structures of our data model. In the following, we focus on the data structures used in the use case applications, which will be described in another paper "Social Big Data: Case Studies" in this issue.

From the observations of various application fields and cross-cutting technology groups, the data model of social big data can be based on data structures with a high degree of abstraction. In this paper, for application description, we will use highly abstract procedures and data structures that do not depend on the programming languages.

*Hierarchical Data Structure.* In the first place, social big data applications analyze spatio-temporal data, that is, data with time and position information. The analysis of such data is, so to speak, "analysis on the ground." For example,

- The maps consist of a grid (or mesh) hierarchy: 80 km, 10 km, 1 km, 500 m, 250 m square grids
- Time series data also have a hierarchical structure of time interval: year, month, week, day, and hour-minute-second

Furthermore, each grid and time interval can be considered as a set of data contained by them.

In this paper, a family whose elements are sets is described as the basis of data structures. For example, an element of a family is a set while a set has numbers, strings, vectors, and tuples as its elements.

We can often observe that social big data applications contain families as well as sets and they involve both data mining and data management. Please note that a family is also suitable for representing hierarchical structures inherent in time and locations associated with social big data.

Consider a concrete example. A map is considered to be a collection of grids or meshes. Here we will consider the widely used grid square system (BIODIC 2019). The index attached to the element in this case is a grid code calculated based on the latitude and longitude of the lower left (southwest) point of the grid.

Furthermore, the grid hierarchy (i.e. upper grid and lower grid) is present: approximate length of one side is 80 km (the first area section, $1^{st}$ grid), 10 km (second area section, $2^{nd}$ grid), 1 km (third area section, the standard grid), and the like. The hierarchy in this case consists of inclusion relations.

The smallest grid determined by the application includes zero or more points (POI). Latitude and longitude values are used as POI identifiers. As the grid includes data with location information such as photos shot and text articles posted therein, the grid can be considered to be a set of such data.

Here, image-oriented social data such as Flicker consist of a set of images and an identifier is attached to each image. Text-oriented social data such as Twitter consist of a set of text articles with identifiers as well.

Figure 10 illustrates a map having a hierarchical structure.

There are hierarchical structures also in general documents, that is, book, chapter, section, paragraph, sentence, phrase, word, and characters. The short text such as tweets dealt with in this study has a hierarchical structure with statements as its elements. That is, each text article is a family of sentences, a sentence is a family of phrases, and a phrase is a family of words. Furthermore, a word is a family of letters. In this case, an identifier is attached to each from article to word.

Figure 11 shows a part of the hierarchical structure in the document.

Similarly, in time series data, each time interval can be regarded as a family of data contained in it, based on the time of the data. Furthermore, the time interval spanning

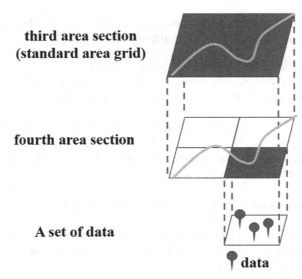

**Fig. 10.** Hierarchical structure of map.

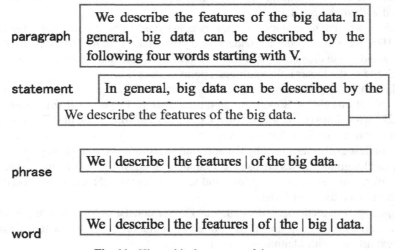

**Fig. 11.** Hierarchical structure of document.

across the oldest data and the most recent data becomes a family of time intervals. In other words, there is also a hierarchy in the time intervals. The time point is the time interval where the start time and the end time coincide.

*Data Structures in Programming Languages.* A variety of data structures are used by programming languages. Next, we will explain how these will be represented by a family. An array is of course represented as a family of elements (singleton sets in this case) and their indexes. A tuple is also represented as a family of elements (or components) and their indexes. If we think of such a tuple itself as an element, we can represent data frames, which are data structures used in frameworks such as Spark.

Objects generally have object identifiers, which distinguish objects from each other. We can represent an object by using a tuple. An object consists of a tuple and its attribute corresponds to a component of such a tuple. An object identifier can be represented as one of attribute values. A method of an object can be represented by an attribute containing an object that consists of an interface and programming codes. Alternatively, the method can be created as a separate object. We will call such an object a method object. In this case, the identifier of the method object should be set as the value of the method (attribute) associated with the object.

Furthermore, let's think about expressing vectors, matrices, and tensors in mathematics as a family. These data structures can be represented naturally by a family of elements and their indexes.

See the appendix for more information on the social big data model.

# 3   Model-Based Approach to Hypothesis Generation

The final purpose of this study (this paper and another) is to provide a framework (i.e., data model, methodology, and enabling technologies) to support the applications using social big data. In order to do so, it is necessary to combine results (individual hypotheses) based on multiple data so as to construct and test more complex hypotheses. Our research objectives are to propose the model which becomes the foundation of integrated analysis and to construct the methodology of hypothesis generation based on the model. In other words, we aim to materialize the "Ishikawa concept."

Then, according to this data model approach, we propose the methodology to generate hypotheses by integrating multiple data sources.

## 3.1   Hypothesis Definition

In the first place, hypotheses should satisfy the following properties:

- A hypothesis must be able to explain as many previous examples of phenomena as possible (universal). This is what must be considered in the first place in order to construct a hypothesis.
- A hypothesis must be able to predict what will happen in the future as to a phenomenon (predictive). This characteristic is related with usefulness of a hypothesis.
- A hypothesis must provide any new knowledge (ampliative).
- A hypothesis must be verifiable (testable).
- A hypothesis must be made as simple as possible (parsimonious). In other words, a hypothesis must be intelligible to the users.
- A hypothesis, whether science- or business-oriented, must reflect interests of stakeholders in a certain field of the contemporary time (interesting).

In general, estimation and prediction are required as the basis of future actions and plans. Here the concept of a hypothesis is broadly contemplated, and the hypothesis includes not only the estimation result and the prediction result but also the model or procedure that produce the hypothesis and the result.

## 3.2 Method of Hypothesis Generation

Conventional data analysis and data mining often generate hypotheses using a single data source, but in the social big data era, applications also have emerged that combine different data sources.

Generally, the following effects can be expected by combining multiple data sources.

- Method 1: A hypothesis can be made only by combining (i.e., making the difference between) existing hypothesizes. In other words, new hypotheses can be made by finding differences between multiple hypotheses like set difference (data management operation)
- Method 2: The accuracy of a hypothesis can be increased by combining (i.e., over-laying) existing hypothesizes. In other words, one hypothesis can be emphasized, confirmed, or verified by another analogous to set intersection (data management operation)
- Method 3: A new hypotheses can be made only by combining (i.e., complementing each other of) existing hypothesizes. In other words, multiple hypotheses complement each other and create a hypothesis like join (data management operation)
- Method 4: Increase the number of candidate hypotheses by combining (i.e., making the sum of) existing hypothesizes like set sum (data management operation)

In this study, mainly the first method is expanded, and the rest of the methods are also explored. Generally, the same or similar data are different from each other in the following aspects:

- Temporal difference
- Spatial (geographical) difference
- Semantic difference
- Difference between a value and its mean value
- Difference between a predicted value and an actual value
- Other differences (e.g., difference in calculation method, observation method, and acquisition method)

First based on preceding researches and our case study experiences (Ishikawa et al. 2018), a methodology called generalized difference method is proposed as follows:

- Difference of a series of data at different times can

  - Determine the change of events
  - Detect motions, mutations, and trajectories related to movement.

- Difference between data in the same location and for the same time generated by different observation or calculation modes can

  - Create a new hypothesis by the difference between the hypotheses.

- Difference between data independently generated in the same location and for the same time can

  - Create a new hypothesis by the difference between the hypotheses.

- Difference in semantic space (concept space) can

  - Find the essential meaning of the concept.
  - Represent differences between concepts and understand the concepts with the represented differences.

  Here, it is assumed that the above data satisfy the following conditions.

- Data are collected for the same targets in the same areas in the same periods.
- Data are compatible with difference calculation, that is, difference calculation is possible between data.

### 3.3 Related Research

We describe researches related to our generalized difference method in the following.

**Traditional Statistics.** One of the goals of traditional statistics is to test hypotheses that have already been created (i.e., declarative hypotheses). In particular, to test the differences between groups with respect to the following aspects: averages, variances, and ratios. In contrast, our proposed method creates a new hypothesis by making differences between two separate hypotheses.

**Method of Mill.** The methodology of hypothesis generation proposed by the philosopher Mill includes methods of agreement, difference, and residual (Holland 1986). In that Mill proposed the difference as an important element in hypothesis generation, it can be said that his methodology is a pioneering advocate of our generalized difference method. However, whereas Mill is focused on the discovery of cause-effect relations, our method generalizes the difference to generation of more generic hypotheses and extends the hypothesis generation by complement (method 3) and sum (Method 4).

**Basic Concept and Theory of Difference.** There are difference equations (i.e., recursion equations) as mathematical concepts related to differences (Mickens 2018). The idea of the recursion equation goes back to the age of Pythagoras and difference equations are now applied to modeling of natural and social phenomena and numerical solution of differential equations.

This study describes the concepts of social big data and hypothesis generation using social big data (i.e., Ishikawa concept). In particular, the basic concept of differences effective for hypothesis generation is introduced (Ishikawa et al. 2018).

**Time Difference.** Comparison of data with time difference (here, simple data such as scalars and vectors are assumed) can show changes in events. Time difference is the most typical difference (Brockwell et al. 2016). There are several possible cases, depending on what is considered as a difference:

- backward difference (forward difference, or central difference)
- difference between measured value and moving average
- difference between moving averages with different periods

In this study, we first deal with backward difference and introduce a use case to evaluate the satisfaction level of sightseeing spots using changes in travelers' impressions (Ishikawa et al. 2018). Next, by using moving averages, which was designed at the beginning of the twentieth century, we introduce our study on phenological observations (Endo et al. 2018). Our study includes the failure diagnosis of spacecrafts by using the temporal change (Yamamoto et al. 2019).

**Real Space Difference.** Instead of simple data as described above, by detecting the difference of more complicated data (for example, an image or a family of pixels) that can be represented by a matrix, moving objects and lesions included in the image are detected. Trajectories related to movement can be discovered as well. These techniques have been developed in areas to use the particular image processing such as automotive engineering (Jimenez et al. 2017) and medicine (Wu et al. 2016).

**Difference Between Hypotheses.** Aiming at integrated analysis in social big data applications, we create new hypotheses by using differences between hypotheses. First, the difference between the hypotheses obtained separately is calculated. The resulting difference is the final hypothesis. In this study we will describe discovery of candidate free Wi-Fi spots (Mitomi et al. 2016) and discovery of lunar craters with central peaks based on the DEM data (Hara et al. 2019). Research on the discovery of genes that cause diseases (Ishikawa 2015) is also included in this method. That is, the genome set is divided into one subset of patients having a particular disease suspected to be caused by a mutation of the genes and another subset of non-patients without the disease and the difference between them is calculated to identify the candidate genes causing the disease.

**Difference in Semantic Space.** The meaning of the concept is considered not in the real space as described so far but in the semantic space (i.e., concept space). The vector space model for information retrieval is an attempt to express the meaning of a document or a word using the vector space that is the basis of linear algebra (Salton et al. 1975). A vector space model consists of a document vector and a word vector. Particularly, as described later in this study, distributed representation of words in Word2Vec (Mikolov et al. 2013) helps find the essential meanings of concepts based on the difference (vector) between concepts (Tsuchida et al. 2017). In addition, expressing the difference of the concepts (e.g. cooking) by an effective way can help understanding the concept itself (Nobumoto et al. 2017, 2019).

**Regression in Machine Learning.** The least squares method, simultaneously invented by Gauss who predicted the trajectory of Ceres (Abdulle et al. 2002) and by others, provides a regression model as an approach of machine learning (Strang 2016, 2019; Hastie et al. 2009). Regression uses observed data and create a straight line, a curve, or flat surface as a model to explain the data. That is, regression creates a model by minimizing the differences between observed values and predicted values.

**Deep Learning.** In deep learning, which recently gathers much attention, the residual sum of squares (RSS) is used as a typical error function. In the propagation of the errors, weights and biases can be updated by recursive equations based on RSS (Hastie et al. 2009) (Strang 2019).

# 4 Conclusion

In this paper, we have introduced "Ishikawa concept" as the basic concept for integrated analysis in the age of social big data. Then, we have introduced the data model suitable for describing integrated hypotheses and have described the methods for hypothesis generation involving different social big data, focusing on *differences*.

**Acknowledgments.** This work was supported by JSPS KAKENHI Grant Number 20K12081, Tokyo Metropolitan University Grant-in-Aid for Research on Priority Areas, and Nomura School of Advanced Management Research Grant.

# Appendix Social Big Data Model

Our Social Big Data model (SBD hereafter) model uses a mathematical concept of a *family*, a collection of sets, as a basis for data structures. Family can be used as an apparatus for bridging the gaps between data management operations and data analysis operations.

Basically, our database is a *Family*. A Family is divided into *Indexed family* and *Non-Indexed family*. A Non-Indexed family is a collection of sets.

An Indexed family is defined as follows:

- $\{Set\}$ is a Non-Indexed family with *Set* as its element.
- $\{Set_i\}$ is an Indexed family with $Set_i$ as its *i-th* element. Here *i: Index* is called *indexing set* and *i* is an element of Index.
- Set is { <time space object> }.
- $Set_i$ is { <*time space object*> }$_i$. Here, *object* is an identifier to arbitrary identifiable user-provided data, e.g., record, object, and multimedia data appearing in social big data. *Time* and *space* are universal keys across multiple sources of social big data.
- $\{Indexed\ family_i\}$ is also an Indexed family with *Indexed family$_i$* as its *i-th* element. In other words, Indexed family can constitute a hierarchy of sets.

Please note that the following concepts are interchangeably used in this study.

- Singleton family ⇔ set
- Singleton set ⇔ element

If operations constructing a family out of a collection of sets and those deconstructing a family into a collection of sets are provided in addition to both family-dedicated and set-dedicated operations, SBD applications will be described in an integrated fashion by our proposed model.

SBD is consisted of Family data management operations and Family data mining operations. Further, Family data management operations are divided into Intra Family operations and Inter Family operations.

1) Intra Family Data Management Operations

    a) Intra Indexed Intersect (*i: Index Db p*($i$)) returns a singleton family (i.e., set) intersecting sets which satisfy the predicate $p(i)$. Database *Db* is a Family, which will not be mentioned hereafter.

    b) Intra Indexed Union (*i: Index Db p*($i$)) returns a singleton family unioning sets which satisfy $p(i)$.

    c) Intra Indexed Difference (*i: Index Db p*($i$)) returns a singleton family, that is, the first set satisfying $p(i)$ minus all the rest of sets satisfying $p(i)$.

    d) Indexed Select (*i: Index Db p1*($i$) *p2*($i$)) returns an Indexed family with respect to $i$ (preserved) where the element sets satisfy the predicate $p1(i)$ and the elements of the sets satisfy the predicate $p2(i)$. As a special case of true as $p1(i)$, this operation returns the whole indexed family. In a special case of a singleton family, Indexed Select is reduced to Select (a relational operation).

    e) Indexed Project (*i: Index Db p*($i$) *a*($i$)) returns an Indexed family where the element sets satisfy $p(i)$ and the elements of the sets are projected according to $a(i)$, attribute specification. This also extends also relational Project.

    f) Intra Indexed cross product (*i: Index Db p*($i$)) returns a singleton family obtained by product-ing sets which satisfy $p(i)$. This is extension of Cartesian product, one of relational operators.

    g) Intra Indexed Join (*i: Index Db p1*($i$) *p2*($i$)) returns a singleton family obtained by joining sets which satisfy $p1(i)$ based on the join predicate $p2(i)$. This is extension of join, one of relational operators.

    h) Select-Index (*i:Index Db p*($i$)) returns *i:Index* of $set_i$ which satisfy $p(i)$. As a special case of true as $p(i)$, it returns all index.

    i) Make-indexed family (*Index Non-Indexed Family*) returns an indexed Family. This operator requires *order-compatibility*, that is, that $i$ corresponds to *i-th set of Non-Indexed Family*.

    j) Partition (*i: Index Db p*($i$)) returns an Indexed family. Partition makes an Indexed family out of a given set (i.e. singleton family either w/or w/o index) by grouping elements with respect to $p$ (*i: Index*). This is extension of "groupby" as a relational operator.

    k) ApplyFunction (*i: Index Db f*($i$)) applies $f(i)$ to *i-th* set of DB, where $f(i)$ takes a set as a whole and gives another set including a singleton set (i.e., Aggregate function). This returns an indexed family. $f(i)$ can be defined by users.

2)  Inter Family Data Management Operations Index-Compatible

    a)  Indexed Intersect (*i: Index Db1 Db2 p(i)*) union-compatible
    b)  Indexed Union (*i: Index Db1 Db2 p(i)*) union-compatible
    c)  Indexed Difference (*i: Index Db1 Db2 p(i)*) union-compatible
    d)  Indexed Join (i: Index Db1 Db2 p1(i) p2(i))
    e)  Indexed cross product (*i: Index Db1 Db2 p(i)*)

3)  Family Data Mining Operations

    a)  Cluster (*Family method similarity {par}*) returns a Family as default, where Index is automatically produced. This is an unsupervised learner.
    b)  Make-classifier (*i: Index set:Family learnMethod {par}*) returns a classifier (Classify) with its accuracy. This is a supervised learner.
    c)  Classify (*Index/class set*) returns an indexed family with class as its index.
    d)  Make-frequent itemset (*Db supportMin*) returns an Indexed Family as frequent itemsets, which satisfy *supportMin*.
    e)  Make-association-rule (*Db confidenceMin*) creates association rules based on frequent itemsets *Db*, which satisfy *confidenceMin*. This is out of range of our algebra, too.

Please note that the predicates and functions used in the above operations can be defined by the users in addition to the system-defined ones such as Count.

# References

Abdulle, A., Wanner, G.: 200 years of least squares method. Elem. Math. **57**(2), 45–60 (2002). https://doi.org/10.1007/PL00000559

AmeBlo. https://ameblo.jp/. Accessed 2019

Apache Spark. https://spark.apache.org/. Accessed 2019

BIODIC. Grid Square System. http://www.biodic.go.jp/english/kiso/col_mesh.html. Accessed 2019

Blogger. https://www.blogger.com/. Accessed 2019

Brockwell, P.J., Davis, R.A.: Introduction to Time Series and Forecasting. STS. Springer, Cham (2016). https://doi.org/10.1007/978-3-319-29854-2_9

DBpedia. https://wiki.dbpedia.org/. Accessed 2019

Deezer. https://www.deezer.com/. Accessed 2019

Delicious. https://del.icio.us/. Accessed 2019

Digg. http://digg.com/. Accessed 2019

Endo, M., Shoji, Y., Hirota, M., Ohno, S., Ishikawa, H.: Best-time estimation for regions and tourist spots using phenological observations with geotagged tweets. Int. J. Inf. Soc. (IJIS) **9**(3), 109–117 (2017)

Endo, M., Hirota, M., Ohno, S., Ishikawa, H.: Best-time estimation method using information interpolation for sightseeing spots. Int. J. Inf. Soc. (IJIS) **10**(2), 97–105 (2018)

Facebook. https://www.facebook.com/. Accessed 2019

FarmVille. https://www.zynga.com/games/farmville. Accessed 2019

Flickr. https://www.flickr.com/. Accessed 2019

G suite. https://gsuite.google.com/. Accessed 2019

Google Cloud Vision API. https://cloud.google.com/vision/?hl=en. Accessed 2019

Google Photo. https://photos.google.com/. Accessed 2019

Hara, S., Yamamoto, Y., Araki, T., Hirota, M., Ishikawa, H.: Discrimination of crater with central hill by machine learning using Kaguya DEM. J. Space Sci. Inf. **8**, 1–10 (2019). (in Japanese)

Hastie, T., Tibshirani, R., Friedman, J.: The Elements of Statistical Learning - Data Mining, Inference, and Prediction, 2 edn. Springer, Cham (2009)

Holland, P.W.: Statistics and causal inference. J. Am. Stat. Assoc. **81**(396), 945–960 (1986)

IEEE, Towards a Definition of Internet of Things (IoT). https://iot.ieee.org/images/files/pdf/IEEE_IoT_Towards_Definition_Internet_of_Things_Revision1_27MAY15.pdf. Accessed 2019

Instagram. https://www.instagram.com/. Accessed 2019

Ishikawa, H.: Social Big Data Mining. CRC Press, Boca Raton (2015)

Ishikawa, H., Endo, M., Sugiyama, I., Hirota, M., Yokoyama, S.: Is it possible for the first three-month time-series data of views and downloads to predict the first year highly-cited academic papers in open access journals? Int. J. Inf. Soc. (IJIS) **8**(2), 59–66 (2016). ISSN 1883-4566

Ishikawa, H., Kato, D., Masaki, E., Hirota, M.: Generalized difference methods for generating integrated hypotheses in social big data (invited paper). In: Proceedings of the 10th International Conference on Management of Digital EcoSystems (MEDES 2018) (2012)

Ishikawa et al.: Social Big Data Practiced in Full Stack JavaScript and Python Machine Learning Library-From Basic Concepts and Techniques to Collection, Analysis and Visualization. Corona Ltd. (2019). (in Japanese)

Ishikawa, H., Yamamoto, Y., Hirota, M., Endo, M.: Towards construction of an explanation framework for whole processes of data analysis applications: concepts and use cases. In: Proceedings of the Eleventh International Conference on Advances in Multimedia, MMEDIA 2019 (Special tracks: SBDMM: Social Big Data in Multimedia) (2019)

JAXA DARTS. https://www.darts.isas.jaxa.jp/index.html.en. Accessed 2019

Jimenez, F.: Intelligent Vehicles: Enabling Technologies and Future Developments. Butterworth-Heinemann, Oxford (2017)

Line. https://line.me/. Accessed 2019

Mechanical Turk. https://aws.amazon.com/jp/mturk/. Accessed 2019

MEDES. Welcome to the International Conference on ManagEment of Digital EcoSystems (MEDES).http://medes.sigappfr.org/. Accessed 2019

Mickens, R.E.: Difference Equations. CRC Press, Boca Raton (2018)

Micro Workers. https://Ttv.Microworkers.Com/index/template. Accessed 2019

Mikolov, T., Chen, K., Corrado, G., Dean, J.: Efficient estimation of word representation in vector space. arXiv:1301.3781 .Accessed 2019

Minecraft. https://minecraft.net/. Accessed 2019

Ministry of Internal Affairs and Communications 2019. Open data. http://www.soumu.go.jp/johotsusintokei/whitepaper/ja/h25/html/nc121210.html. Accessed 2019

Ministry of Land, Infrastructure, Transport and Tourism Meteorological Agency, Information on phenological observation (2019). https://www.data.jma.go.jp/sakura/data/index.html. Accessed 2019

Mitomi, K., Endo, M., Hirota, M., Yokoyama, S., Shoji, Y., Ishikawa, H.: How to find accessible free wi-fi at tourist spots in Japan. In: Spiro, E., Ahn, Y.-Y. (eds.) SocInfo 2016. LNCS, vol. 10046, pp. 389–403. Springer, Cham (2016). https://doi.org/10.1007/978-3-319-47880-7_24

Nobumoto, K., Kato, D., Endo, M., Endo, M., Hirota, M., Ishikawa, H.: Multilingualization of restaurant menu by analogical description. Proceedings of the 9th Workshop on Multimedia for Cooking and Eating Activities (CEA 2017) (2017)

Nobumoto, K., Hirota, M., Kato, D., Ishikawa, H.: Multilingualization of cooking by analogical description. J. Jpn. Soc. Fuzzy Theory Intell. Inf. **31**(1), 526–533 (2019). (in Japanese)

ODbL. https://opendatacommons.org/licenses/odbl/index.html. Accessed 2019

Office. https://www.officeppe.com/. Accessed 2019

Olshannikova, E., Olsson, T., Huhtamaki, J., Karkkainen, H.: Conceptualizing big social data. J. Big Data **4**(1), 1–19 (2017). https://doi.org/10.1186/s40537-017-0063-x. Accessed 2019

OpenStreetMap. https://www.openstreetmap.org/. Accessed 2019

Peng, D.: Reproducible research in computational science. Science **334**(2), 1226–1227 (2011)

Photobucket. https://photobucket.com/. Accessed 2019

Pinterest. http://www.pinterest.com/. Accessed 2019

RingCentral. https://www.ringcentral.com/. Accessed 2019

Salton, G., et al.: A vector space model for automatic indexing. Commun. ACM **18**(11), 613–620 (1975)

Skype. https://www.skype.com/ .Accessed 2019

Slashdot. https://slashdot.org/. Accessed 2019

Smith, D.D., Eggen, M., Andre, R.S.: A Transition to Advanced Mathematics. Brooks/Cole Pub Co., Lexington (2014)

Spotify. https://www.spotify.com/. Accessed 2019

Strang, G.: Introduction to Linear Algebra. Wellesley-Cambridge Press, Cambridge (2016)

Strang, G.: Linear Algebra and Learning from Data. Wellesley-Cambridge Press, Cambridge (2019)

TripAdvisor. https://www.tripadvisor.com/. Accessed 2019

Tsuchida, T., et al.: Semantic operation for area and landmarks using Word2Vec. In: Proceedings of DEIM Forum 2016. (in Japanese)

Twitter. https://twitter.com/. Accessed 2019

W3C, Linked Data. https://www.w3.org/wiki/LinkedData. Accessed 2019

W3C, SPARQL Query Language for RDF. https://www.w3.org/TR/rdf-sparql-query/. Accessed 2019

WeChat. https://www.wechat.com/. Accessed 2019

Weibo. http://jp.weibo.com/. Accessed 2019

WhatsApp. https://www.whatsapp.com/. Accessed 2019

Wikipedia. https://www.wikipedia.org/. Accessed 2019

Wikipedia. ChaCha. https://en.wikipedia.org/wiki/ChaCha_(search_engine). Accessed 2019

Wikipedia. DBpedia (2019). http://wiki.dbpedia.org/. Accessed 2019

Wikipedia. Flickr (2019). https://en.wikipedia.org/wiki/flickr Accessed 2019

Wikipedia. Instagram (2019). https://en.wikipedia.org/wiki/instagram. Accessed 2019

Wikipedia. Mahalo (2019). https://en.wikipedia.org/wiki/mahalo.com. Accessed 2019

Wikipedia. Tim Barners-Lee. https://en.wikipedia.org/wiki/tim_berners-lee. Accessed 2019

Wikipedia. Twitter (2019). https://en.wikipedia.org/wiki/twitter. Accessed 2019

WordPress. https://wordpress.com/

Wu, G., Shen, D., Sabuncu, M.R.: Machine Learning and Medical Imaging. Academic Press, New York (2016)

Yamamoto, Y.: The beginning of DARTS lunar and planetary science, Japan's lunar and planetary exploration and science data archive, No.3, PLAIN News 190, 2009 (in Japanese) http://www.isas.jaxa.jp/docs/PLAINnews/190_contents/190_2.html Accessed 2019

Yamamoto, Y., Ishikawa, H.: Anomaly detection with hotelling t-square method for raw housekeeping telemetry. In: International Symposium on Space Technology and Science (2019)

Yamamoto, Y., Ishikawa, H.: Data management in Japanese planetary explorations for big data era. In: Proceedings of the 10th International Conference on Web Intelligence, Mining and Semantics (WIMS2020) (2020)

Yelp (2019). https://www.yelp.com/. Accessed 2019

YouTube (2019). https://www.youtube.com/. Accessed 2019

# Social Big Data: Case Studies

Hiroshi Ishikawa[1]([⊠]) and Yasushi Miyata[2]

[1] Tokyo Metropolitan University, Tokyo, Japan
`ishikawa-hiroshi@tmu.ac.jp`
[2] Hitachi, Ltd., Tokyo, Japan
`yasushi.miyata.bz@hitachi.com`

**Abstract.** Based on the concepts and theory that we have introduced in another paper "Social Big Data: Concepts and Theory" in this issue, we will concretely explain hypothesis generation and integrated analysis through use cases in this paper.

**Keywords:** Social big data · Hypothesis generation · Integrated analysis · Tourism · Science · Disaster mitigation

## 1 Case Studies in Social Big Data

We describe use cases related to tourism, science, and disaster mitigation. Tourism is increasingly expected as an industry responsible for the future development of Japan. The Japanese Government aims to attract sixty million foreign visitors in 2030 [Japanese Government 2019]. Some researchers in lunar and planetary science aim to discover interesting structures on the moon (e.g., central peak craters) to use real-world data, which are observed by lunar orbiters and archived for open use. We use applications related to tourism and science to present the hypothesis generation based on differences and integrated analysis while we use one tourism application to present the hypothesis generation based on emphasis.

The disaster mitigation is a familiar and serious problems for us since we are surrounded by risks such as earthquakes, tsunamis, and typhoons. This application is explained as a use case of hypothesis generation based on mutual complementation with multiple hypotheses and integrated analysis.

Six cases for hypothesis generation based on differences are introduced, followed by one case for hypothesis generation based on emphasis and another for hypothesis generation based on mutual complementation.

This paper will describe the meaning of the procedure used in each use case. The meanings of the operations used in the procedure description will be explained therein. We use the following background colors and bounding box for each category of social big data operations for illustration:

- Relational (set) data management operation
- Family data management operation
- Data mining operation

A. Hameurlain et al. (Eds.): TLDKS XLVII, LNCS 12630, pp. 80–111, 2021.
https://doi.org/10.1007/978-3-662-62919-2_4

## 2  Tourism Application: Bargain Spot Discovery

There are a lot of tourist-related applications. One of tourism-related works [Fujii et al. 2019] classifies users of social media sites Twitter and Flickr into visitors and residents based on the places where each of the users most frequently posts articles or photos. Based on the attributes (visitor or resident) of users, the work analyses the differences of behaviors with respect to their routes. Another tourist-related work [Miura et al. 2018] aims to predicate the genders of visitors based on places which they frequently visit.

Here we describe a tourism application, that is, search for bargain spots by evaluating emotions which are calculated based on social data. This application uses differences to generate hypotheses (i.e., Hypothesis Generation Method 1). We have described the hypothesis generation method 1 in the Sect. 3.2 in another paper "Social Big Data: Concepts and Theory" in this issue.

Some people expect that a certain spot will be joyful before the visit but find it "disappointing spot" after the visit. On the contrary, others do not expect it, but find it unexpectedly "bargain spot."

Therefore, we measure such a change in emotions with respect to each person and collectively process these changes to find "bargain spots" (i.e., joyful spots) or "disappointing spots."

[Integrated Hypothesis]
It is possible to calculate value (satisfaction level) of places for individuals by using social data.

Procedures for generating a hypothesis are shown below [Toyoshima et al. 2017].

For a place of interest (POI) in a grid where more than a certain number of tweets are posted, we collect the tweets posted serially before and after the visit.

Next, we decide the emotion of each tweet (NEG from POS, that is $-1$ to $+1$) using a table corresponding a word with its emotion polarity.

The following are some words and their emotional scores (i.e., polarity).

| Word | (Japanese) | score |
|------|------------|-------|
| Happy | (うれしい, Ureshii) | 1.00 |
| Say hello | (よろしく, Yoroshiku) | 0.68 |
| Health | (健康, Kenkou) | 0.44 |
| Angel | (天使, Tenshi) | 0.37 |
| Passive | (消極, Shoukyoku) | -0.35 |
| Landslide | (地滑り, Jisuberi) | -0.40 |
| Careless | (油断, Yudan) | -0.60 |
| Sad | (悲しい, kanashii) | -1.00 |

First, evaluation of $Tweet_{pre}$ posted within one day before the visit of a place to which a poster is currently paying attention is made using the function $Evaluate\text{-}Emotion$. Next, the evaluation of $Tweet_{post}$ posted at the location the poster is really visiting is similarly made. The difference between both evaluations is made and whether "+" change or "−"

change is determined by using each threshold (positive number $Th_+$, negative number $Th_-$) as in the inequalities (1.1) and (1.2) follows:

- $\boxed{\text{Evaluate-Emotion}}\ (Tweet_{pre}) - \boxed{\text{Evaluate-Emotion}}\ (Tweet_{post}) > Th_+$     (1.1)

- $\boxed{\text{Evaluate-Emotion}}\ (Tweet_{pre}) - \boxed{\text{Evaluate-Emotion}}\ (Tweet_{post}) < Th_-$     (1.2)

The value (satisfaction level) of the place is determined by aggregating the results of emotional changes of many different users for a certain place.

Specifically, we calculate the ratio of the total number of " +" changes over the total number of " +" and "-" changes and rank the spots by that value to find "bargain spot." Similarly, we use the total number of "-" changes instead of the total number of " +" changes as the numerator to discover a "disappointing spot." In this case " +" and "-" changes correspond to two separate hypotheses.

Figure 1 illustrates the change of the tweet's emotional score along the course of time.

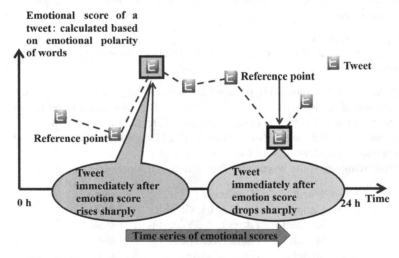

**Fig. 1.** Change of the tweet's emotional score along the course of time.

[Integrated Analysis]

To calculate individual's expectation degree, a method is devised based on *reference points* in prospect theory of behavioral economics, which differ among individuals (See Box "Behavioral Economics"). That is, not the absolute evaluation value of the individual but the change of the evaluation value (that is, the difference) in the individual is taken. Also, in terms of avoidance of losses in behavioral economics, it is particularly important for users to find "bargain spots" or "disappointment spots" in advance.

Furthermore, with respect to weather as open data, we select separate subsets of tweets by sunny days and rainy days and calculate satisfaction levels for each subset to find "bargain spots" for separate weathers. By calculating the differences between two hypotheses on separate data, it is possible to know collective emotional changes on the same spot depending on weathers. For example, on sunny days the satisfaction level is high around Shibuya crossing, but on the rainy days the satisfaction level drops. Meanwhile the satisfaction level is higher around Takeshita street in Harajuku near Shibuya than in Shibuya crossing on rainy days.

Figure 2 illustrates changes in the emotional scores of tweets depending on weathers.

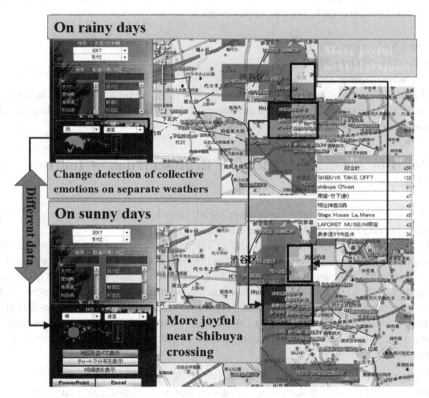

**Fig. 2.** Changes in the emotional scores of tweets depending on weathers.

## 〖Box〗 Behavioral Economics [Behavioral Economics 2019]

Behavioral economics is proposed under the premises different from those of traditional economics. In the first place, behavior economics is based on the premise that people do not necessarily act rationally with respect to economics. Traditional economics, on the other hand, assume that the economic person (i.e., Homo *economicus*) acts rationally.

For example, in the behavioral economics a person has the following biases. That is, the person (i.e., Homo *sociologicus*).

- Evaluates utility (value) subjectively.
- Emphasizes aversion of loss rather than equivalent gain.
- Focuses on present or the near future rather than the distant future.
- Is socially susceptible.

Furthermore, if only freedom of choice is guaranteed, a person can be guided with just a few tricks called *nudge* such as recommendation.

The researchers who contributed to the construction of behavioral economics have recently received the Nobel Prizes in Economics.

- Daniel Kahneman (2002)
- Richard H. Thaler (2017)

If analysis of social big data is to be recaptured from the point of view of behavioral economics, understanding that there are biases in the subjects in social big data, to take advantage of such biases is considered rather than to eliminate them.

## 3  Tourism Application: Meaning Representation of Tourism Resource Name

We describe another tourism application which uses hypothesis generation based on differences (i.e., Hypothesis Generation Method 1).

For example, Tokyo Tower is popular in Tokyo as a tourism resource, but whatever corresponds to Tokyo Tower in Osaka? Or the Yokohama Bay Bridge is situated in Yokohama, what is equivalent to it in Kobe. Quantitatively answering these questions, for example, would be useful for a destination management organization to increase the value of its relevant community area as a tourist destination [Tourism Culture 2019]. A technique called Word2Vec (See Box "Word2Vec") suitable for meaning representation as vectors in natural language processing is used in order to extract the features of these tourism resource names.

[Integration Hypothesis]

By learning the vocabulary that appears in tweets (social data) containing names of many tourism resources (open data) in consideration of the proximity of each other on the text, it is possible to extract the features associated with the tourism resource names. Furthermore, operations such as addition and difference can be performed on the obtained tourism resource names [Tsuchida et al. 2016].

Here we represent a tweet as a tuple. The Tweet database has the following schema:

Tweet <Tweet ID, user ID, posted time, GeoTag, text body>

The tourism resource name according to the following procedure (hypothesis generation) is learned:

```
(ApplyFunction
  (union
    (select Morphological Analyzer (Twitter) w contain tourism resource
      name fetch 500)
    (select Morphological Analyzer (Twitter) w not contain tourism resource
      name fetch 500))
  Word2Vec))
```

Here *Morphological Analyzer* parses a tweet and returns a set of words. *Union* makes the sum of the sets in the same way as SQL. *Word2Vec* is a kind of machine learning algorithm. We collect location-based Twitter data (social data) for a certain period and use the data to learn the meanings of words although geolocational information is not used in this case.

In the above and hereafter procedures, "w" is an abbreviation for "where" denoting conditions for data selection. The procedures consist of functions as well as their compositions and sequences. Please see the Appendix in another paper in this issue for individual operations.

[Integrated Analysis]

First, a list of tourism resource names is prepared using open data. Next the list is used to search the social data as conditions. That is, we prepare the same numbers of social data with tourism resource names and social data without them in order to learn the vocabulary (i.e., the meanings of words). The resultant meanings are subject to the operations such as addition and subtraction.

We make a list of tourism resource names by using tourism resource data (open data) published by the Ministry of Land, Infrastructure, Transport, and Tourism of Japan (MLIT) and related data available through travel sites such as TripAdvisor. From the tweets collected over about 8 months, 500 tweets with the tourism resource names in this list are fetched, and the same number of tweets without the tourism resource names are also fetched. All the fetched tweets are fed into the algorithm Word2Vec to learn the meanings of the words contained by them (See Box "Word2Vec"). That is, Word2Vec is sequentially applied to a set of morphemes that make up each tweet. As hyperparameters of Word2Vec, 400 for dimensions of vectors, Skip-gram for the model, hierarchical softmax function for normalization, and five for the window size are determined by the preliminary experiment (omitted in the above procedure).

The validity of the results is confirmed by using information on the Web. As the measure of similarity between meanings (i.e., word vectors), cosine similarity (the cosine measure) is used.

Let us take the following Eq. (2.1) as an example:

$$. = X - \text{"Yokohama"} + \text{"Kobe"} \tag{2.1}$$

The Eq. (2.1) denotes a concept in Kobe, which corresponds to $X$ in Yokohama. Here if we set? to $Y$ in the Eq. (2.1), then we obtain the following Eq. (2.2):

$$X - \text{"Yokohama"} = Y - \text{"Kobe"} \tag{2.2}$$

The Eq. 2.2 denotes the invariant meaning of a concept which is independent of places such as Yokohama and Kobe.

In other words, we assume that the essential meaning of the concept represented by both hands in the Eq. (2.2) can be obtained by the difference between the concepts represented as word vectors in the semantic space as shown in the above Eq. (2.2). For example, the expression "Yokohama Chinatown" – "Yokohama" denotes the concept or essential meaning of "Chinatown" in general. In this formula, if $X$ = "Yokohama Chinatown", then "Nanjing Town" in Kobe as $Y$ is obtained as a tourist resource name (word) most similar to the given name $X$. Also, if $X$ = "Yokohama Bay Bridge", then "Akashi Kaikyo Bridge" in Kobe is found as the most similar name.

This case is an example of synchronous analysis using social data and open data sequentially in terms of selecting social data using open data as criteria for selection.

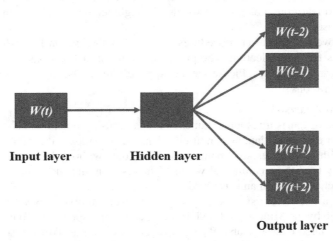

**Fig. 3.** The way how Word2Vec (Skip-gram model) works.

**【Box】 Word2Vec**

Word2Vec [Mikolov et al. 2013] used in this case is a simple kind of three-layer neural network of input layer, middle layer and output layer. The analyst specifies the dimension of the middle layer (hidden layer). The dimension corresponds to the number of neurons. In the learning phase, for the word $w (t)$ in the input layer, the weights of the middle layer are calculated so that the probability of the word $w (t \pm i)$ *appearing* near the word $w (t)$ is high in the output layer. These weights are regarded as the feature vector of the word. Linear algebraic operations (e.g., sums, differences) can be performed between feature vectors obtained by Word2Vec.

Fig. 3 illustrates the Skip-gram model of Word2Vec.

## 4    Tourism Application: Estimation of the Best Time for Seeing Cherry Blossoms

We describe another tourism-related work [Endo et al. 2017], which is classified as integrated analysis based on social data and open data (i.e., Hypothesis Generation Method 2) as well as differences between data (i.e., Hypothesis Generation Method 1).

Cherry blossoms and autumn leaves are among the things that symbolize the sceneries of Japan where the four seasons are clearly distinctive. They are also Japanese things attracting foreign travelers. It is useful information for foreign travelers when the best time of the full bloom of cherry blossoms can be estimated. At present, many websites provide related information in the form of guidebooks. However, the frequency of these updates is often low. The local governments, tourist organizations, and travel agencies provide information about the destination of tourists, but not associated with each other. That is, it is difficult to efficiently collect "now" information about tourist destinations helpful for travelers although tourists want real-time and local-specific seasonal information posted on web sites.

Therefore, providing current, useful, and real-world information for travelers by capturing the change of information in accordance with the season and temporal zone of the tourist region is important for the travel industry. We define "now" information as information for tourists as well as disaster mitigation necessary for travelers during travel, such as best flower-viewing times, festivals, and local heavy rains.

Here we assume that tourist have the following bias.

(Bias) Tourists are interested in estimations closer to the present than predictions that are far away.

The district meteorological observatories of Japan Meteorological Agency (JMA) provide information about flowering and full bloom of flowers such as Sakura (cherry blossoms), and flowering of hydrangea [Ministry of Land, Infrastructure, Transport and Tourism Meteorological Agency 2019]. These data are called phenological observation (information) in JMA. These are open data as well as real-world data. This report is about one place for every weather district, that is, point with a specimen tree to observe such as Chiyoda-ku, Tokyo. Therefore, for example, it represents information of the entire Tokyo (represented by the observation point) but not necessarily faithfully represents the information of the finer point (for example Shinjuku Gyoen National Park in Tokyo). Therefore, we decide to estimate the full bloom of cherry blossoms with various granularity from any area of interest based on social data (tweets) to the place for phenological observation provided by JMA [Endo et al. 2017].

We propose a method to estimate the best time for phenological observations for tourist such as the best-time viewing cherry blossoms and autumn leaves in each region by particularly addressing phenological observations assumed for "now" information in the real world. Tourist information for the best time requires a peak period to view blooming flowers. Furthermore, the best times differ depending on regions and locations. Therefore, it is necessary to estimate the best time of phenological observation for each region and location. Estimating the best-time viewing requires the collection of a lot of information having real-time properties. For this research, we use Twitter data posted by many users throughout Japan.

Phenological observations, such as flowering (Yoshino Sakura), chirps of birds (Japanese nightingale), and insects (small cicadas) are included in data of the first observation dates as open data by 58 weather stations located in Japan (as of 2017).

As an example, we describe a case for cherry blossoms (Sakura). It is also an event that specialists observe cherry blossoms and blooms. Preprocessing includes reverse geocoding and morphological analysis as well as database storage for collected data.

The Japan Meteorological Agency (JMA) carries out phenological observations of Sakura, which yields two outputs, that is, the flowering date and the full bloom date of the observation target. JMA uses one specimen tree for observations in each target area, which produces open data. The flowering date of Sakura is the first day of blooming of 5–6 or more buds of flowers of a specimen tree. The full bloom date of Sakura is the first day of a state in which about 80% or more of the buds are open in the specimen tree.

We used moving averages for analyzing time-series data of tweets posted per day. The standard lengths of time we used for the simple moving average are seven-day moving average and one-year moving average as well as five-day moving average. Since geo-tagged tweets tend to be more frequent at weekends than on weekdays, a moving average of seven days (one-week periodicity) is taken as one of estimation criteria. The phenomenological observation is based on the one-year moving average as the estimation criterion since there are many "viewing" events every year, such as "viewing of cherry blossoms," "viewing of autumn leaves," and "harvesting period."

In addition to the seven-day moving average and the one-year moving average, we also use the moving average of the number of days depending on each phenological target. In this study, we set the number of days of moving average from specified biological period of phenological target. For Sakura, the number of days from flowering until full bloom is biologically known to be about 5 days. Therefore, Sakura in this study uses a five-day moving average as a standard.

Morphological analysis divides the collected geo-tagged tweet into morphemes. We use the MeCab morphological analyzer [MeCab 2019]. For example, the text "桜は美しいです" ("Cherry blossoms are beautiful" in English) is divided into morphemes (" 桜 cherry blossom" / noun), ("は -" / particle), ("美しい beautiful" / adjective), ("です is" / auxiliary verb), and ("。" / symbol).

We use the simple moving average calculated by the following formula (3.1) using the number of data going back to the past from the day before the current date of the best-time viewing:

$$X(Y) = (P_1 + P_2 + \ldots + P_y)/Y \tag{3.1}$$

$(Y)$: $Y$-day moving average.

$Pi$: Number of data of $i$ days ago.

Our method for estimating the best-time viewing counts the number of extracted data and calculates a simple moving average, yielding an estimation of the best flower-viewing time. The method defines a word related to the best-time viewing as the target word. The target word can include Chinese characters, hiragana, and katakana, which represent an organism name and seasonal change.

Next, we calculate a moving average for the best-time viewing judgment. The method calculates a simple moving average using data aggregated daily by the number of extraction data.

The time series of the number of social data and the time series of the number of open data show pseudo correlation in a broad sense with respect to bursts (daily units). This makes it possible to do the following.

- We can know the exact viewing time from social data only by constructing a proper model.

- We can know the full bloom time of finer-size places (e.g., Shinjuku Gyoen National Park) than target places for the phenological observation provided by weather observatories.
- We can estimate the full bloom time of flowers not included in open data (for example, sunflowers).

If the number of tweets on each day exceeds the one-year moving average as in the inequality (3.2), then the Condition 1 holds:

$$P_1 \geqq X(365) \tag{3.2}$$

For the Condition 2, we use the following in Eq. (3.3) with respect to both phenological moving average dependent on biological species and seven-day moving average for one-week periodicity.

$$X(A) \geqq X(B) \tag{3.3}$$

In case of cherry blossoms, we set $A$ and $B$ to five days and seven days, respectively. In other words, this inequation determines the date on which the moving average of a short number of days exceeds the moving average of a long number of days.

The Condition 2 holds if the inequality (3.3) continuously holds for the number of days, which is made equal to or more than half of the moving average of a short number of days. In the case of cherry blossoms, 5 days / 2 = 2.5 days 3 days is the consecutive number of days. That is, if the 5-day moving average exceeds the seven-day moving average by 3 days or more, it shall be the date satisfying the Condition 2.

We describe data for analysis. We collected geo-tagged tweets posted in Japan from 2015/2/17 to 2016/6/30. The data include about 30 million items. We conducted the estimation experiment to ascertain the best-time viewing cherry blossoms and used the target words: "Sakura" or "cherry blossom," which has a variety of spellings such as "桜", "さくら" and "サクラ" in Japanese. The experimental target area is Tokyo. Our proposed method determines the best-time viewing duration in 2015.

[Integrated Hypothesis]

It is possible to estimate the best time viewing time for Sakura by using different data generated by our genialized difference method from the original time-series data of tweets based on three different periods of moving averages (5, 7, and 365 days).

The Condition 1 holds on the day when a dark gray bar exceeds the dotted line, one-year average (See Fig. 4). The Condition 2 holds on the day when the solid line five-day average exceeds the broken line seven-day average for more than 3 days. Therefore, we estimated the duration 3/23 to 4/3 each of which satisfies both the Condition 1 and the Condition 2 as best-time viewing indicated by light gray area according to the following method:

ApplyFunction (ApplyFunction (Partition
(select    $DB_{tweet}$    Date    (2014,    2015)    w    within    *"Tokyo"*    &
*MorphologicalAnalyzer* (*Text*) contain (*Sakura*))
       *Date*) count) *Best-time-viewing-time* sequential

Here the function *Best-time-viewing-time* determines the duration as a temporal data mining operator, which is applied to one element of the set of counts of tweets per day after another as specified by the option *sequential*.

[Integrated Analysis]

If phenological observation data like Sakura (open data) are available, then check of the full bloom judgment using the open data is done to verify the estimated results. That is, if corresponding phenological observation data about Sakura (open data) are contained by the data released by JMA, the validity of the result is verified by using the data.

For narrower regions (e.g., Shinjuku Gyoen National Park), tweets are searched on the condition of a tourism resource name (Shinjuku Gyoen National Park), time-series data are created, and the date of full bloom is obtained. The estimation result in this case is verified by using other social data (e.g. Flicker images) or the related Web pages.

However, we cannot estimate itself for places such as small local park where enough tweets as to cherry blossoms are not posted. Therefore, if we want to estimate such a case, we need to interpolate the number of tweets by using the data of its surrounding places. Interpolation methods include Kriging (See Box "Kriging").

This case generates hypotheses based on differences between different periods of moving averages (that is, represented by the above inequalities). It is also an example of synchronous analysis verifying the results obtained in social data by open data or other social data (i.e., Hypothesis Generation Method 2). We have described the hypothesis generation method 2 in the Sect. 3.2 in another paper in this issue.

Figure 4 illustrate time-series data as to the number of tweets including cherry blossoms posted in Tokyo in 2015, which are counted daily. In addition, data of 1-year moving average, 7-day moving average, and 5-day moving average are also displayed.

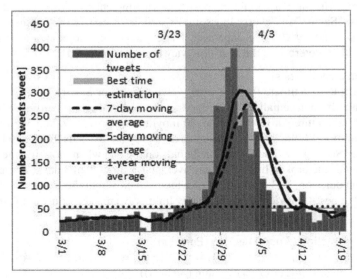

**Fig. 4.** Results of the best time to see, as estimated for Tokyo in 2015.

**【Box】 Kriging**

The spread of SNS has made it possible to acquire real-time data that reflects real-world events. Social data with location information (i.e., the latitude and longitude information) is very useful in spatial and temporal analysis. Generally, however, the proportion of data with position information over entire data posted to various SNS is small. For this reason, there are situations where space-time analysis becomes difficult due to a shortage of data to be analyzed depending on the area and location.

Therefore, an interpolation method is used to estimate the value of the point to be observed based on the values observed at surrounding points. For example, AMeDAS (Automated Meteorological Data Acquisition System), a local meteorological observation system of the Japan Meteorological Agency, performs automatic observation of precipitation, wind direction, wind speed, temperature, and sunshine time in order to monitor weather phenomena such as rain, wind, snow. AMeDAS is installed at approximately 1,300 locations (approximately 17 km apart) throughout Japan. However, since it is observed at discrete points (observation point), the value of the weather point that is not observed is calculated by using the corresponding values of AMeDAS at observation points surrounding the point. Thus, to derive unknown values at a point from the known values around the point is referred to as interpolation.

Here we introduce Kriging [Oliver et al. 1990], which is one of the interpolation methods. Kriging is a geostatistical tool that has been developed to predict the mineral contents of the target area in the field of geology. At present, spatial data analysis is being applied to various fields. The application to space-time analysis is also expected in social data.

As an example, we show an interpolation example of tweets related to cherry blossoms from March to April 2017 at tourist spots in Tokyo (Mount Takao, Showa Memorial Park, Shinjuku Gyoen National Park, Rikugien Garden). $\lambda_{i,}$ in Variogram is calculated based on the number of tweets target word "Sakura" (i.e., Cherry blossoms in Japanese) posted within a 100m-square grid using the power model. Spatial interpolation of tweets posted the tourist spot is performed by Kriging using the calculated variogram as in the formula (3.1):

$$Z(S_0) = \sum\nolimits_{i=1,N} \lambda_i Z(S_i) \qquad (3.1)$$

$S_0$: prediction point.
$N$: number of observation points.
$\lambda_i$: weight at point $i$.
$Z(S_i)$: number of tweets observed at point $i$.

The values on the horizontal axis denote the dates and those on the vertical axis denote the number of tweets posted on each date. Each black bar in the graph is the number of tweets per day containing the name of the tourist spot and the target word. On the other hand, the gray bar in the graph is the result of interpolation based on Kriging of the tweets including the target word around the spot. An example of Kriging-based interpolation is shown in Fig. 5.

It is difficult to identify the peak period without interpolation since Mt. Takao has a small number of tweets where the name of the tourist spot and the target word co-occur. By using interpolation, we can not only grasp the trend through the analysis period, but also capture the peaks of the winter cherry blossoms and the late-flowering cherry blossoms that could not be caught only from the tweets where the tourist spot name and the target word co-occur.

As for Showa Memorial Park and Shinjuku Gyoen National Park, we have succeeded in capturing the peak period without interpolation. However, interpolation has captured the peaks of the winter cherry blossoms in Showa Memorial Park and Shinjuku Gyoen National Park in early March, and those of a rare kind of yellow cherry blossoms in Shinjuku Gyoen National Park in late April. This suggests that effective use of spatial interpolation in social data analysis enables acquisition of rare information that is characteristic of the tourist spots targeted for analysis.

Rikugien Garden has more data to be extracted at the tourist spot itself than the surrounding areas with respect to information related to the cherry blossoms, so the interpolation effect on the peak period to Rikugien Park is small. However, it is possible to obtain the amount of the steady-state information generated from the place name and shop name by interpolation. Therefore, it is possible to capture more accurate peak period estimation and characteristic events by considering the amount of information in steady state analysis.

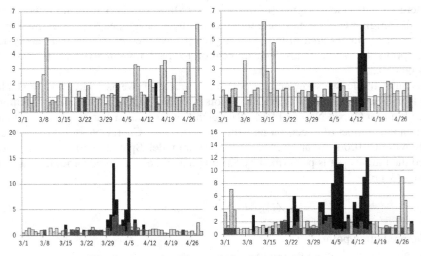

**Fig. 5.** Example of interpolation based on Kriging.

As mentioned above, analysis of social data can be connected to multilateral and high-precision analysis by using spatial interpolation. Of course, it is necessary to fully verify the correctness of the interpolation result, such as further analysis of the interpolation result after understanding the nature of the data set to be analyzed.

In addition to Kriging interpolation of the geostatistical methods introduced here, there are also interpolation methods called deterministic methods. These methods consider only the distance between the prediction point and the observation point, and do not consider the spatial arrangement between these points. They include IDW (Inverse Distance Weighted), Natural Neighbor, Spline, and Trend.

# 5   Tourism Application: Discovery of Free Wi-Fi Candidate Spot for Installation

We describe a case study, finding candidate access spots for accessible Free Wi-Fi in Japan [Mitomi et al. 2016]. This case is classified as integrated analysis based on differences between hypotheses generated from two kinds of social data (i.e., Hypothesis Generation Method 1).

This section describes our proposed method of detecting attractive tourist areas where users cannot connect to accessible Free Wi-Fi by using posts by foreign travelers on social media.

Our method uses differences in the characteristics of two types of social media:

- *Real-time*: Immediate posts, e.g., Twitter
- *Batch-time*: Data stored to devices for later posts, e.g., Flickr

Twitter users can only post tweets when they can connect devices to Wi-Fi or wired networks. Therefore, travelers can post tweets in areas with Free Wi-Fi access spots for inbound tourist or when they have mobile communications. In other words, we can obtain only tweets with geo-tags posted by foreign travelers at such places. Therefore, areas where we can obtain huge numbers of tweets posted by foreign travelers are identified as places where they can connect to accessible Free Wi-Fi and /or that are attractive for them to sightsee.

Flickr users, on the other hand, take many photographs by using digital devices such as digital cameras and smartphones regardless of the availability of networks, but whether they can upload photographs on-site depends on the conditions of the network. As a result, almost all users can upload photographs after going to cafes, returning to their hotels or home countries. However, geo-tags annotated to photographs can indicate when and where they were taken. Therefore, although it is difficult to obtain comprehensive information (activities, destinations, or routes) on foreign travelers from Twitter, Therefore, Flickr can be used to observe such information on foreign travelers as activities, destinations, or routes.

In this case, we are based on our hypothesis of "a place that has a lot of Flickr posts, but few Twitter posts at the same time must have a critical lack of accessible Free Wi-Fi." We extracted areas that were tourist attractions for foreign travelers, but from which they could not connect to accessible Free Wi-Fi by using the differences of these characteristics of social data.

Our method for analysis aims to discover places that meet the following two conditions as candidate access spots for accessible free Wi-Fi:

- Spots which have no accessible Free Wi-Fi
- Spots which attract a lot of foreign tourists

We use the number of photographs taken at locations to extract tourist spots. Many people might take photographs of subjects, such as landscapes based on their own interests. They might then upload those photographs to Flickr. As these were locations at which many photographs had been taken, these places might also be interesting places

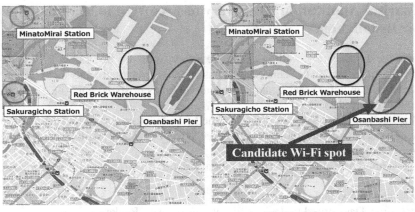

**Twitter dense grids**          **Flickr dense grids**

**Fig. 6.** Differences of highly dense areas of Tweets (left) and of Flickr photos (right).

for many other people to sightsee or visit. We have defined such places as tourist spots. We specifically examined the number of photographic locations to identify tourist spots to find locations where photographs had been taken by a lot of people. To achieve this, we mapped photographs with photographic locations onto a two-dimensional grid based on the locations at which they had been taken. Here we created an individual cell as a grid that was 30 square meters. We then counted the number of Flickr users in each cell. We regarded cells with greater numbers of users than the threshold as tourist spots. Similarly, we counted the number of Twitter users in each cell. We regarded cells with greater numbers of users than the threshold as tourist spots with free Wi-Fi available.

[Integrated Hypothesis]

Based on different data generated from Twitter and Flickr by using our generalized difference method, the fragment collects attractive tourist spots for foreign visitors but without accessible free Wi-Fi currently (See Fig. 6):

$DB_{t/visitor}$ ← Tweet DB of foreign visitors obtained by using durations of their stays in Japan;

$DB_{f/visitor}$ ← Flickr photo DB of foreign visitors obtained by using their habitations;

$T$  ← Partition (*i:Index grid* $DB_{t/visitor}$ $p(i)$); This partitions foreign visitors tweets into grids based on geo-tags; This operation returns a indexed family.

$F$ ← Partition (*j:Index grid* $DB_{f/visitor}$ $p(j)$); This partitions foreign visitors photos into grids based on geo-tags; This operation returns a indexed family.

*Index1* ← Select-Index (*i:Index T Density(i)* $>=$ *th1*); *th1* is a threshold. This operation returns a singleton family.

*Index2* ← Select-Index (*j:Index F Density(i)* $>=$ *th2*); *th2* is a threshold. This operation returns a singleton family.

*Index3* ← Difference (*Index2 Index1*); This operation returns a singleton family.

We determined the thresholds *th1* and *th2* for minimum densities by conducting preliminary experiments.

[Integrated Analysis].

The analysis takes advantage of the differences in characters of the two kinds of social data.

The users of Flicker take photographs of things or landscapes of interest and upload the photos to the site. If there is an internet connection on the spot, you can upload it, but otherwise upload it at another place such as a hotel or restaurant with internet connection. The photograph posted to Flickr at least includes the photographer's interest with information on the shooting time and location added. This is called Hypothesis 1.

On the other hand, Twitter users post what they want to announce such as interests, opinions, impressions on the spot. In other words, the location where tweets are posted has at least the Internet connection environment. This is called Hypothesis 2.

First, select only foreigners visiting Japan from Twitter and flicker users. As for Twitter, if the registered language of the user and the language used for description by the user matches and the user stays in Japan in a short period, this user is added to the set of inbound travelers. In the case of Flicker, only the users whose residence is outside Japan are added to the set of inbound travelers.

We count the number of unique users in each 30m-square grid by considering the Wi-Fi signal strength and leave grids above the threshold. We perform this separately with Twitter and Flicker. Then we make differences between two hypotheses (i.e., Hypothesis 1 "minus" Hypothesis 2) on each grid and focus on the grids which remain as the result. Such grids will be interesting to foreign travelers, but they do not have any or sufficient internet access. This is newly made Hypothesis 3. The validity of this result is confirmed by a field survey.

In short, this case is an example of synchronous analysis to produce an integrated hypothesis by making differences between hypotheses utilizing two social data in parallel.

We collected more than 4.7 million data items with geo-tags from July 1, 2014 to February 28, 2015 in Japan. We detected tweets posted by foreign visitors by using the method proposed by Saeki *et al.* [Mitomi et al. 2016]. The number of tweets that was posted by foreign visitors was more than 1.9 million. The number of tweets that was posted by foreign visitors in the Yokohama area was more than 7,500. We collected more than 5,600 photos with geo-tags from July 1, 2014 to February 28, 2015 in Japan. We detected photos that had been uploaded by foreign visitors to Yokohama by using our proposed method. Foreign visitors posted 2,132 photos in Yokohama. For example, grids indexed by *Index3* contain "Osanbashi Pier." Please note that the above description doesn't take unique users into consideration.

From the analysis of Flicker and Twitter, it is shown that Osanbashi Pier is a candidate location for free Wi-Fi installation (at least during the experiment).

## 6   Tourism Application: International Cuisine Notation System Based on Analogy Between Similar Cuisines

Here we describe a use case using hypothesis generation based on differences (i.e., Hypothesis Generation Method 1).

When foreign travelers visit a restaurant, it may not be possible for them to grasp the outline of the cuisines even if they look at the menu. This is a case where dining options are described in the menu with only Japanese. For example, even if they try to search for cooking information on the Internet, it is not always possible to use the Internet. In such a situation, the travelers cannot order cuisines they want to eat.

In recent years, Japan has been focusing on promoting foreigners travel to Japan. According to the survey of Japan Tourist Agency of the Ministry of Land, Infrastructure, Transport and Tourism (MLIT), what foreign travelers mostly expected before visiting Japan is to eat Japanese foods. It can be known that foreign visitors are strongly interested in Japanese foods. However, they often find difficulties in the Japanese language and ordering foods and drinks.

If a restaurant has a free Wi-Fi in place, the problem of the Japanese language can be solved by machine translation and the problem related to foods and drinks is also expected to be solved by using Internet search. However, it is often considered that the simple translations of the cuisine name and its description from the mother tongue are not sufficiently accurate and that the clerks cannot understand the cuisine the travelers want.

Here to describe the menu in more than one language in advance is considered an effective way for restaurants to receive foreign visitors. However, whether manual or machine, translation tends to be inaccurate. Furthermore, it is difficult to judge whether the translation result is accurate without prior knowledge. Therefore, the menu described in more than one language is important, but its realization is rather difficult.

Therefore, we propose an international cuisine notation system by which foreigners can guess cuisines easily from their familiar and similar cuisines [Nobumoto et al. 2019].

In this study we create this representation automatically by using the data of the user-generated recipe sites such as Cookpad, which is recently popular in Japan [Cookpad 2019]. Cookpad includes not only recipes of Japanese cuisines, but also those of cuisines in the world.

[Integration Hypothesis]

In this research, we propose a notation system using analogy to make it easy to extend the domestic restaurant menu to multiple language versions as an integration hypothesis. We propose a notation system based on the differences between similar cuisines of two countries (for example, Japan and Korea) as in the Eq. (5.1):

$$"Okonomiyaki" (Japanesestylepancake)$$
$$= "Chijimi" (Koreanstylepancake) - "leek" + "cabbage" \quad (5.1)$$

The left side of the equation 1 indicates any one cuisine of a certain country. The right side is a mathematical expression using the operators (+, -) on the cuisine name of different countries similar to the left side one and the ingredients that are the differences between those two cuisines. This notation system has two advantages in that readers can easily understand cuisines and restaurants can easily translate cuisines. With these advantages, the menu of the restaurant can be easily extended to the multiple language versions. Using this scheme, it is possible to provide an international menu as in Fig. 7.

**Fig. 7.** Example of International menu provided by our notation system.

The notation method proposed in this study is supposed to make translation easier than from conventional sentences. This is, "Chijimi", "leek", and "cabbage" are just words, but not statements. Therefore, the interpretation of statements is not necessary and the notation can be translated in a domain targeted to cuisines.

[Integrated Analysis]

Here we propose an automatic generation method of this notation system. This method generates the expressions in the following procedure using the recipe data of the user-generated recipe site.

Step 1: Generate feature vectors of cuisines.

Here we describe the method for making features of cuisines using recipe specific words. Cooking is considered to consist of various elements such as ingredients, cooking process, taste, and utensils. Therefore, in this research, words specific to the recipe are extracted from the recipe data, and they are classified into categories such as ingredients and cooking process. Then, for each category, we generate a feature vector whose component is the word frequency. The procedure for feature vector generation is shown below.

(1)  Creation of lists of international cuisines

The list of cuisines of each country used in this study is prepared in advance. We collect the cuisine names of each country from Web sites and books and make a list of $L$ cuisines. The cuisine of another country (the leftmost item of the right side of the Eq. 1) similar to the cuisine to be explained (left side of the Eq. 1) is to be explored from this list. Hereafter, the cuisine we want to explain is referred to as a query.

(2) Extraction of recipe-specific words.

In the present study, words which frequently appear in the sentences for the procedure of cooking, and less frequently appear in the general sentences are defined as recipe-specific words. We use Wikipedia pages in addition to the recipe data in order to extract such words. We define a score $SC_{df}$ with respect to the recipe specificity of a word $w$, which appears in both cooking procedure of the recipe data and the sentences of Wikipedia by the following Eq. (5.2).

$$SC_{df}(w) = df_{recipe}(w)/df_{wp}(w) \qquad (5.2)$$

Here $df_{recipe}(w)$ is the number of cooking procedures in the recipe data containing the word $w$ and $df_{wp}(w)$ is the number of Wikipedia pages containing the word. We make words with top 500 $SC_{df}$ recipe-specific words. Such recipe-specific words are manually classified into categories such as ingredients and cooking procedures.

(3)    Feature vector generation method

Here we describe the method of generating feature vectors of cuisine names using the generated list of cuisines of one country considering the weight of the cuisine. This vector is characterized by the frequencies of categorized recipe-specific words. Using the category $c$ included in the $C$ kinds of categories ($1 \leq c \leq C$), a recipe-specific word $w_{c,m}$ in $c$ ($1 \leq m \leq M$), cuisine name $l$ of a country ($1 \leq l \leq L$), we generate feature vector $v_a$ ($c, l$) by the following formulas (5.3) and (5.4).

$$v_a(c, l) = (a_1, a_2, ..., a_m, ..., a_M) \qquad (5.3)$$

$$a_m = df\left(w_{c,m,l}\right)/|N_l| \qquad (5.4)$$

Here. $df\left(w_{c,m,l}\right)$ is the number of recipe data which contain the cuisine name $l$ in the recipe name and contain the recipe-specific word $w_{c,m,l}$ in the sentences for the cooking procedures. $|N_l|$ is the total number of recipe data which contain the cuisine name $l$ in the recipe name.

In the above equation, by replacing $l$ by the cuisine name $q$ as the query, a feature vector $v_a$ ($c, q$) is generated similarly.

Step 2: Extract similar cuisines.

We measure the similarity between each cuisine name in the cuisine name list and the query using the generated feature vectors. The importance of factors such as ingredients and cooking process are different in characterizing the cuisine. For example, ingredients are considered more important than cooking utensils. Therefore, in this study, we determine which category is more important for the extraction of similar cuisines by preliminary experiments. Similarity calculation is done by using this importance as a weight of each vector is performed and a similar cuisine is finally extracted. As similarity between the cuisine name $l$ and query $q$ in the category $c$, $sim_c$ ($l, q$) is defined by using the cosine measure between the feature vectors $v$ ($c, l$) and $v$ ($c, q$). Using $sim$ ($l, q$) and the category weight $\alpha c$, as similarity between each cuisine name $l$ and query $q$, $sim_{all}$ ($l$, $q$) is obtained by the following formula (5.5):

$$sim_{all}(l, q) = \Pi_{c=1,C} \; sim_c(l, q)^{\alpha c} \tag{5.5}$$

The importance used here is obtained by preliminary experiments. The obtained cuisine name $l$ with the highest $sim_{all}$ ($l$, $q$) is extracted as a cuisine name similar to the query $q$.

Step 3: Output differences.

We extract differences of cuisine elements similar to query elements and output them as expressions. In this study, we restrict elements to be extracted to the ingredients. The generated feature vector of the ingredient category is based on the frequency of each ingredient. Therefore, by making differences between a feature vector of a cuisine and that of similar cuisine in the ingredient category, features frequent only in either of $l$ and $q$ are extracted. We output ingredients as the difference between the query $q$ and the selected cuisine name $s$ obtained as a cuisine similar to the query as an expression. Using the feature vectors $v(s)$ and $v(q)$, the vector $v_{all}$ ($s$, $q$) for extracting ingredients as differences between $s$ and $q$ is generated by the following formula (5.6).

$$v_{diff}(s.q) = v(s) - v(q) \tag{5.6}$$

Based on the descending order of the absolute value of the top $P$ ingredients $w_p\left(0 \leq p \leq P\right)$ from the resultant $v_{diff}(s, q)$ is extracted as the difference between the cuisine $s$ and query $q$.

These ingredients are used to generate the output shown in the Eq. (5.1). Let $r$ be the expression on the right side of Eq. (5.1). $r$ is initialized with $s$. It is generated by concatenating $w_p$ according to the following expressions (5.7).

$$
\begin{aligned}
r &\leftarrow r + w_p\left(a_p < 0\right) \\
r &\leftarrow r \quad \left(a_p = 0\right) \\
r &\leftarrow r - w_p\left(a_p > 0\right)
\end{aligned}
\tag{5.7}
$$

Here $a_p$ is the value of the ingredient $p$.

The proposed method was realized using about 17.10 million recipe data of Cookpad and 6 subjects evaluated the performance of the method by using 50 outputs in Korean and Italian for 25 Japanese cuisines as queries. The evaluation with respect to the correctness of the expressions was based on 5 levels (1 to 5). The average was 2.7 and the number of the good evaluations ($>= 3$) was 22. The correctness is proportional to the number of the ingredients as the differences.

# 7 Scientific Application: Automatic Discovery of Crater with Central Peak

Scientific data are a kind of real-world data. By taking an example of research conducted by our team including JAXA researchers using scientific data which are also open data, we explain integrated analysis [Hara et al. 2019]. We use hypothesis generation based on differences between original data and their rotations (i.e., Hypothesis Generation Method 1).

A detailed map of the surface of the moon was provided by the JAXA launched lunar orbiter KAGUYA (SELENE) [JAXA KAGUYA 2019]. Of course, KAGUYA's purpose goes beyond making a map of the moon. The goal is to collect data that will help elucidate the origin and evolution of the moon. In order to further pursue such purposes, it is important to examine the internal structure of the moon.

The NASA Apollo program placed the seismometers on the lunar surfaces and collected the moonquake data. Based on the fact that moonquake events from the same hypocenters have similar seismic waves, the moonquake events can be classified into those with distinctive hypocenters. However, the previous classification was mostly done manually and visually. So, there remain a lot of unclassified moonquake events. One of our research works [Kikuchi et al. 2017] aims to automatically classify moonquake events by using machine learning methods such as neural networks and SVM (support vector machine) and has found the former method more efficient than the latter. Another research of ours [Kato et al. 2018] takes different approaches without using seismic waves and shows that it is possible to classify moonquake events by using features such as the distances between the moon and the planets alone.

Another method is to launch a spacecraft to directly explore the internal structure of the moon. However, it is not sufficient to land the spacecraft anywhere on the moon. That is naturally because there are limited resources such as budgets that can be used for lunar exploration. In other words, it is necessary to determine the effective point as the target of the spacecraft based on the evidence. In this way, making an effective plan based on evidence under limited resources is generally called EBPM (Evidence-Based Policy Making) (See Box "EBPM").

On the other hand, whether large or small, a lot of craters exist in the moon. Among them, special crater with a structure called "central peak" (hereinafter referred to as "central peak craters") is present (See Fig. 8). The central peak is exposed on the moon and lunar crustal substances are also exposed therein. Therefore, it is likely that central peak craters scientifically have important features. In other words, the exploration of the surface of the central peak makes it possible to analyze the surrounding internal crustal materials in a relatively easy way. By this, it is expected that not only the origin of the crater and central peak can be estimated, but also the surface environment of the past lunar surface and the process of crustal deformation of the moon can be estimated.

But with respect to the central peak crater as the exploration target, conventionally the confirmation of existence of the central peaks has been visually done by the experts. So, the number of craters known as central peak craters is rather small. This problem can be solved by automatic discovery and cataloguing of central peak craters to significantly increase the number of central peak craters as candidate exploration points.

Thus, in this case with creating the catalog of central peak craters as our final goal, a specific technique for automatic discovery of central peak craters has been proposed. This case uses DEM (Digital Elevation Model) of the lunar surface as results observed by the lunar orbit satellite "KAGUYA" of JAXA [JAXA KAGUYA 2019]. Paying attention to the image characteristics of DEM, we apply CNN (Convolutional Neural Network,

See Box "Convolutional Neural Network") as one technique for deep learning, which is recently in the limelight as AI, to construct the discrimination model. We evaluate discriminability of the central peak crater by the model by experiments.

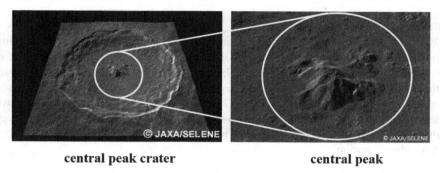

**central peak crater**                    **central peak**

**Fig. 8.** Example of central peak crater.

[Integration Hypothesis]
The central peak crater is identified by the following two-step procedure.

1. Crater extraction on the moon by RPSD method
- Craters are extracted by using the method called RPSD (Rotational Pixel Swapping for DTM) for digital terrain models. Here, DTM (Digital Terrain Model) is a digital terrain model similar to the digital elevation model (DEM).
- The RPSD method focusses on the rotational symmetry when rotating the image of the DEM at a certain point (i.e., central point). That is, RSPD uses the fact that the negative gradient property from the rim of the crater to the center in the lunar DEM does not change with rotation of craters. In other words, we make the difference between the original candidate crater and the rotated one (corresponding to the difference in the observation mode for the same object) and confirm that the feature about rotational symmetry does not change in order to discriminate craters. In a word, this method corresponds to Hypothesis Generation Method 1 in which hypotheses (craters) are found by focusing on differences obtained by different means for the same object (candidate craters).
2. CNN-based automatic discrimination of central peak crater from extracted craters
- In general, in the discrimination phase for each layer of deep learning, each output node multiplies the input values by weights, takes their sum, and adds their bias to the sum, and then outputs the result in the forward direction.
- In the learning phase of deep learning, as a problem of minimizing the error between the output of discrimination and the correct answer, the values of weights and biases are updated by differentiating the error function with respect to the weight and bias of each layer.

[Integrated Analysis].
First, using RPSD, we extract the DEM data of each candidate crater and provide them with a label (non-crater, non-central peak crater, and central peak crater) to create

training data. We learn CNN model thus using the training data and discriminate the central peak craters by using the CNN model. By recall ratios obtained by experiments focusing on how much correct answers are contained in the results, the possibility that CNN is an effective technique in the central peak crater determination is confirmed.

## 【Box】 EBPM

EBPM uses honestly and clearly the current most valuable evidence when choosing among multiple policy options [OECD 2019]. In the context of social big data, it is rephrased as to enable effective policy planning by applying an integrated analysis method to social big data, and grasping the behavior of a group (person, thing) based on quantitative and qualitative evidences. In other words, quantitative and qualitative understanding of where and how much demand and necessity exist in advance by survey analysis can lead to the success of effective measures and investments in important areas such as administration.

## 【Box】 Convolutional Neural Network (CNN)

First the relationships between data mining, machine learning, and artificial intelligence as neighboring technical fields are commented on. Data mining aims to discover knowledge and patterns using methods such as classification and clustering. On the other hand, machine learning has many overlaps with data mining in terms of methods, but it focuses on the learning process of models (classifiers) for making judgments and recognition. In addition, artificial intelligence focuses on reproducing intellectual functions (such as reasoning and judgment) performed by humans on a computer. In the above sense, it can be said that deep learning is just in the common domain of machine learning and artificial intelligence.

In general, CNN [Chen et al. 2014] [LeCun et al. 2015], which is a method of deep learning, first applies one or more filters from the original input (mainly an image) to obtain different types of feature quantities. The process is called convolution. In this case, the filter value corresponds to the weight. Values obtained in the result of the convolution are called feature map. Furthermore, the result of adding a bias to the values of this feature map is output through a function called an activation function (for example, a sigmoid function, a ramp function).

The values output in this way are aggregated together with multiple surrounding values. This process is called pooling. One of the most frequently used aggregation methods is the method of maximizing called maximum pooling. The pooling process has a role to compress information (i.e., subsampling). The aggregation result is output as it is.

CNN is multilayered by preparing multiple pairs of convolutional layer and pooling layer. Therefore, it is called deep learning.

Furthermore, these results are finally combined with all nodes and output. Among the output values, for example, the node number (corresponding to the label) having the largest value is the judgment result.

Let's look at CNN from another point of view. The filter in CNN corresponds to one channel. In general, CNN can be regarded as multi-channel analysis. Although the original data (individual data) is one, different feature quantities can be obtained through each channel. CNN finally combines these and outputs the discrimination result corresponding to the label. In other words, CNN can be said to be *micro* integrated analysis in that it makes copies of different data (features) from the same data source and combines them. By contrast, the integrated analysis described so far is *macro* integrated analysis in the sense of combining multiple data sources.

Figure 9 illustrates how CNN works.

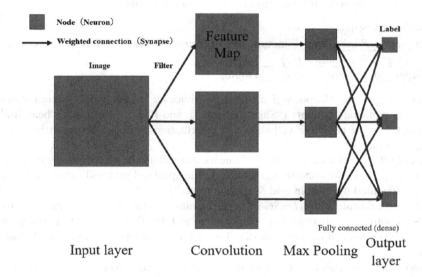

**Fig. 9.** The way how CNN works.

## 8 Tourism Application: Influence of Topics to Regions

So far, cases using the method of generating hypotheses using differences between different hypotheses or data have been specifically described. Here, the case of emphasizing or confirming hypotheses by superposition of different hypotheses (i.e., Hypothesis Generation method 2) is explained using tourism as a subject.

We investigate what concepts (e.g., tourism resource names, phenological observations) are used in relation to a certain topic (e.g., Tokyo Skytree). Further, we analyze how the topic relates to its surroundings if location information is used. We analyze social data (Twitter) and use other social data (e.g., Flickr) for confirmation as well. This case is also an example of synchronous analysis in sequence.

[Integrated Hypothesis]

Regional biases exist in terms used in social data. Therefore, we can discover words strongly related to a topic and geographically identify areas containing a large amount of such related words in a region close to the topic [Tsuchida et al. 2017].

The procedure for hypothesis generation is as follows:

Here we represent a tweet as a tuple.

First, we create a cluster by the clustering algorithm called DBSCAN [Ester et al. 1996][Miyata et al. 2018] [Miyata et al. 2020].

cluster (select *Morphological Analyzer* (*Twitter*) w contain *topic*) $\boxed{DBSCAN}$ *Eps MinP*;

We do the following for each grid contained in each cluster:

Related words$_{grid}$     ←
$\boxed{biasedLexRank}$ (ApplyFunction (select *Morphological Analyzer* (*Twitter*) w within grid & contain *topic*)
$\boxed{Make\_co\text{-}occurrence\_network}$) *topic*;

For example, the *Morphological Analyzer* divides a sentence that "Sakura is beautiful" into syntactic elements ("Sakura" / noun), and ("は"-/ position), ("beautiful" / adjective), ("is") / adjective verbs), (".." / punctuation marks). The result is a set of syntactic elements.

Like SQL, select returns a set of elements that satisfy the selection criteria after w (i.e., where). Here, the condition "included in the specified grid and include a specific topic" is specified by "within grid & contain topic."

The clustering algorithm *DBSCAN* performs clustering using *Eps*, a threshold parameter that controls the distance between clusters and *MinP*, a threshold parameter that controls the number of data in a cluster. The result of clustering is a family of clusters (sets).

ApplyFunction executes the specified function ("make_co-occurrence_network") for each elements of the family.

A specific tourism resource name (in this case, Tokyo Skytree) is set as a topic, and geo-tagged tweets containing the topic are clustered using *DBSCAN* on a grid basis. Next, a word network (graph) is created based on the co-occurrence relationships of the words contained in the social data (i.e., tweets) posted in each grid that composes the cluster. Furthermore, for the network, the importance is propagated from a specific topic (e.g., Tokyo Skytree) by a method called *biasedLexRank* [Lei et al. 2013], and the degree of association between words and topics is calculated. Then we select related words with high importance and analyze them.

[Integrated Analysis]

We find the top 20 related words (e.g., cherry blossoms) in each grid included in the cluster and collect tweets containing the words. By analyzing such tweets, the influence relationship of the topic (tourism resource name) to the grid can be understood.

Other social data (e.g., Flicker images and Wikipedia articles) are used to verify the validity of the results. As a result, it can be confirmed that the identified grid includes the places where Tokyo Skytree and cherry blossoms can be seen together in this case.

This case is an example of synchronous analysis using multiple social data sequentially in the sense that the result obtained from analysis using one social data is confirmed with other social data. In other words, first estimation results (Hypothesis 1) are emphasized or ensured by other estimation results (Hypothesis 2) or the fact as evidence.

Figure 10 illustrates grids where many tweets containing cherry blossoms as related words obtained by using Tokyo Skyree as a topic are posted, and photographs are posted therein as a proof.

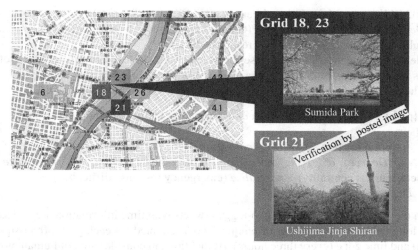

**Fig. 10.** Discovery of grids where we can enjoy Tokyo Skytree (topic) and cherry blossoms (related word) at the same time.

# 9 Disaster Mitigation Application: Discovery of Risky Evacuation Route

Here hypothesis generation using different data complementarily (i.e., Hypothesis Generation Method 3) will be described with disaster mitigation as a subject.

When a large earthquake occurs, the movement of people from the current location (i.e., dense area) to the evacuation facility creates new dense areas. Furthermore, such situations may interfere with evacuation itself. The degree of crowding is expected to be higher if it goes through a traffic route of importance. Also, it is estimated by local governments that a certain area is originally high with respect to *emergency response difficulty* at the time of disaster. So we extract high risk routes on the basis of congestion degree, determined by utilizing tweets (social data), the road networks from Open Street Map (open data), and evacuation facilities (open data), published by the Ministry of Land, Infrastructure, Transport and Tourism as well as emergency response difficulty at the time of disaster (open data), published by the Tokyo Metropolitan Government [Kanno et al. 2016].

[Integration Hypothesis]

A combination of social data (Twitter) and open data (road network, evacuation facilities, and emergency response difficulty) can be used to analyze evacuation routes with high risk.

$INDEX_{(c,e)} \leftarrow$ *Make-crowded-evacuation-area* ($DB_{tweet}$, *Gaussian*)
$FAMILY_{path} \leftarrow$ Make-Indexed Family ($INDEX_{(c,e)}$ pgRouting)
*Degree of risk* $\leftarrow$ *normalize* (congestion degree) + *normalize* (betweenness centrality) + *normalize* (emergency response difficulty)

$FAMILY_{path} \leftarrow$ Make-Indexed Family ($INDEX_{(c,e)}$pgRouting).
*Degree of risk* $\leftarrow$ *normalize* (congestion degree) + *normalize* (betweenness centrality) + *normalize* (emergency response difficulty).

Here $DB_{tweet}$ denotes the database for tweets. Make-Indexed Family makes a set of routes for each index of crowded area ($c$) and evacuation area ($e$) in $INDEX (c,e)$.

The procedure is as follows:

{path} $\leftarrow$ Path from dense area $c$ to evacuation facility $e$; Find a set of paths.
(sort
   (ApplyFunction {path} *Risk calculation*
      (*Degree of risk*: *normalize* (congestion degree) + *normalize* (betweenness centrality) + *normalize* (emergency response difficulty))
   *Degree of risk*)

In the whole area of interest, geo-tagged tweets with time information are collected for a long time, and the number of unique users is counted for each grid (500m-square mesh) and time zone (every three hours). At that time, in consideration of human movement at the grid boundary, we use the result of smoothing using *Gaussian* filter among nine neighboring grids including the target grid in order to count the users. The dense area is decided by this value.

Next, we will consider the people movement from the determined dense area as the departure point to the evacuation facility as the destination point, which are the open data provided by MLIT (See Box "Evacuation Facilities and Emergency Response Difficulty"). First, the route is modeled in a graph using the road information of obtained from OSM open data. Next, a set of routes for moving from a dense area to an evacuation facility is searched. We use pgRouting [pgRouting 2019] for the search.

Furthermore, the risk of the route is calculated as follows. First, the density (i.e., congestion degree) of routes is calculated based on the estimated number of people in the dense area, the number of evacuation facilities in the vicinity of the dense area, and the number of roads from the dense area to the evacuation facility as one kind of open data. Next, we calculate the betweenness centrality of the route from the node near the dense area to the node near the evacuation facility that appears on the graph (network) model constructed from second open data. Furthermore, we determine the degree of emergency response difficulty of the route based on the degree of emergency response difficulty at the time of disaster as third open data (See Box "Evacuation Facilities and Emergency Response Difficulty") provided by Tokyo Metropolitan Government. Congestion degree, betweenness centrality, and emergency response difficulty of a route are respectively normalized and summed to calculate the overall risk of the route.

Figure 11 illustrates an example of detecting a high-risk route in Shinjuku area.

[Integrated Analysis].

From the point of view of integrated analysis, one social data and three open data are combined to calculate three indices, and the results are combined to calculate the

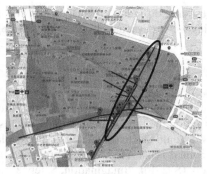 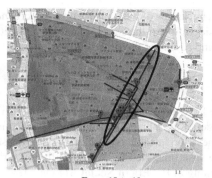

From 05 to 06                     From 18 to 19

**Blue Area : Shinjuku 3-Chome**    **Green Area : Shinjuku 4-Chome**

**Fig. 11.** Detection of high-risk route in Shinjuku area (surrounded by ovals).

degree of risk of the route. In other words, this case is an example of synchronous analysis that combines the discovery of routes based on social data and open data, and the aggregation of hazard levels based on social data and open data. In a word, in this case, hypotheses are generated by combining different hypotheses as results complementarily (i.e., Hypothesis Generation Method 3).

The validity of the analysis result on the degree of risk of the obtained route is confirmed by the information from the local public sector [Shinjuku Station Area Disaster Prevention Measures Council 2019].

## 【Box】 Evacuation Facilities and Emergency Response Difficulty

(a) Evacuation facility [Ministry of Land, Infrastructure, Transport and Tourism 2019]
    The Ministry of Land, Infrastructure, Transport and Tourism maintains basic information about land such as topography, land use, public facilities as GIS data. Some of the data are provided as open data in XML format in accordance with the Basic Law for Promotion of Use of Geospatial Information. Evacuation facility information is also included therein.
(b) Emergency response difficulty [Tokyo Metropolitan Government Bureau of Urban Development 2019]

The Tokyo Metropolitan Government conducts regional risk measurement surveys approximately every five years. In the seventh survey, the risk for earthquakes in each area was measured for 5,133 town districts in urbanized areas of Tokyo, regarding the collapse of buildings and fires. In this survey, the following dangers due to earthquake shaking are measured at every town. The data are provided by XLS.

- Building collapse risk (risk of building collapse)
- Risk of fire (risk of fire spread due to fire occurrence)
- Overall risk (risk of building collapse and spread of fire)

- The degree of risk considering "emergency response difficulty," that is, danger in consideration of the ease (or hardness) of activities such as evacuation, fire extinguishing, and rescue at the time of disasters)

## 10  Conclusion

We have explained various use cases such as tourism, science, and disaster mitigation in detail as examples of integrated analysis based on the three methods for hypothesis generation introduced in another paper. Lastly, we would like to add there is a spectacular use case imagined by a science fiction writer named Isaac Asimov, who predicted the coming of the Era of Social Big Data realistically (See Box "Imagination, Science, and Technology").

### 【Box】  Imagination, Science, and Technology

Some writers of science fiction imagine technologies or concepts that are not realized at the time of writing the works, but would lead to the realization of the same thing later in history. For example, French-born science fiction writer Jules Verne [Wikipedia Jules_Verne 2019] is known for writing "From the earth to the moon" and "Twenty Thousand Leagues Under the Sea." As important props of the stories in those works, Verne introduced the prototypes of rockets and submarines. Close to the present age, British-born science fiction writer Arthur C. Clarke [Wikipedia Arthur_|C._Clarke 2019] advocated the concept of geostationary satellites in a contribution to the scientific magazine "Wireless World" in 1945. And there is Isaac Asimov [Wikipedia Isaac_Asimov 2019] as a science fiction writer in the United States, which is lined up with Clark. Asimov wrote a series of works on robots (such as "I, Robot"). In the works he introduced three laws of robotics or artificial intelligence (AI), which is currently attracting attention.

On the other hand, Asimov's works include another series called *foundation*. In this group of works, which began writing about *70 years ago*, it predicts the invention of new disciplines using modern big data and social data [Zeng2015] [Szakaly 2017]. The field of study developed in those works is, of course, a fictitious field of study (called *psychohistory* in the works), but the main character named Seldon that appears in the works states there are several principles that can be said to be equivalent to the premises of social big data. Extractions related to such principles and their modern interpretations are described below.

Please note that the italic words are changed from the original ones or newly inserted by the author.

- *"It is assumed that data* are sufficiently large for valid statistical treatment."
  It can be said that this expresses the concept of big data itself. It goes without saying that big data are a prerequisite for model learning.
- "He *(Seldon)* kept one *(i.e., pad computer)* beneath his pillow for use in moments of wakefulness."

At the time the first story in this series was written, computers were not so popular yet. Now, in order to process big data at high speed, it is indispensable to use parallel computing and GPU (Graphics Processing Unit) in addition to the efficient sequential computing.

- "As each item *(i.e., variable)* was mentioned, new symbols sprang to life at his touch, and melted into the basic function which expanded and changed."
Selection of variables is an important step in prediction. The more attributes are considered, the more accurate the prediction will be in general. It is necessary to consider variables as additional candidates, which are highly independent of each other and have sufficient contribution ratios as well.
- "It will end well; almost certainly so for the project; and with reasonable probability for you *(i.e., not in the all-or-nothing manner)*."
In general, multiclass, multilabel, and probabilistic attribution are fundamental to the problem of determining attribution to data class (or category).
- "Within another half year he would have been here and the odds would have been stupendously against us – 96.3 plus or minus 0.05% to be exact."
Predictions always have uncertainty. The confidence interval is used in statistics.
- "I have tried to analyze his workings, but you know how risky it is to introduce the vagaries of an individual in the psychohistoric equations."

Hypotheses are statistical properties as a group and cannot be used to predict the behavior of a specific individual.

The talented author's imagination may be to vividly portray the ideal form of the future that has not yet been seen in the age of the works, as if it were a reality. It can be said that Asimov is one of such talented writers.

**Acknowledgments.** This work was supported by JSPS KAKENHI Grant Number 20K12081, Tokyo Metropolitan University Grant-in-Aid for Research on Priority Areas, and Nomura School of Advanced Management Research Grant.

# References

Behavioral economics. https://www.behavioraleconomics.com/resources/mini-encyclopedia-o20 19f-be/prospect-theory/ Accessed August 2019

Chen, X.-W., Lin, X.: BigData Deep Learning: Challenges and Perspectives 2014 IEEE Access **2**

Cookpad. https://cookpad.com/ Accessed 2019

Endo, M., Shoji, Y.S.S., Hirota, M., Ohno, S., Ishikawa, H.: Best-time estimation for regions and tourist spots using phenological observations with geotagged tweets. Int. J. Informat. Soc. (IJIS) **9**(3), 109–117 (2017).

Ester et al.: A density-based algorithm for discovering clusters a density-based algorithm for discovering clusters in large spatial databases with noise. In: Proceedings of the Second International Conference on Knowledge Discovery and Data Mining, pp. 226–231 (1996).

Fujii,S., Hirota, M., Kato, D., Araki, T., Endo, M., Ishikawa, H.: Analysis of the difference of movement trajectory by residents and tourists using geotagged tweet. In: Proceedings of the 11th International Conference on Advanced Geographic Information Systems, Applications, and Services (GEOProcessing2019) (2019).

Hara, A., Yamamoto, Y., Araki, T., Shibata, M., Ishikawa, H.: Identification of moon central peak craters by machine learning using Kaguya DEM. J. Space Sci. Informat. Japan, 8, pp. 1–10 (2019). (in Japanese). https://doi.org/10.20637/JAXA-RR-18-008/0001

Japanese Government, Tourism Vision to Support the Future of Japan. https://www.kantei.go.jp/jp/singi/kanko_vision/pdf/honbun.pdf. Accessed 2019

JAXA, KAGUY(SELENE) Data Archive. https://darts.isas.jaxa.jp/planet/pdap/selene/index.html. Accessed 2019.

Kanno, M., Ehara, Y., Hirota, M., Yokoyama, S., Ishikawa, H.: Visualizing high-risk paths using geo-tagged social data for disaster mitigation. In: Proceedings of the 9th ACM SIGSPATIAL Workshop on Location-based Social Networks (2016)

Kato, K., Yamada, R., Yamamoto, Y., Shibata, M., Yokoyama, S., Ishikawa, H.: Investigation of orbit parameters to classify the deep moonquake source. J. Space Sci. Informat. Japan **7**, 43–52 (2018). (in Japanese). https://doi.org/10.20637/JAXA-RR-17-009/0005

Kikuchi, S., Yamada, R., Yamamoto, Y., Hirota, M., Yokoyama, S., Ishikawa, H.: Classification of unlabeled deep moonquakes using machine learning. In: Proceedings of the 9th International Conferences on Advances in Multimedia (MMEDIA 2017) (2017).

LeCun, Y., Bengio, Y., Hinton, G.: Deep learning, vol. 521, pp. 436–444 (2015). https://doi.org/10.1038/nature14539

Lei, K., Zeng, Y.F.: A novel biased diversity ranking model for query-oriented multi-document summarization Appl. Mech. Mater. **380–384**, 2811–2816 (2013). https://citeseerx.ist.psu.edu/viewdoc/download?doi=10.1.1.835.1759&rep=rep1&type=pdf Accessed 2019

MeCab. https://taku910.github.io/mecab/. Accessed 2019

Mikolov, T., Chen, K., Corrado, G., Dean, J.: Efficient estimation of word representation in vector space. arXiv: 1301.3781. Accessed 2019

Ministry of Land, Infrastructure, Transport and Tourism, National Land Numerical Information Download Service, Evacuation Facility Data. https://nlftp.mlit.go.jp/ksj/gml/datalist/KsjTmplt-P20.html. Accessed 2019

Ministry of Land, Infrastructure, Transport and Tourism Meteorological Agency, Data on phenological observations. https://www.data.jma.go.jp/sakura/data/index.html. Accessed 2019

Mitomi, K., Endo, M., Hirota, M., Yokoyama, S., Shoji, Y., Ishikawa, H.: How to find accessible free Wi-Fi at tourist spots in Japan. In: Spiro, E., Ahn, Y.Y. (Eds.) Informatics Social. SocInfo 2016. Lecture Notes In Computer Science, vol. 10046. Springer, Cham (2016)

Miura, R., Hirota, M., Kato, D., Araki, T., Endo, M., Ishikawa, H.: Predicting user gender on social media sites using geographical information. In: Proceedings of the ACM 10th International Conference on Management of Digital EcoSystems (MEDES2018) (2018)

Miyata, Y., Ishikawa, H.: Accelerating analysis of frequently gathered data with continuous density based clustering. In: Proceedings of 10th ACM International Conference on Management of Digital EcoSystems (MEDES2018) (2018)

Miyata, Y., Ishikawa, H.: Concept drift detection on data stream for revising DBSCAN cluster. In: Proceedings of the 10th International Conference on Web Intelligence, Mining and Semantics (WIMS2020) (2020)

Nobumoto, K., Hirota, M., Kato, D., Ishikawa, H.: Multilingualization of cooking by analogical description. J. Japan Soc. Fuzzy Theory Intell. Informat. **31**(1), 526–553 (2019). (in Japanese)

OECD, Evidence in Education: Linking Research and Policy. https://www.oecd.org/education/ceri/evidenceineducationlinkingresearchandpolicy.htm. Accessed 2019

Oliver, M.A., Kriging, W.R.: A method of interpolation for geographical information systems. Int. J. Geographic Inf. Syst. **4**, 313–332 (1990)

pgRouting. https://pgrouting.org/. Accessed 2019

Shinjuku Station Area Disaster Prevention Measures Council, Shinjuku Rule. https://www.city.shinjuku.lg.jp/content/000201844.pdf. Accessed 2019

Szakaly, A.: 7 Data science principles introduced by Asimov in the foundation (2017). https://Eas ymarketingmath.Com/2017/01/7-data-science-principles-asimov/. Accessed 2019

Bureau of Urban Development Tokyo Metropolitan Government, Emergency response diffi-culty. https://www.toshiseibi.metro.tokyo.jp/bosai/chousa_6/download/kikendo_06.pdf?1802. Accessed 2019

Tourist culture, tide management of destination management, No. 234 (July 2017). https://www.jtb.or.jp/wp-content/uploads/2017/07/bunka234.pdf. Accessed 2019

Tooshima, M., Kato, D., Endo, M., Shoji, Y., Hirota, M., Ishikawa, H.: Finding spots that disbelief based on differences in polarity of microblogging. In: Proceedings of the 9th Forum on data engineering and information management (DEIM) (2017). (in Japanese)

Tsuchida, T.: On calculation of the meanings of the areas and landmarks using Word2Vec. In: Proceedings of the 8th Forum on Data Engineering and Information Management (DEIM) (2016). (in Japanese)

Tsuchida, T., Kato, D., Endo, M., Hirota, M., Araki, T., Ishikawa, H.: Analyzing relationships of words using BiasedLexRank from Geotagging Tweets. In: Proceedings of ACM International Conference on Management of Digital EcoSystem (MEDES2017) (2017)

Wikipedia, Arthur C. Clarke. https://en.wikipedia.org/wiki/Arthur_C._Clarke. Accessed 2019

Wikipedia, Isaac Asimov. https://en.wikipedia.org/wiki/Isaac_Asimov. Accessed 2019

Wikipedia, Jules_Verne. https://en.wikipedia.org/wiki/Jules_Verne. Accessed 2019

Zeng, D.: Crystal Balls, Statistics, Big Data, and Psychohistory: Predictive Analytics and Beyond. IEEE Intell. Syst. **30**(2), 2–4 (2015). https://doi.org/10.1109/MIS.2015.24. Accessed2019

# Data Analysis in Social Network: A Case Study

Mou De[1,2(✉)], Anirban Kundu[1,2], and Nivedita Ray De Sarkar[1,2]

[1] Netaji Subhash Engineering College, Kolkata 700152, India
mou.latu@gmail.com, anik76in@gmail.com,
nivedita.raydesarkar@gmail.com
[2] Computer Innovative Research Society, Howrah 711103, West Bengal, India

**Abstract.** Authors propose a structural design of social networks to study architecture of social networking site and its working principles. Typical social networking sites have three-tier architecture which induces higher searching time for user queries. Our proposal presents a load balancing module for protecting user enquiries before spreading them to data server. In this chapter, query optimization of user queries for faster results has been discussed. Experimentation results exhibit possibilities of data (user queries) failure reduction due to external disturbances. Authors have analyzed large scale data of social network through graph for reducing data loss and minimal network failure to maintain scale free growth in Social network. Properties of interface module and growth coefficient are to be analyzed to exhibit benefits of proposed system architecture for balancing load from web server to data server through Hash table cache, Log table and index control module with scale-free query optimization.

**Keywords:** Social network (SN) · Query optimization · Social architecture · Distributed network · Data analysis

## 1 Introduction

SNs provide virtual connections among users by the use of specific domains according to users' choice like sports, cinema, music, and so on. A user is interconnected with SN using share, like, post and joins on particular domains to build their social relationships. User is able to like/follow other profiles unless it is blocked. Users also send friend requests to other persons for connecting to outer world based on particular choices [1–4]. Each social networking site [5–8] needs authenticated/valid users (registered users on particular site and their profiles are visible to public users) who are treated as existing users. Interaction between users through the friendship request using SN makes the relationship/ networking [9–12]. User exchanges their views with other users on SN platform to create a virtual network connectivity using web server and data server working on behalf of users.

User data analysis [13] has a major impact for maintaining data security and network connections among users of SN [14, 15]. In SN [16, 17], user networks are not always structured [18], and do not maintain specific patterns for communication purpose. It is necessary for flawless platform to understand and analyze [19–21] SN data according

© Springer-Verlag GmbH Germany, part of Springer Nature 2021
A. Hameurlain et al. (Eds.): TLDKS XLVII, LNCS 12630, pp. 112–136, 2021.
https://doi.org/10.1007/978-3-662-62919-2_5

to need of user in minimal time [22, 23] maintaining user data reliability [24], and data security [25, 26].

Users share their photos, videos, files in SN with others without maintaining privacy. SN platform has to take care of data security and privacy issue to protect user data from being tampered by others maintaining privacy [27]. User privacy is a major criterion in SN as number of users is increased on daily basis. A user has shared own data with other users. Shared data is visible to the world through SN providing secured interfaces, policies, and data storage for keeping user's privacy. User has to follow some privacy policies [28] so that they can restrict to expose their personal information to outer world [29, 30]. SN provides an authentication procedure to maintain data ownership of a user. Users' exchange and share personal information without awareness of being exposed. User data could be hacked and misused by anyone. Proper verification of a user login could establish a secured connection between data server and user to handle private data. Extensible database and distributed framework [31] are needed to manage huge scalable data of users. SN database has been designed for faster query optimization, query processing, and crash recovery to store and retrieve user data [32]. Freedom of communication for particular users can enhance social, political, and economic environment [33, 34].

Our aim is to show an efficient procedure through which SN interacts with help of web servers and data servers. A user log-in facility is incorporated in web server using proper authentication. User data is transmitted to web server for further processing. User data has been analyzed using load balance module for checking query patterns to send to the particular data server for evaluation.

Scope of the research work includes analyze real time user data to check system performance using process waiting time, response time and completion time in CPU and memory.

Motivation of the research work is the index-controlled load balancing to be applied for optimizing time complexity in case of data analysis in social network.

Novelties of our proposed design framework are as follows:

– Interface module ($I_M$) is a subset of Webserver_Selection, Load Balancer ($L_B$), Data Flow ($D_F$) and Index Control ($I_C$).

Growth coefficient is dependent on number of elements of Hash table cache, Log table, Load balancer, Dataflow and Index control which are subsets of Interface module.

Rest of the chapter is organized as follows: Sect. 2 briefly mentions about the related works; Sect. 3 describes design framework in details; Sect. 4 represents mathematical explanations; experimental results have been depicted in Sect. 5; finally, Sect. 6 concludes our research work.

## 2  Related Works

In this section, we have dealt with distributed network [35], social network, existing architecture, and new architecture for better results. Exchange of information from one-end to another are called network. Connection between multiple nodes for sharing data is a type of networking. Physical and virtual connections are used to share user information. Social networks [36] are very popular and useful for common people, politician, business person, company, etc. Each type of user could create & show profile on social network. Known and unknown persons are connected through "friendship" on SN in a geographically distributed manner. Performance of SN depends on geographical distribution [37] of networks, and time complexity. Growth [38] of a SN is dependent on network connection, distributed framework [39], user response, and query optimization.

Existing system structures and its working procedures in response of particular group of users have been studied. In existing architecture of SN, we see a typical three layer concept. A user directly sends request to a server dedicated to SN. Web server receives request and accordingly it passes query to "avatar" node. Then, "avatar" node decides active server. Query passes to specific databases according to availability of active servers. A cache [40] is used for buffering users' queries from "avatar" node to database. Results are thrown to the users after processing queries in database.

Load balance [41, 42] helps to manage network traffic for large scale social network, and it manages to store & retrieve users' data. Load balance synchronizes [43] data flow from the webserver to the data server. Server loads are controlled using load balancing to maintain data flow [44] in SN. Specific server is assigned to each user according to the queries and stored resultant data after execution of certain queries. Similar types of user queries are served using particular servers with increasing number of users. Load balance [45, 46] technique is incorporated to avoid query optimization delay and stabilizes SN assigning new servers for serving particular user queries. Communication delay due to network traffic is avoided by load balancing technique.

Distributed server concept is used in SN platform to increase network performance, efficient data storage [47] and query optimization with minimal delay. Information is classified [48] based on real-time users' choice by analyzing 'like', 'opinion', 'share' in SN. Data mining [49] and data analysis [50] approach have been used to find out key information from pool of data in data server. Analysis of SN through data mining depends on users' psychology, behavior, statistics, sociology for classifying and grouping important information.

## 3 Design Framework

In this section, we have presented how a large scale data is handled by social networking site for analyzing the architecture of any social network. We have studied time complexity management using online social networks to understand SN architecture. We have analyzed real time users' data for checking balanced load from one module to another module maintaining users' data reliability and privacy. Earlier version of this chapter has been published in [51].

The entire procedure of sending and receiving data from user to server-end and vice versa is described in this section (refer Fig. 1) using distinct algorithms (Algorithm 1 to Algorithm 6). User sends query to interface module which is designed for verification of user data for next level of processing and further executions. Authentication of a particular user (existing or new) is verified by interface module. Entire user log is maintained by interface module. Interface module transfers verified data to selection manager module.

Hash table cache and log table are parts of selection manager. Selection manager selects web server for processing queries.

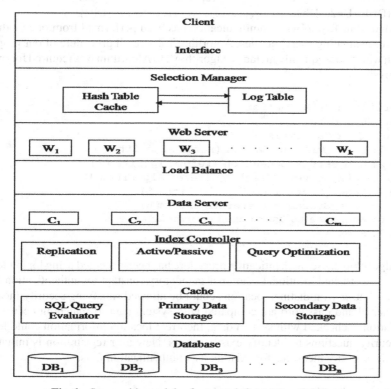

**Fig. 1.** Server-side modular framework for proposed design.

Selection manager has two parts, such as hash table cache and log table. Hash table cache monitors all web servers for maintaining detailed statistics. It passes request and makes a copy of location details of particular web server as required. Hash table cache keeps record of frequently used web services.

Hash table cache information is stored in log table which maintains system (web server) log details. Log table module keeps each user's transaction details as a log file. Load balancer module is designed to control flow of data from web server to data server. Load balancer module also selects data server to process query of user. Web server module serves request of each client. Each web server consists of many servers as follows:

$$N1 = \{w10, \ w11, \ w12, \ w13, \ \ldots, \ w1n\}$$

$$N2 = \{w20, \ w21, \ w22, \ w23, \ \ldots, \ w2n\}$$

$$N3 = \{w30, \ w31, \ w32, \ w33, \ \ldots, \ w3n\}$$

A copy of data is replicated on cache. Database is mainly used for storing data tables for each user.

Databases are represented as follows: Dbs = {Db1, Db2, Db3, ..........................., Dbn}

In Algorithm 1, step-wise communication has been performed from one module to another for evaluating users' queries. Algorithm 1 is overall procedure of our proposed approach which subsequently includes Algorithm 2 to Algorithm 6 as required for overall data analysis.

```
Algorithm 1: Data_Analysis
Input: User data
Output: Query analysis
Step 1: User _Authentication (refer Algorithm 2)
Step 2: Web_Server_Selection (refer Algorithm 3)
Step 3: Data_Server_Selection (refer Algorithm 4)
Step 4: Index_Control (refer Algorithm 5)
Step 5: Data_Storager (refer Algorithm 6)
Step 6: Response to user based on data analysis
Step 7: Stop
```

In Algorithm 2, user authentication procedure has been executed using login identification, password, and location. Location is mandatory constant for authentication in our approach. A user with distinct locations could be allowed satisfying security measurement. User-id and password are compared with system data. If matching occurs, then user location is checked with system data. Incorrect location information could lead to raise security questions to identify existing users. New user registration is initiated in case all the security measures for existing user authentication fails.

```
Algorithm 2: User_Authentication
Input: User Data
Output: User data validation
Step 1: Void Validate_User (int User_id, String Password, String
User_Location)
Step 2: If (User_id! = Null && Password ==User.Password)
Step 2.1: Check (User_Location)
If (User_Location ==Location)
Then User exists
Else
Error message: Location does not match
Step 2.2: Check security question to identify user
Step 3: Else
Error message: User does not exit
Step 4: Register (new user)
Step 5: Stop
```

In Algorithm 3, details of web server selection are received by "selection manager" for checking availability of web servers according to users' queries. Data has been sent to hash table cache of selection manager. Data is being searched within hash table cache. Data log and server log are maintained by hash table and log table respectively. Log table preserves web server location details, and web server crash reports. User log details like query patterns, user locations, login time are kept using hash table cache. Hash table cache channels user queries to a particular web server for proceeding further. Web server passes user queries to load balance the module for processing in data server.

**Algorithm 3: Web_Server_Selection**
```
Input: User data
Output: Data log maintain, server log maintain, selection of par-
ticular web server
Step 1: Selection_manager (hash_table_cache) = data
Step 1.1: Search (hash_table_cache, data)
Step 1.2: If(data == hash_table_cache.data)
Step 2: hash_table_cache(data)
Step 2.1: If(data(checked) == TRUE)
Select(web_server)
Step 2.2: Else
Search(available web server)
Step 3: update(hash_table_cache.data) //keeps all details of web
server
Step 4: hash_table_cache maintains user log
Step 5: Log table keeps track of web server crash report service &
location details of web server
Step 6: Web server takes query for further processing
Step 7: Web server passes query to next module
Step 8: Stop
```

Load balance module has selected data server for execution of users' queries as shown in Algorithm 4. A user query is fetched from Algorithm 3 and sent to load balance module for execution. Availability of data server has been checked by Load balance module. Data server is being selected by load balance module according to availability and type of queries.

**Algorithm 4: Load_Balance_Data_Server_Selection**
```
Input: User_Query
Output: Data server selection
Step 1: Load_balance(Query)
Step 2: Select Data server to pass query
Step 3: Data_Server_Selection(table, query)
Step 3.1: for (query Q search Data_server)
Step 3.1.1: If(query == table.query)
Select the data server
Step 3.1.2: Else
Data server not selected
Step 3.2: Create the table for received data
Step 4: Data server process the query
Step 5: Stop
```

Algorithm 5 exhibits step-wise checking of active server and process users' queries. Data is being searched by "Index_control" module in cache & database as required. Index_control module searches active data servers to process user queries. Data server finds data in cache to evaluate user queries. Database is searched for particular data table in case of inadequate data in cache. Error message is delivered to index_control module to find next available data server for evaluate user queries.

```
Algorithm 5: Index_Control
Input: Data, data server selection
Output: Processed Query
Step 1: Search (active data server)
Step 2: If (data server == active)
Step 2.1: Search (table for processing query)
Step 2.2: If (data == cache.data)
Evaluate query
Step 2.3: Else if (cache.data == Not Found)
Check table in database
Step 2.4: Else
Error: Table is not present in Database
Step 3: Stop
```

Query evaluation and data storage procedures have been described in Algorithm 6 using cache for frequent data update. The cache is being searched for user query evaluation, and further database is updated. In case, user data is not found in cache, database is searched for evaluation. After evaluation, cache and database are updated, and result is returned to the users.

```
Algorithm 6: Data_Storage
Input: Processed query, cache, Database
Output: Query evaluation, store data
Step 1: Update_Cache(table, query)
Step 2: for(query q, user.query)
Step 2.1: If (query.data == table.data)
Execute query;
Update Database;
Return result;
Step 2.2: Else
Search table in Database for evaluate query;
Update Database;
Update cache;
Step 3: Stop
```

## 4   Mathematical Explanations

**Motivation of Theorem 1:** Motivation of Theorem 1 is to establish relations between Interface module and web server selection, Load balance, Data flow, Index control with respect to their functionality.

***Theorem 1:*** **Interface module $(I_M)$ is a subset of Webserver_Selection, Load Balancer $(L_B)$, Data Flow $(D_F)$ and Index Control $(I_C)$.**

*Proof:*

$$\text{Set of clients} \implies C_S = \{C1, C2, \ldots\ldots, Cn\}$$

$$\text{Interface Module } (I_M) \implies UserValidation(U\_Validity)$$

$$U_{Validity} \in I_M$$

$$\because U_{Validity} = \{Uid, Upassword, ULocation\}$$

$$\therefore \{Uid, Upassword, ULocation\} \in I_M$$

$$\text{WebServer\_Selection}(WS_{Select}) \implies Hashtablecache(\text{HT}_{cache})(Domain_{type})$$

$$\text{WebServer\_Selection}(\text{WS}_{Select}) \implies Logtable(L_T)(access_{history}, crash_{info}, replication_{info})$$

$$\because \text{WS}_{Select} \subseteq I_M$$

$$\therefore \{\text{HT}_{cache}, L_T\} \subseteq I_M$$

$$\therefore \{Domain_{type}, access_{history}, crash_{info}, replicate_{info}\} \subseteq I_M$$

$$\therefore \{Domain_{type}, access_{history}, crash_{info}, replicate_{info}\} \subseteq \{Uid, Upassword, ULocation\}$$

$$\text{Load Balancer } (L_B)$$

$$\text{Data Server}(D_S) = \{DS_1, DS_2, DS_3, \ldots\ldots\ldots\ldots.DS_n\}$$

$$\text{Data Flow}(D_F)$$

Load balance module maintains the flow of data. It selects when and how the data will hits on the data server to process the query.

$$(L_B) \cap (D_F) \rightarrow (D_S)$$

$$\text{WS}_{Select} \cap L_B \cap D_F \rightarrow D_S$$

$$\{\text{HT}_{cache}, L_T\} \cap L_B \cap D_F \rightarrow D_S$$

$$\because \text{WS}_{\text{Select}} \subseteq I_M$$

$$\therefore \{\text{HT}_{\text{cache}}, L_T\} \cap L_B \cap D_F \subseteq I_M$$

$$\text{Index Control}(I_C) = \{Replication_{info}, ServerSearch_{info}, Query_{optimization}\}$$

$$\text{Cache} = \{Query_{evaluate}, Data_{storage}\}$$

$$\text{Cache} \subseteq \text{Database}(D_B)$$

$$\because (I_C) \in \text{Cache}$$

And, $(I_C) \in \text{Database}(D_B)$

$$\therefore (I_C) \in \{\text{Cache}, \text{Database}\}$$

$$\because D_S \cap I_C = \text{WS}_{\text{Select}}$$

$$\therefore \{\{\text{HT}_{\text{cache}}, L_T\} \cap L_B \cap D_F \cap I_C\} = \text{WS}_{\text{Select}}$$

$$\therefore \{\{\text{HT}_{\text{cache}}, L_T\} \cap L_B \cap D_F \cap I_C\} \subseteq I_M$$

Hence, it has been proved that Interface module $(I_M)$ is a subset of Web-server_Selection, Load Balancer $(L_B)$, Data Flow $(D_F)$ and Index Control $(I_C)$.

*(End of proof)*

**Explanation of Theorem 1:** $C_S$ is set of clients/users who can login into interface module $(I_M)$ for validation which depends on the value of *Uid*, *Upassword*, *ULocation*. Therefore, *Uid*, *Upassword*, *ULocation* are elements of $I_M$. Web server Selection module has two properties such as hash table cache and log table. Hash table cache works for caching and checks domain type of user request. Log table keeps track of access history, crash information, and web server replication. Web server selection module is an element of interface module. Load balancer module $(L_B)$ maintains the data flow and data processing in data server. Index controller module processes data queries. Index control module keeps the record of data server replication, server searching information as well as query optimization. Therefore, interface module is a subset of web server selection, load balancer, index control. Cache and database work for query evaluation and data storage. So cache and database are elements of index control module.

**Motivation of Theorem 2:** Motivation of Theorem 2 is to establish relations between growth coefficient and web server selection, Load balance, Data flow, Index control which are subset of Interface module.

***Theorem 2:*** **Growth coefficient is dependent on number of elements of Hash table cache, Log table, Load balancer, Dataflow and Index control which are subsets of Interface module.**

Proof:

We quantify popularity of a collection C of social networking sets.

We use concept of growth coefficient.

For a collection of C of social networking sets $d_s \subset \mu$. $\mu$ is a social networking space.

We define $n^{th}$ growth coefficient of C as follows:

$$G_C^{(n)} \alpha \, No\_of\_Elements$$

$$G_C^{(n)} \alpha \, D_F$$

$$L_B G_C^{(n)} \alpha \, L_B$$

$$G_C^{(n)} \alpha \, HT_{Cache \, HIT}$$

$$\therefore G_C^{(n)} = max_{ds \in \mu} No\_of\_Elements\{\{\{HT_{cache} L_T\} \cap L_B \cap D_F \cap I_C\} \subseteq I_M$$

where, No_of_Elements = Number of elements

$$d_s = DS_1, DS_2, DS_3, \ldots \ldots \ldots DS_n$$

Hence, it is proved that growth coefficient is dependent on number of elements of Hash table cache, Log table, Load balancer, Dataflow and Index control which are subset of Interface module.

(*End of proof*)

**Explanation of Theorem 2:** C is a collection of social networking sets. C sets $d_s proper subset of$ $\mu$, $\mu$ is a social networking space and we have defined $G_C^{(n)} = max_{ds \in \mu} No\_of\_Elements\{\{\{HT_{cache} L_T\} \cap L_B \cap D_F \cap I_C\} \subseteq I_M$. Growth coefficient $(G_C^{(n)})$ is dependent on number of elements of Hash table cache, Log table, Load balancer, Data flow and Index control which are also subset of Interface module.

Therefore,        we        can        derive        from
$G_C^{(n)} = max_{ds \in \mu} No\_of\_Elements\{\{\{HT_{cache} L_T\} \cap L_B \cap D_F \cap I_C\} \subseteq I_M$

## 5  Experimental Results

Our experiments have been executed in real time. In this context, 100 server systems have been considered for analyzing results.

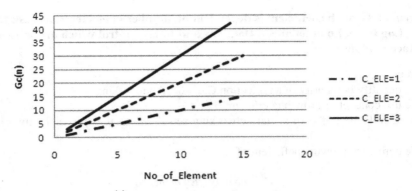

**Fig. 2.** $G_c^{(n)}$ vs. Number of Element with 'C_ELE' values.

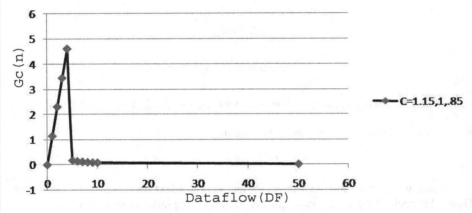

**Fig. 3.** Gc(n) vs. Dataflow with 'α' values.

## 5.1   Data Analysis for Overall System Network

In Fig. 2, growth coefficient is dependent on number of elements as user. Growth coefficient is increased according to increasing value of number of elements. We have introduced a constant value "Current Element" (C_ELE) for stabilizing value of growth coefficient.

In Fig. 3, $G_C^{(n)} \infty D_F$

∴ We have index = 1, index = 0, & index = −1

∴ Case 1: $Current_{value_{DF}} < Threshold_{DF}$

∴ $G_c^{(n)} \alpha D_F$

Case 2: $Current_{value_{DF}} == Threshold_{DF}$

Case 3: $Current_{value_{DF}} > Threshold_{DF}$

∴ $G_c^{(n)} \alpha 1 / D_F$

A set of damping factors {1.15, 1, 0.85} is being introduced for stabilizing proposed growth coefficient ($G_c^{(n)}$).

In this context, growth coefficient is dependent on values of damping factors, such as:

Over damped ($\alpha > 1$), critical damped ($\alpha = 1$), and under damped ($\alpha < 1$).

**Over damped-**Over damped situation in proposed design is the delay at the time of data flow without turbulence.

**Critical damped-**Critical damped situation is considered as data flow that decays in fastest possible time without going into turbulence.

**Under damped-**Under damped situation in proposed system is experienced having turbulence with growth decreasing amplitude of the growth coefficient ($G_c^{(n)}$).

In Fig. 4, two situations (Case1 and Case 2) are shown for increasing or maintaining growth coefficients.

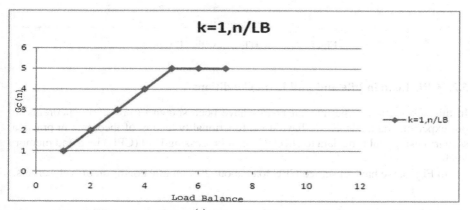

**Fig. 4.** $G_C^{(n)}$ vs. LB with 'k' values.

Case 1: Growth coefficient is increased, only if number of servers is increased. It means load is increased in a directly proportional manner with respect to growth of our system load.

Case 2: In certain point of time, growth coefficient becomes stagnant due to limitation of maximum system load. Therefore, we have introduced constant 'k' to overcome system turbulence. 'k' is considered as stabilization factor in following expression:

$$G_c^{(n)} \alpha L_B$$

$$\therefore k = n / LB_{value}$$

$\therefore$ Constant 'k' is represented as follows:

$$k = n / LB_{value}$$

In Fig. 5, we have shown growth coefficient which is indirectly proportionate with respect to hit ratio of hash table cache. Constant 'H' is introduced for stabilizing growth coefficient ($G_C^{(n)}$) of our proposed system.

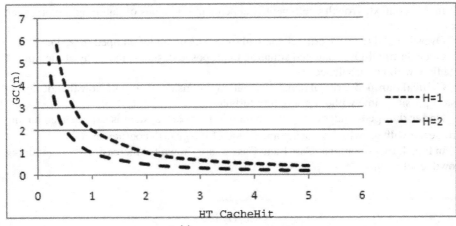

**Fig. 5.** $G_C^{(n)}$ vs. $HT_{cache}$ with 'H' values.

## 5.2 CPU Load in Idle and Full Load Conditions

In this sub-section, experimental results have been shown to prove our theorems. In our experimental analysis, we have done functionality testing of theorems in practical scenario using real time data to check Central Processing Unit (CPU) load and memory load.

In Fig. 6, we have observed CPU load about 20% in idle condition of web servers.

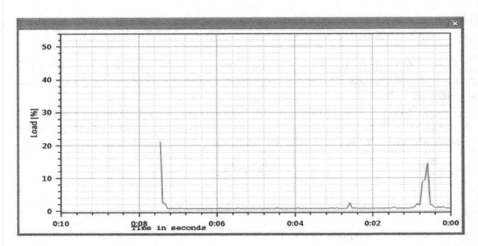

**Fig. 6.** CPU load vs. Time in idle condition of Web server

In Fig. 7, we have restricted CPU load about 80% to 85% in full load condition when 1000 users are accessing our web servers.

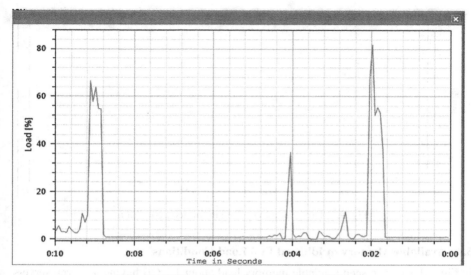

**Fig. 7.** CPU load vs. Time in full load condition

## 5.3 Memory Load in Idle and Full Load Conditions

In Fig. 8, we have seen memory load near about 40%–45%. Web server in idle condition means no users are requesting for execution within our server systems.

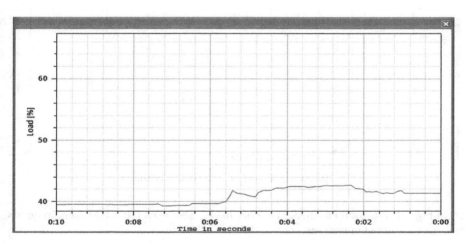

**Fig. 8.** Memory load vs. Time in idle condition

In Fig. 9, we have observed memory load about 80%.1000 users' requests are being executed in web servers. Memory load is increased up to 70%–80% for initial load condition. After certain time period, our system has been stabilized with respect to memory load at around 60%.

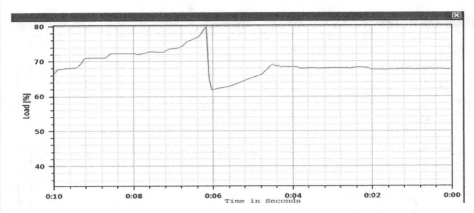

**Fig. 9.** Memory load vs. Time in full load condition

## 5.4 Available Memory in Idle and Full Load Conditions

In Fig. 10, we have seen available memory load about 1.2 GB having idle web servers without users' requests.

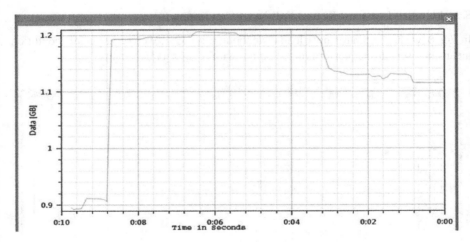

**Fig. 10.** Available load vs. Time in idle condition

In Fig. 11, maximum available memory load is about 0.8 GB. 1000 users' requests have been executed in web servers.

## 5.5 Used Memory Load in Idle and Full Load Conditions

In Fig. 12, we have observed used memory load in respect of time when web servers are not executing users' requests. In certain case, it ranges between 0.0 GB to 0.2 GB.

In Fig. 13, we have seen used memory load in respect to time when web server is running with 1000 users' requests. Graph shows a peak value of about 1.4 GB.

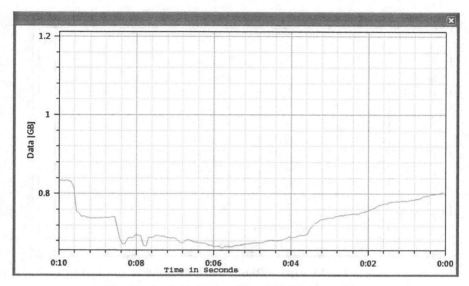

**Fig. 11.** Available load vs. Time in full load condition

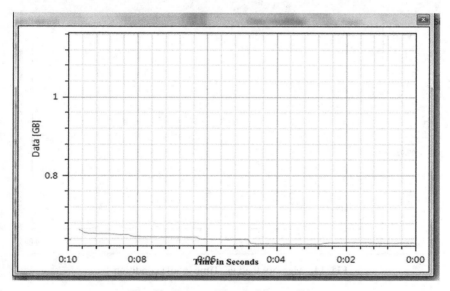

**Fig. 12.** Data vs. Time in idle condition

## 5.6  Used Space in Memory in Idle and Full Load Conditions

In Fig. 14, it has been shown that used space in memory is about 95.925% while our web server is not running over certain time period.

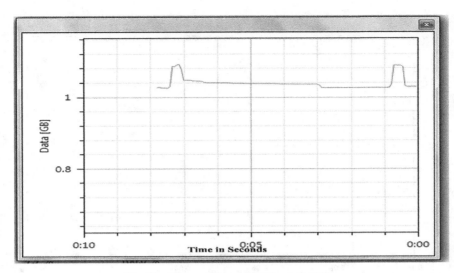

**Fig. 13.** Data vs. Time in full load condition

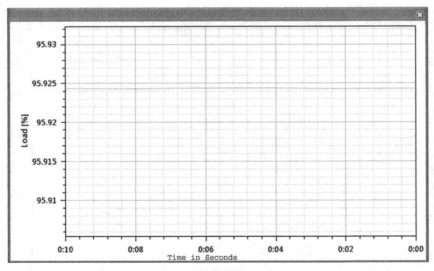

**Fig. 14.** Memory load vs. Time in idle condition

In Fig. 15, it has been observed that used space in memory in respect of time is reached a maximum of 95.94% while web servers are running with 1000 users' queries.

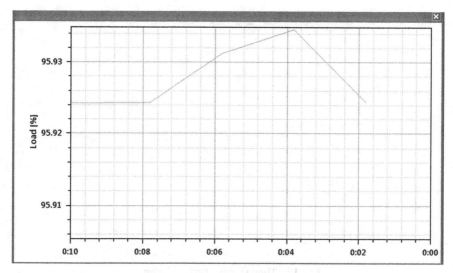

**Fig. 15.** Memory load vs. Time in full load condition

## 5.7 JMeter Based Data Analysis

This sub-section includes analysis of load balance using throughput, average, & deviation. In this context, we have used maximum 1000 users' requests at a time. JMeter is used for load testing in proposed Web server framework.

In Fig. 16, throughput of our web server-based systems has been demonstrated in respect of time. As per Fig. 16, system throughput has been gradually increased up to certain limit, and then throughput follows a downward direction.

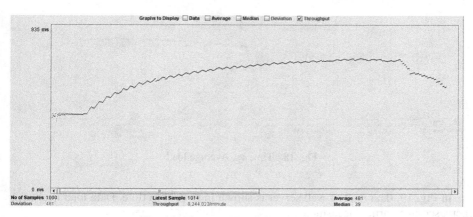

**Fig. 16.** Time vs. Throughput of system

In Fig. 17, Standard deviation of proposed system is depicted in respect of time.

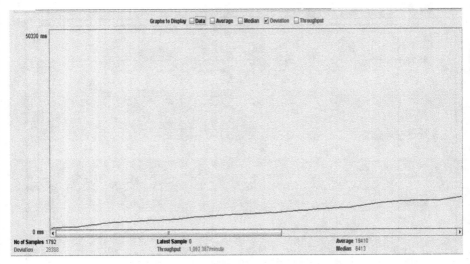

**Fig. 17.** Time vs. Standard deviation

In Fig. 18, average load of web server is being demonstrated. Average load is always increased in a particular fashion.

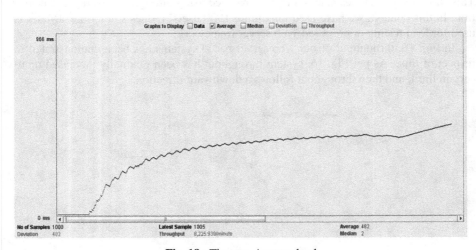

**Fig. 18.** Time vs. Average load

In Fig. 19, data load of web server is shown in respect to time. Data load is always increased in a particular fashion.

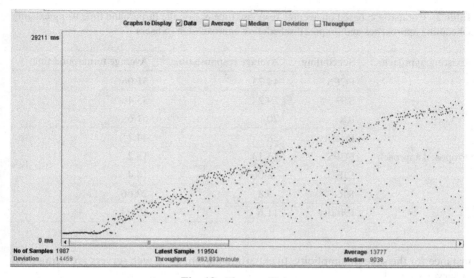

**Fig. 19.** Time vs. Data

## 5.8 Comparison Based on Average Response Time and Average Turnaround Time

In [51], a comparison between existing system and proposed system has been demonstrated based on number of steps required, user request directions, and load balancing issues.

**Table 1.** Comparison based on average response time & average turnaround time using existing scheduling approaches and proposed scheduling approach for 5 users

| Existing approach | Scheduling | Average response time | Average turnaround time |
|---|---|---|---|
| | FCFS | 13.4 | 19.2 |
| | SJF | 8.4 | 14.2 |
| | RR | 6 | 22.6 |
| | Priority | 13.6 | 19.8 |
| Proposed approach | FCFS | 2.6 | 10.2 |
| | SJF | 2.6 | 10.2 |
| | RR | 1.2 | 12 |
| | Priority | 1.4 | 6.6 |

In Table 1 & Table 2, tabular charts have been shown to compare existing scheduling approaches and proposed system-based scheduling approaches for five users and fifteen users respectively. Arrivals of all processes (users) have been considered at $0^{th}$ time

**Table 2.** Comparison based on average response time & average turnaround time using existing scheduling approaches and proposed scheduling approach for 15 users

| Existing approach | Scheduling | Average response time | Average turnaround time |
|---|---|---|---|
| | FCFS | 44.73 | 51.06 |
| | SJF | 29.2 | 35.46 |
| | RR | 20 | 61.6 |
| | Priority | 38 | 44.2 |
| Proposed approach | FCFS | 13.13 | 15.2 |
| | SJF | 8.06 | 14.4 |
| | RR | 5.8 | 23.66 |
| | Priority | 11.6 | 17.93 |

instance for the sake of simplicity. In experimentation, three web servers are being used at server-side.

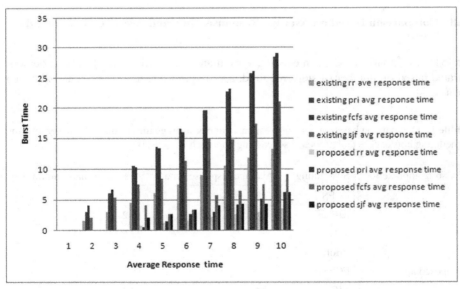

**Fig. 20.** Average response time vs. Burst time in existing approaches and proposed approach for 15 users

In Fig. 20, average response time for each existing scheduling approaches (FCFS, SJF, RR, PRI) and proposed scheduling are shown based on 15 users' requests, considering no difference in arrival time. Distinct approaches are being monitored with respect to burst time and average response time. According to the performance, response time of RR scheduling is considered as best among other scheduling approaches since RR is taking minimum time compared to other approaches.

## 6  Conclusion

Authors have identified an advanced architecture of social network having efficient properties compared to typical architecture of social networks. Our architecture exhibits load balancing for buffering user queries before transmitting to data server. In analytical study, we have introduced algorithms and graphs comparing existing system structures with real time data. Web server selection module, load balancer module, data flow module and index control module have been observed as subset of the interface module. Further, growth coefficient of design framework is reliant on number of element of hash table cache, log table, load balancer, dataflow and index control. Authors have verified system performance using data analysis. Load testing of design framework has been accomplished using "JMeter". Real time users' data analysis has been demonstrated using CPU scheduling algorithms. "JMeter" and "OpenHardware" have been utilized for checking CPU and memory loads. Graphs are shown to exhibit deviations in system performances compared to existing systems.

## References

1. https://www.facebook.com/notes/facebook-engineering/under-the-hood-building-out-the-infrastructure-for-graph-search/10151347573598920
2. Farrington, N., Andreyev, A.: Facebook's data center network architecture. In: IEEE Optical Interconnects Conference, pp. 49–50 (2013)
3. Greenberg, A.G., et al.: VL2: a scalable and flexible data center network. In: ACM SIGCOMM Conference, pp. 51–62 (2009)
4. Tramp, S., Frischmuth, P., Ermilov, T., Shekarpour, S., Auer, S.: An architecture of a distributed semantic social network. Semant. Web, IOS Press 5(1), 77–95 (2014)
5. Barrigas, D., Barrigas, H., Barata, M., Furtado, P., Bernardino, J.: Overview of Facebook scalable architecture. In: ACM International Conference on Information Systems and Design of Communication (ISDOC), pp. 173–176 (2014)
6. Madey, G., Freeh, V., Tynan, R., Gao, Y., Hoffman, C.: Agent-based modeling and simulation of collaborative social networks. In: 9th Americas Conference on Information Systems (AMCIS), Tampa, FL, USA, p. 237 (2003)
7. Mislove, A., Marcon, M., Gummadi, K.P., Bhattacharjee, B.: Measurement and analysis of online social networks. In: Proceedings of the 7th ACM SIGCOMM Conference on Internet Measurement (IMC), pp. 29–42 (2007)
8. Boyd, D.M., Ellison, N.B.: Social network sites: definition, history, and scholarship. J. Comput.-Mediated Commun. 13, 210–230 (2008)
9. Barabasi, A.L., Albert, R.: Emergence of scaling in random networks. Science 286(5439), 509–512 (1999)

10. Newman, M.: The structure of scientific collaboration networks. Proc. Natl. Acad. Sci. (PNAS) **98**(2), 404–409 (2001)
11. Amaral, L.A.N., Scala, A., Barthelemy, M., Stanley, H.E.: Classes of small-world networks. Proc. Natl. Acad. Sci. (PNAS) **97**, 11149–11152 (2000)
12. Awan, A., Ferreira, R.A., Jagannathan, S., Grama, A.: Distributed uniform sampling in unstructured peer-to-peer networks. In: Proceedings of the 39th Annual Hawaii International Conference on System Sciences (HICSS), Kauia, HI, USA, p. 223c (2006)
13. Kundu, A., Xu, G., Ji, C.: Structural analysis of cloud classifier. Int. J. Cloud Appl. Comput. (IJCAC), IGI Global Publication, **4**(1), 63–75 (2014). ISSN: 2156-1834. EISSN: 2156-1826. https://doi.org/10.4018/ijcac.2014010106
14. Farasat, A., Gross, G., Nagi, R., Nikolaev, A.G.: Social network analysis with data fusion. IEEE Trans. Comput. Soc. Syst. **3**, 88–99 (2016)
15. Bonchi, F., et al.: Social network analysis and mining for business applications. ACM Trans. Intell. Syst. Technol. **2**(3), 1–37 (2011)
16. Peng, S., Wang, G., Xie, D.: Social influence analysis in social networking big data: opportunities and challenges. IEEE Netw. Issue **99**, 12–18 (2016)
17. Varlamis, I., Eirinaki, M., Louta, M.: A study on social network metrics and their application in trust networks. In: International Conference on Analysis of Social Networks and Mining (ASONAM), pp. 168–175 (2010)
18. Yuan, X., Wang, Z., Liu, Z., Guo, C., Ai, H., Ren, D.: Visualization of social media flows with interactively identified key players. In: IEEE Conference on Visual Analytics Science and Technology (VAST), Paris, France, pp. 291–292 (2014)
19. van Ham, F., Schulz, H.-J., Dimicco, J.M.: Honeycomb: Visual Analysis of Large Scale Social Networks. In: Gross, T., Gulliksen, J., Kotzé, P., Oestreicher, L., Palanque, P., Prates, R.O., Winckler, M. (eds.) INTERACT 2009. LNCS, vol. 5727, pp. 429–442. Springer, Heidelberg (2009). https://doi.org/10.1007/978-3-642-03658-3_47
20. Henry, N., Fekete, J.D.: Matlink: enhanced matrix visualization for analyzing social networks. In: Proceedings of INTERACT, pp. 288–302 (2007)
21. Hoff, P.D., Raftery, A.E., Handcock, M.S.: Latent space approaches to social network analysis. J. Am. Stat. Assoc. **97**(460), 1090–1098 (2002)
22. Benevenuto, F., Rodrigues, T., Cha, M., Almeida, V.: Characterizing user behavior in online social networks. In: Proceedings of the 9th International Conference on ACM SIGCOMM Internet Measurement Conference, pp. 49–62 (2009)
23. Gionis, A., Junqueira, F., Leroy, V., Serafini, M., Weber, I.: Piggy backing on social networks. In: Proceedings of the 39th International Conference on Very Large Data Bases (VLDB Endowment), Trento, Italy, vol. 6, no (6), pp. 409–420 (2013)
24. Timm, D.M., Duven, C.J.: Privacy and social networking sites. new directions for student services, Wiley Periodicals, Wiley Inter Science, 124 (2008). https://doi.org/10.1002/ss.297
25. Centola, D.: Failure in complex social networks. J. Math. Sociol. **33**, 64–68 (2009)
26. Turner, D., Levchenko, K., Snoeren, A.C.: Stefan savage: california fault lines: understanding the causes and impact of network failures. In: SIGCOMM, pp. 315–326. ACM, New Delhi, India (2010)
27. Guo, L., Zhang, C., Yue, H., Fang, Y.: PSaD: a privacy-preserving social-assisted content dissemination scheme in DTNs. IEEE Trans. Mob. Comput. **13**(12), 2903–2918 (2014)
28. Zhou, B., Pei, J.: Preserving privacy in social networks against neighborhood attacks. In: Proceedings of the 24th IEEE International Conference on Data Engineering (ICDE 2008), Cancun, Mexico, pp. 506–515 (2008)
29. Gill, P., Jain, N., Nagappan, N.: Understanding network failures in data centers: measurement, analysis, and implications. In: SIGCOMM, pp. 350–361. ACM, Toronto, Ontario, Canada (2011)

30. Chewae, M., Hayikader, S., Hasan, M.H., Ibrahim, J.: How much privacy we still have on social network? Int. J. Sci. Res. Publ. **5**(1), 1–5 (2015)
31. Kundu, A., Ji, C., Liu, R.: Software-as-a-service using heterogeneous distributed system for user specific applications. Int. J. Cloud Appl. Comput. (IJCAC), IGI Global Publication, **4**(1), 15–32 (2014). ISSN: 2156-1834. EISSN: 2156-1826. https://doi.org/10.4018/ijcac.201 4010102
32. Gross, R., Acquisti, A.: Information revelation and privacy in online social networks (The Facebook case). In: Proceedings of the 2005 ACM Workshop on Privacy in the Electronic Society, WPES 2005, Alexandria, Virginia, USA, pp. 71–80 (2005)
33. Bao, Z., Zhou, J., Tay, Y.C.: sonSQL: an extensible relational DBMS for social network start-Ups. In: Ng, W., Storey, V.C., Trujillo, J.C. (eds.) ER 2013. LNCS, vol. 8217, pp. 495–498. Springer, Heidelberg (2013). https://doi.org/10.1007/978-3-642-41924-9_43
34. McGoldrick, D.: The limits of freedom of expression on facebook and social networking sites: a UK perspective. Hum. Rights Law Rev. **13**(1), 125–151 (2013)
35. Kundu, A.: Heterogeneous Cloud Architecture. Scholars' Press, pp. 1–172 (2014)
36. Zeitel-Bank, N., Tat, U.: Social media and its effects on individuals and social systems. In: Portoroz Slovenia International Conference, Slovenia, pp. 1183–1190 (2014)
37. Madey, G., Freeh, V., Tynan, R.: The open source software development phenomenon: an analysis based on social network theory. In: Americas Conference of Information Systems (AMCIS), Dallas, TX, pp. 1806–1813 (2002)
38. Liben-Nowell, D., College, C., Kumar, R., Novak, J., Raghavan, P., Tomkins, A.: Geographic routing in social networks. Natl. Acad. Sci. U. S. Am. **102**(33), 11623–11628 (2005)
39. Kundu, A., Ji, C., Liu, R.: Cloud Based Heterogeneous Distributed Framework. In: Advances in Intelligent Systems and Computing, Intelligent Informatics, Engineering, vol. 182, pp. 471–478 (2013). https://doi.org/10.1007/978-3-642-32063-7_50
40. Jacobson, V., Smetters, D.K., Thornton, J.D., Plass, M.F., Briggs, N.H., Braynard, R.L.: Networking named content. In: Palo Alto Research Center Palo Alto, CA, USA, vol. 55, no (1), pp. 117–124 (2012)
41. Backstrom, L., Huttenlocher, D., Kleinberg, J., Lan, X.: Group formation in large social networks: membership, growth, and evolution. In: 12th ACM SIGKDD International Conference on Knowledge Discovery and Data Mining (KDD), Philadelphia, PA, pp. 44–54 (2006)
42. Nilizadeh, S., Jahid, S., Mittal, P., Borisov, N., Kapadia, A.: Cachet: a decentralized architecture for privacy preserving social networking with caching. In: International Conference on Emerging Networking Experiments and Technologies, pp. 337–348 (2012)
43. Kundu, A., Luan, L., Liu, R.: Synchronisation of data transfer in cloud. Int. J. Internet Protoc. Technol. (IJIPT), Inderscience Publication, Europe, **8**(1), 1–24 (2014). ISSN: 1743-8209 (Print). ISSN: 1743-8217 (Online). https://doi.org/10.1504/ijipt.2014.060856
44. Sarkar, S., Kundu, A.: An indexed approach for multiple data storage in cloud. In: Satapathy, S.C., Mandal, J.K., Udgata, Siba K., Bhateja, V. (eds.) Information Systems Design and Intelligent Applications. AISC, vol. 433, pp. 639–646. Springer, New Delhi (2016). https://doi.org/10.1007/978-81-322-2755-7_66
45. Yahya, W., Basuki, A., Jiang, J.: The extended dijkstra's-based load balancing for open flow network. Int. J. Electr. Comput. Eng. (IJECE) **5**(2), 289–296 (2015)
46. Wang, R., Butnariu, D., Rexford, J.: Open flow-based server load balancing gone wild. In: Hot-ICE 2011 Proceedings of the 11th USENIX Conference on Hot Topics in Management of Internet, Cloud, and Enterprise Networks and Services, USENIX Association Berkeley, CA, USA, p. 12 (2011)
47. Sarkar, S., Kundu, A., Banerjee, A.: Evaluation of reliable data storage in cloud using an efficient encryption technique. In: Handbook of Research on Cloud Computing and Big Data Applications in IoT. IGI Global Publications, Chapter 12, pp. 229–242 (2019)

48. Kundu, A., Xu, G., Ji, C.: Analysis on cloud classification using accessibility. Int. J. Cloud Appl. Comput. (IJCAC) **4**(3), 44–53 (2014)
49. Nandi, G., Das, A.: A survey on using data mining techniques for online social network analysis. Int. J. Comput. Sci. Issues (IJCSI) **10**(6), 162–167 (2013)
50. De Sarkar, N.R., Kundu, A., De, M., Bera, A.: Agent based noise detection using real time data analysis towards green environment. Int. J. Green Comput. (IJGC), IGI Global Publication, **8**(2), 37–58 (2017). ISSN: 1948-5018. eISSN: 1948-5026
51. De, M., Kundu, A., De Sarkar, N.R., Bera, A.: Design of social network: a new approach. In: The 8th International ACM Conference on Management of Digital Eco Systems (MEDES'2016), Hendaye, France, pp. 1–4 (2016)

# Smart Services Using Voice and Images

Alexander I. Iliev[1,2(✉)] and Peter L. Stanchev[2,3]

[1] UC Berkeley Global, Berkeley, CA, USA
ailiev@berkeley.edu
[2] Institute of Mathematics and Informatics, Bulgarian Academy of Sciences, Sofia, Bulgaria
[3] Kettering University, Flint, USA
pstanche@kettering.edu

**Abstract.** In this chapter, we will emphasize on some of the most prominent advances in smart technologies that formulate the smart city ecosystem. Furthermore, we will be highlighting the automation of numerous developments based on the extraction and analysis of digital media, using speech and images. At present, there is a multitude of practical systems used for personalization and recommendation of different media. On the other hand, there are assorted types of services in different areas that are directly benefiting from these advancements. Most of them were created with human-machine interaction methodology in mind, where people had to interact with the machines in various ways. In the past this type of interaction has been completed through the use of conventional interfaces such as a mouse and a keyboard, where the user had to type a response manually, which was in turn recorded by the machine for subsequent analysis. Therefore, in order to simplify these types of interactions and lead to improvement of services, new methodologies must be studied, discovered and developed so as to improve services such as recommendation and personalization services.

**Keywords:** Smart systems · Emotion recognition · Voice recognition · Image recognition

## 1 Introduction

Smart services provide addition value for both service providers and consumers. The continuous growth of data according to different sources [1, 2] leads to an increasing necessity of novel and adequate technologies that can structure and analyze vast amounts of new data every day. This inevitably leads to the need of creating smart machines that have a profound impact on our daily lives. The increase of computational power as well as minimization of electronics in every field is also a factor in the complex equation of smart technology development. Simply put, there are too many factors that can contribute to the advance of smart devices, smart cars, smart homes and even smart cities in a global Internet of Things system. This is why the topic of smart system development in multiple areas is the focus of this chapter.

Despite all of this, technology is not the main driver behind the need to develop more advanced concepts for smart cities. Technology merely serves the need we have.

© Springer-Verlag GmbH Germany, part of Springer Nature 2021
A. Hameurlain et al. (Eds.): TLDKS XLVII, LNCS 12630, pp. 137–154, 2021.
https://doi.org/10.1007/978-3-662-62919-2_6

Recent studies [3] by the United Nations Population Fund suggest that by the year 2030 approximately 66% of the world's population (or about 5 billion people) will live in urban areas. According to this report, in 2014 this number was 54% (about 3.3 billion people). By the growth of the world's population and the increase of smart technologies and devices worldwide, it is inevitable that more and more smart technologies should emerge in years to come.

ACM Transactions on Internet of Things (ACM TIOT) is a new ACM journal that will publish novel research contributions and experience reports in several research domains whose synergy and interrelations enable the IoT vision. TIOT focuses on system designs, end-to-end architectures, and enabling technologies, and on publishing results and insights corroborated by a strong experimental component.

Voice is easy to capture, retain and process. These characteristics of voice make it an extremely attractive source for gathering intelligence. Thus, the reason why we will spend some time in this chapter to discuss smart technologies based on speech signals. Nowadays it is an absolute necessity to study and use speech and images as a source of automation. It is an advanced way to think about future developing technologies. The amalgamation between Digital signal processing (DSP) and Artificial Intelligence is the expected way of solving sophisticated smart technology problems and is already happening. Through the usage of DSP, we can contrive complex feature vectors as inputs to machine learning algorithms in order to complete specific smart tasks. The informational capability of speech signals remains undisputed.

## 2  Smart Systems Through Voice

In today's world we are constantly bombarded by an ever-growing information flow. It is all around us in everything we do. The steady increase of options in every aspect of our lives requires an exponential growth of information gathering and processing. Making simple choices when selecting food in our local shops, selecting the right doctor based on specific criteria or choosing an entertainment tonight are some of the many choices we are up against on a daily basis. These, among many other choices must be made by all of us in order to fit the modern paradigm we live in. The selection process must therefore be aided by the implementation of smart algorithms for nearly every aspect of our lives. We see the growth of smart systems implemented in different industries such as the automobile industry, banking, healthcare, insurance, security, shopping, and entertainment to name a few. For many of these algorithms data is collected from human activity that usually is the basis for deducing specific behavior using deep learning methods. In many cases, these behavioral patterns are typical for different people and in these cases personalization of services becomes possible. The data sources used for this kind of activity is usually gathered silently in the background. Amazon is constantly gathering information on the latest products we search for or the ones we already bought. Google and Facebook built their enormous empires around personalizing ads based on search records and habits we have when interacting with their systems. These services are based on textual information we typed when searching for people, services or products. Based on this kind of search there is a way of creating new technology and services to aid us in the sea of choices we are up against.

Depending on the task, the designer of such system can collect information from different layers of speech such as:

1. *Who is talking: that is a trivial speaker recognition task. This can also be specific to gender recognition only (men, woman or a child) or more specific as to what individual is talking from a number of speakers in the room;*
2. *What a speaker is saying: this is known as speech recognition and it aims to collect a specific verbal message from each speaker. In many cases a smart system can be tuned to gather specific words that a speaker is using to deduce some logic from the speech. In this layer of information, the systems can even be tuned to map specific verbal messages and words to specific people, if there are several speakers in the particular environment, thus combing the first two points above;*
3. *How was the voice message conveyed: this captures yet another extremely important layer of information from speakers? By capturing the way each speaker is talking we can gather important information about each person's behavior and mood. This type of information is especially valuable for smart system development in areas such as security, customer service interaction, banking, etc.*

Speech recognition is a very developed and extremely interesting field when it comes to implementing the result of it in today's Smart Systems. It is often that we see researchers using the Mel-frequency cepstral coefficients (MFCCs) to extract specific attributes for speech recognition, and then using methods like Dynamic Time Warping (DTW) in combination to capture some interesting patterns and achieve voice command/speech recognition as a result [4]. In their research, the authors mention some of the different techniques to be incorporated in the field of gender recognition. Pre-emphasis filtering is applied to the speech signal and as a result the magnitude of the higher frequencies was increased in order to improve the overall SNR Ratio. This signal was then passed through a so-called framing technique wherein it is divided into N samples with M distance between them (M < N). Then after Hamming window was applied, a Discrete Fourier Transform (DFT) was performed in order to convert the signal from time to frequency domain and access to magnitude frequency spectrum was obtained. The MFCC recognizes the linguistic and relevant content and discard every other signal. Access to the Mel spectrum was given through the use of triangular shaped filters or Mel Filter Banks. The signal was then transformed back into time domain by using Discrete Cosine Transform (DCT) and then at the final stage data energy and spectrum were collected. Feature matching, DTW is used to compare 2-time series to measure their similarity. The input signal is compared to the variables to determine the accurate output.

Another interesting and very practical example of a smart system that determines *what the speaker is saying* is described in [5]. There, a smart system was developed, which could help people with disabilities, senior citizens or be installed in every household to simplify our lives by aiding us control our home appliances with voice commands. The project was implemented at a fairly low cost and was claimed to be energy efficient. It utilizes a Texas Instruments TMS320 DSP processor along with a microphone, and when specific conditions are met, it sends a signal via Universal Asynchronous Receiver-Transmitter (UART) hardware to the XBee Transmitter (Tx), which is an embedded solution that provides wireless end-point connectivity to different devices. Voice Recognition is done via Zero Crossing with Peak Amplitude (ZCPA) – a method measuring the number of times a given frequency is crossing the zero line. This helps distinguishing between various commands. The XBee Tx transmits the signals via the UART module. Any device that has the UART interface can interact directly with the XBee RF module and will receive the signal through the XBee Receiver (Rx). The XBee Rx has a microcontroller attached to it receives the transmitted control characters and compares them against a set of specific ones. If there is a match, the microcontroller will switch the corresponding relay on or off, thus controlling the state of the appliance.

In another example [6], the gender of a specific speaker is determined based on a speech sample using a one-dimensional Convolutional Neural Network (CNN). CNNs are commonly used for image recognition, but in this case, it was used for gender classification. Voice is firstly passed through a pre-emphasis filter, as it is susceptible to noise interference. Voice samples sometimes can contain a lot of redundant data and thus grow to be too long. Feature extraction is a methodology we use to collect and then reduce the number of samples into a more manageable set of features. When dealing with speech we often used a combination of different MFCCs and even Short-Term Fourier Transform (STFT) techniques in order to extract various attributes. This helps in producing a training set wherein we can use feature selection techniques to extract variables that resemble the target variable. Evolutionary Search algorithms like PSO and Wolf Search are employed as well. Then using Classification Techniques, labeling the samples is achieved by using test samples to identify if the speaker is a male or a female, thus verify the validity of the results.

In [7], an attempt to show the importance of emotion recognition in speech is displayed. There are many kinds of emotions, so the challenge is to label and train for each and every emotion. Depending on implementation different set of emotions can be considered and each emotion represents a separate label. These labels comprise of three general types based on the way speech was conducted or more specifically: acted, elicited, and neutral. Any speech has to undergo the usual digital signal processing where it is: converted to digital signal, quant sized, pre-processed, and windowed, then feature extraction followed by selection techniques are used. There are different types of features to be selected for this purpose:

1. *Prosodic Features*: these are perceived by humans such as intonations and rhythms. An example may be when we put an emphasis on certain words while talking;
2. *Spectral Features*: MFCCs converted to frequency domain and then energy calculated using Mel Filter Banks, Linear Prediction Cepstral Coefficients (LPCC) that contain vocal tract feature specifics; Gammatone Frequency Cepstral Coefficients (GFCC) these are obtained by a similar technique as in the MFCC extraction, but using Gammatone filter-bank instead of Mel-filter bank; Log-Frequency Power Coefficients (LFPC) mimic logarithmic filtering characteristics of the human auditory system;
3. *Voice Quality Features*: These are unintentional features that can be used to differentiate emotions in speech. Properties such as jitter, shimmer, Harmonics to Noise Ratio (HNR) can be paramount in the quest of constructing the perfect feature vectors and determine the emotional state of the speaker. A correlation between voice quality and emotion was previously suggested by [8];

4. *Teager Energy Operator (TEO) based features* [9]: these are used to detect stress features in our speech. In essence, speech is produced by non-linear vortex-airflow interference in the human vocal system. While producing a sound in a stressful situation the muscle tension of the speaker is affected, which results in an alteration of the airflow.

## 3   Smart Services in the Medical Field Through Voice

Smart Systems based on voice have been implemented in a vast number of areas and one of the most important one is the medical field. An interesting product that is monitoring patients by using Digital Signal Processing (DSP) and Deep Learning (DL) is described in [10]. This paper proposed a method that is improving reaction time of medical staff when dealing with disabled people when using technological advancements related to IoT. For that purpose, a Raspberry Pi (RPi) based system has been developed in order to serve people with disabilities. The system is activated via voice and is interpreting them through the usage of a Support Vector Machine (SVM) then generating signals for medical personal as a result. This research was applied in a real-world medical scenario. RPi boards gained popularity for many reasons related to how compact they are, their low-price range, as well as the powerful capabilities that they have. Their size makes them suitable for many mobile and IoT applications. Some of the specifications for the $4^{th}$ generation RPi in 2020 are: 1, 2 or 4 GB memory, with a Broadcom Quad core CPU - Cortex-A72 (ARM v8) 64-bit SoC@1.5 GHz processing power.

Python scripts have been written to enable the voice recording of the signals. The main communication interface was implemented using an LCD touchscreen [11]. These small devices are built with minimization in mind, so they use micro SD cards as hard drives, from which a mini version of Linux system called Raspbian is running. These features make this portable device a very attractive, nice and easy-to-use plug-and-play device. In order to extract and collect the features, the Discreet Cosine Transform (DCT) was used [12]. SVM was employed for classification [13] while feeding voice waveform parameters into the input of the system. The signal was firstly sent to the DCT section, so that frequency features were extracted and then provided to the second stage for classification into the SVM. The Montreal Affective Voices (MAV) dataset was utilized in this product [14], since it comprised of an assorted set of voice samples covering wide range of emotions for training, validation and testing. The following nine emotions were of interest: happiness, sadness, anger, disgust, surprise, fear, pain, pleasure and neutral. All of the samples were exemplified in 90 non-verbal voice samples.

Naturally, when it comes to selecting the features a good performance should be the first thing in mind. On the other hand, not having the minimum set of features, as well as when they are too many, it may hurt the recognition rate and consequently it may result in poor performance both as a computational load as well as bad results. One way to counter that is to run a number of tests in the training stage in order to test performance with different feature combination as well as varying a number of hyper parameters. Unless the input signal is comprised of pixels and feeds hundreds and even thousands of features, normally an optimized feature vector consists of up to about 100 features. In the case of this particular work, the authors reported running tests with different number of features containing 15 to 50 different frequency components. It is shown that SVM significantly surpasses the performance of the K-nearest neighbors (KNN) algorithm when it's using the 25 DCT feature set. Furthermore, the true positive and false positive rates are analyzed, as well as the precision and recall for both MAV and Real-time datasets [10, 15].

In an intriguing research titled: "Wearable IoT sensor-based healthcare system for identifying and controlling chikungunya virus" [16], the authors propose a novel technique for identifying and controlling the outbreak of chikungunya virus (CHV). IoT and fog-based healthcare system is discussed from a new angle, in light of the disease. CHV spreads quickly in geographically affected areas as claimed by the authors, and these areas are usually not well prepared for in-time diagnosis and treatment, hence new methods are needed using modern technological advancements. Cloud computing along with mobile technologies and wearable Internet of Things (IoT) sensors are well suited to provide tangible solution. The dangers of the CHV virus that had been running rampant in many parts of the world are discussed and a differentiation between the Zika and the CHV Virus is also provided. This smart system is typically divided in 3 layers, the first being the *Sensor Layer*. This layer collects data from various sensors that have been taken from the user's body, environment sensor, drug sensor, and climatic sensor. It passes on the information to the second layer that is the *FOG Layer*. The classification process is implemented. Firstly, the collected data is being processed and a classification whether the person is infected or not is performed. There is another algorithm that follows to collect the information from the concerned user's cell phone and sends out messages to the medical professionals in case of a medical concern. The third layer is the *Cloud Layer*. It completes all the rest of the functionality that was not presented in the FOG layer. It stores all the data and transmits it to hospitals or government agencies. It follows all necessary security protocols.

In another work titled "BSN-Care: A Secure IoT-Based Modern Healthcare System Using Body Sensor Network" [17], the researchers mention the prediction that by the end of 2050, 22% of the world's population would comprise of older citizens. As such, Health monitoring system takes an important stance in day-to-day activities. The article also talks about different BSN Care systems already in the market. Code blue developed by Harvard University, and Alarm-net developed by University of Virginia are among the few BSN Care systems already on the market. This smart system has biosensors attached to different parts of the users' body as they measure and send various data. A Local Processing Unit (LPU) identifies the data and acts on it according to some pre-set specifications. For example, if the Beats Per Minute (BPM) is less than 120, the LPU doesn't do anything, but if the BPM is above 120, it notifies the family members of this anomaly. If BPM is more than 130, and if the person lives alone, it notifies the emergency services. Obviously, security is a big part of such system and this paper identifies the different security points in the system. To name a few: Data Privacy, Data Integrity, Localization, Data Freshness are some of these points. Authentication is performed in two levels: the first level comprises of BSN Server issuing security credentials to LPU to initiate a secure channel. The second level is an authentication process where the system gives the LPU a random number; a shadow to initiate security measures. This way, if an attacker tries to modify or extract information, the system can detect it.

## 4 Smart Systems in Robotics Using Voice and Emotion Recognition

The topic of robotics and control systems is becoming more and more popular in recent years. To make the robots be more human-like we have to be able to talk to them in order to facilitate more natural environment for human-machine interaction. Commands are therefore given to robots by voice, then a signal-processing unit interprets them, and action is taken. Convolutional Neural Networks (CNNs) are usually used for training batches of images in order to find objects in images, so it is unusual to use CNN based systems with speech as presented in [18]. There, the authors used voice to detect emotion in companion robots through CNN. The system was implemented in Python via the main two libraries: Keras and Tensorflow used as backend. A brief description of the emotional content extraction from voice was presented in this paper. When it comes to choosing the appropriate number of emotions however, various researches are using a different subsets based on their ability to obtain specific datasets or simply based on the application of their work. Cowie and Cornelius performed one of the fundamental works in that area in 2003 [19], in which they suggested the so-called "big-six" emotions, namely: anger, happiness, sadness, fear, surprise, and disgust. Bhatti M. et al. later confirmed their work in 2004 [20], but very frequently we see that smaller emotional datasets are suggested such as in [21], in which only four emotions were used or: anger, happiness, sadness, and neutral. As reported in [18], the "big-six" emotional set was used as described in [19], and the reported accuracy of their system was 71.33%.

A big boost in this idea was also driven by Google in their research in the Audio Set project, where an analysis on over 2 million video records taken from YouTube was performed so that a large dataset was created consisting of over 600 audio events. In that research Google was using the Mel-Frequency Cepstral Coefficients (aka MFCCs) as feature detection, extraction and classification parameters from audio. They used GMM based classifier and their work is summarized in [18, 22].

The input layer consisted of $400 \times 12$ input neurons. In its core, a conventional CNN system of at least one convolutional layer, after the input layer, followed by pooling, then activation done by a *ReLU* unit, then followed by *Max Pooling*. The research mentioned in [18] used 20 such convolutional layers. The *ReLU* function can be thought of as a way of normalization as it is activation function that turns all negative numbers into zeros. All the rest are positive numbers multiplied by one. This alone will make our network learn non-linear problems.

In their implementation, the researchers used 200 kernels used with size $5 \times 5$. After the feature extraction stage is complete, a typical CNN network ends with the classification stage in which flattening is used, where all the outputs gathered thus far from the network are reorganized into a single flat vector. This layer is immediately followed by a fully connected (or dense) layer consisting of 1000 neurons, which will give us all of the learning we have done so far from all of the neurons. Let's point out that their number had already decreased through applying the convolution. It is at the end of that stage where the previously mentioned six emotions were presented as options at the output. Typically, a *softmax* function is used here that will squash the results to match the classifiers at the end so that we get probabilities for our classes. Then using an argmax function the most probable emotion is chosen at the final stage. At the end, the authors reported that after training the CNN with a set of 200 sound samples the results had a satisfactory performance.

## 5  Smart Systems in Robotics Using Voice Jitter

Emotion recognition is one of the most fundamental layers when it comes to natural communication. Sensing Emotion from Voice Jitter was proposed in [23]. In their research, the authors provide an interesting concept that involves the usage of voice jitter. This means that instead of using complete voice samples the authors used smaller pieces of speech to make their analysis. As it turns out from this research, short timeframes of speech would suffice with a relatively good confidence to be able to determine emotions from speech. This can be very convenient especially when you have to collect specific speech samples for training and testing. Labeled speech datasets for emotion recognition can be costly so this method provides an alternative to this problem. In turn, the solution not only makes the collection of samples easier, but the calculations in recognizing different emotions are also less costly. All in all, the researchers recorded thirty student volunteers aged between 20 and 25 years each speaking 3 motional states (angry, happy and sad), and there was one sample per recording for each emotion from each speaker (90 recordings in total). Each recording was between 7–15 s. That alone shows how small of a dataset was used in order to perform these experiments and make tangible conclusions.

In more details, here is what this system included:

- **Step 1**: in this step *initialization* of the process was performed, which included recording of all the samples from all the users, one for each emotion as already described, then voice samples were categorized in groups. Framing of each recorded voice sample followed then jitter was calculated [24]. After using a vocoder, the portions that carried voice samples were separated from the noise. The first signal frame of each voice portion was then convolved with a 250 ms Hamming Window. For each of the voice frames, jitter coefficients were calculated.
- **Step 2**: this was called *feature clustering* step in which the features were collected and grouped together. In this stage Vector Quantization (VQ) [25] was used for the K-Means clustering machine learning method. This step was necessary in order to make the task more manageable by introducing a vector codebook for the emotion clustering part. At the end of this stage, for each of the voice features an assignment of each of the three emotional clusters was performed.
- **Step 3**: this step was called *feature matching* in which, a test cluster was 'matched' to each of the training clusters. In order to compare the distances between each jitter and the Cepstral Coefficient (CC) in the testing part of the process, from the trained samples in the codebook, the mean Euclidian distance has been adopted as distance measurement.
- **Step 4**: in this so-called *co-efficient computing* stage, the jitter-based coefficient calculations have been revealed. The Mel scale has been utilized in this stage, as applied to each frame, by using thirteen triangular overlapping kernels on each frame in order to recreate the spectrum needed. It is in this stage where the authors mention that

the jitter seemingly reduces the long-term effects of the changes in fundamental frequency $F_0$, the pitch (the perceived frequency). The *jitter* is described to be a small fluctuation of the pitch since it is rising or falling during voice production (as oppose to *shimmer*, which captures an amplitude instability). The relative jitter was referred to as *co-efficient*, which was found relevant for usage in this research instead of the CCs.

The recordings were originally completed in two languages and the average accuracy results for English were: 70.04 for happy, 67.10 for angry, and 70.53 for sad. The performance measure used was true acceptance, through Equal Error Rate (EER). Furthermore, the authors compared the Cepstral Constraint system, and the Jitter based system to MFCC and LPCC as described here [25, 26]. In addition, the authors found that, when the number of users is higher, then the EER is lower. In general, this method provides a low-cost framework base, with overall good accuracy for further exploration. In conclusion, emotion recognition based on jitter from voice had a comparable, if not even better performance than in the cases when conventional MFCCs were used.

## 6 Smart Systems in Entertainment Using Emotions

One of the areas that can greatly benefit from the advancements of smart system development is the entertainment industry. This, not only includes the advancements in personalization and recommendation based on previous experience of the user with the system (concepts that were heavily productized in recent years), but it must also take into account the specific needs of the user at the right time, which can be done either directly or indirectly. This need is especially prominent because of the growth of world media all around the globe. Hundreds and even thousands of new media is created on a daily basis, which makes the problem harder to solve. The solution to this kind of problem is never easy and it can be executed in many different ways. But what makes it smart is the interaction between human and machine. More specifically, the closer the communication between users and autonomous systems to natural person-to-person communication, the better and more natural that system will be. This means that an extra step must be taken in improving that communication. For example, we have seen automated systems with which we speak or show gestures, then some action is usually taken by the system. That is the very first level in human-machine interaction – a direct communication conveying a specific need. However, this may be too intrusive at times and may not have the desired effect by the user, as the communication may not be as natural. The reason for this is that some users get very self-conscious when they are filmed or knowingly recorded. In these kinds of cases, the message might get obscured and may not have the desired effect. But what if a system is introduced where these recordings can be done in the background with a one-time consent of the user (only the first time)? Then in these cases in addition to having something more powerful, we can also have a system that is very natural.

Some research has already been pointing in that direction, as seen in [27]. In this work the authors propose a service-oriented architecture (SOA) for connecting speech to digital information libraries. The scientists use emotion detection from speech as the main method for meeting individual needs, which can be applied explicitly to content recommendation. Some basic speech criteria and strategies have been previously set out for the task in [28]. Six distinct states of emotion were incorporated there: happy, sad, angry, fear, surprise, and neutral. Discussed were also some of the most important prosodic features extracted and collected in both time and frequency domains. The work was later extended in a more practical case for a recommendation system [29], using gender separation based on voice. One of the most promising features in emotion recognition from speech signals was shown to be the Glottal Symmetry (GS) [30, 31]. This fact was investigated in [28]. Figure 1 [32], depicts a plot of a typical Glottal Symmetry for four emotions. It can be seen that different emotional conditions can be clearly separated. The idea of using GS as feature domain has been extensively tested with an Optimum-Path Forest classifier as shown in [33]. Furthermore, Gaussian Mixture Model (GMM) have also been used with prosodic features, in addition to Tonal and Break Indices (ToBI) [34] and Inter-Sentence time domain statistics [35]. A nice review of all of these algorithms and other various features was provided in [36].

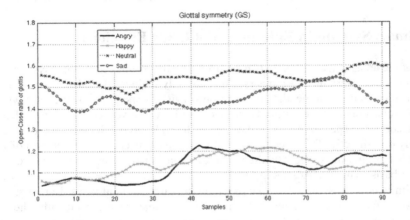

**Fig. 1.** Glottal Symmetry (GS) using four emotions [32]

In another study [37], an attempt to extract the sentiment from five books using "The Game of Thrones" was made through Natural Language Processing (NLP), implemented via Python's NLTK package (Natural Language Processing Toolkit). The result was a novel content discovery system, which was exclusively based on human behavior. The idea could easily be applied to any TV or electronic book series as well as movies libraries or music players as described next.

In [38], a music-based approach has been proposed. It is also based on emotion recognition using voice. In their published work the authors use the following five emotional states: happiness, anger, boredom, sadness, and anxiety. Preprocessing is performed for each of the training and testing datasets in order to remove silent sections in the corpus. This was done implementing the Rabiner-Sambur algorithm. To segment the speech in order to obtain the voiced sections a trivial end-point detection algorithm was carried out. For silence removing a Short-Time Energy (STE) and a Zero-Crossing

Rate (ZCR) were performed for better accuracy. Then feature extraction was performed. The feature domain solely included Mel Frequency Cepstral Coefficients (MFCCs). They are nonlinearly spread following a logarithmic law in the higher frequencies and are linearly spread in the lower frequencies. They are based on the human auditory hearing and are used quite frequently in the world of perceptual coding. This non-linear scale is also known as Mel-Frequency scale and is implemented using filter banks to obtain the MFCCs. Subsequently training with the newly composed feature vectors was done using two different classifiers. The testing determined the performance of the system and the result was directly applied to selecting a specific musical piece from a preselected musical databank. The authors used the Berlin database, which is a well-transcribed emotional database, comprised of voice sounds. In their speech samples the authors used a gender balanced ten-speaker dataset (five male and five female) of different age. The datasets included 1–5 s long samples. The two classifiers used were GMM and SVM. The results from the confusion matrixes for both showed successful accuracy [38].

In conclusion, SVM model showed better results with average accuracy at about 82%, while the GMM model with Maximum Likelihood (ML) showed a bit over 76% average accuracy when detecting emotions.

## 7    Smart Services for Finding Similarity in Images

More than 80% of our sensory experiences are visual. Similarity access and their conversion into high-level semantic features using fuzzy production rules, derived with the help of an image mining technique is given in [39]. Image recognition is used in the search of products or objects, by firstly identifying the objects, and then searching the network for similar patterns (IoT) [40].

**Fig. 2.**  The bridge crossing Arno in Arezzo

Similarity among the series of the water lily pond grudges at Giverny painted by Claude Monet is studied in [41]. Many mysteries have been solved regarding the Da Vinci's Mona Lisa painting. The bridge in the paining was found crossing the Arno in Arezzo - near the city. In Fig. 2 is my photograph of the bridge. I was able to find similarity with the bridge from the painting. In [42] retrieval by contrast and harmony is presented. Examples for search by light-dark, cold-warm and simultaneous contrast are given.

## 8    Smart Services for Extracting Higher-Level Visual Features

A tool for extracting higher-level visual features for art painting classification based on MPEG-7 descriptors was implemented in the system "Art Painting Image Color Aesthetics and Semantics" [43]. The analysis of the significance of the received characteristics and finding regularities between them can be used as discriminating semantic profile of the art paintings. It can predict several characteristics such as: the artists' names, movements, themes, techniques, etc. The system allows also creating some datasets, containing extracted attributes or selected part of them labelled with chosen profile such as artist name, movement, scene-type. These datasets are used for further analysis by data mining tools for searching typical combinations of characteristics, which form profiles of artists or movements, or reveal visual specifics, connected to the presented theme in the images. Example for this is given in Fig. 3.

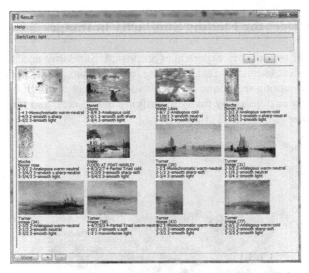

**Fig. 3.** Result of retrieval from the image base with parameter: "Dark/light contrast = Light" (includes "smooth light" and "monointense light")

## 9    Smart Services for Image Data Mining

In the field of image data mining, an approach for extending the learning set of a classification algorithm with additional metadata is developed [44]. It is used as a base for the assignment of appropriate names to find regularities. The analysis of the correspondence between connections established in the attribute space and existing links between concepts can be used as a test for the creation of an adequate model of the observed world. Meta-PGN classifier is suggested as a possible tool for establishing these connections. This approach is applied on the field of content-based image retrieval of art paintings by designing system architecture for the extraction of specific feature combinations, which represent different sides of artists' styles, periods and movements [45]. The system interacts with the user, displaying those parts of the mental model that are utilized in the name generation process. This interaction is used to further improve and extend the mental model.

## 10  Smart Services for Artist Identification

Artist identification has been an interesting task for centuries. Machine learning algorithms are used to solve this problem [46]. An artist's profile is obtained through an artist's merged images enhanced with layer and transparency tools. The machine learning J48 algorithm is utilized for classification. Cohen's Kappa, F-measure, and Matthew's correlation coefficient statistics are applied to compare the results obtained.

## 11  Smart Services for Autonomous Cars

Autonomous cars [47], or cars that run without human control, have been developed over the past several decades, starting in 1977. Currently, we have autonomous cars still in experimental and development stage that have driven autonomously thousands of miles. Some autonomy systems are already being used in the cars such as: Cruise Control, Anti-Lock Brakes. Some systems are just starting to be used: Stability and Traction Control, Pre-Accident Systems, Traffic Jam Assist, Self-Parking Systems. V2V (vehicle to vehicle) communication systems, are designed to prevent crashes in a number of scenarios such as: Intersection assist; Left-turn assist, Do-not-pass warning; Advance warning of a vehicle braking ahead; Forward-collision warning; Blind-spot/lane-change warning.

Computer vision and image processing are one of the main elements used in the autonomous car. Among them is Lidar technology (Light Detection and Ranging). It consists of puck-shaped device that creates a high-resolution map of the environment in real time. Some of the most important algorithms are for Lane Detection, Speed Bump Detection, Traffic Sign Detection, Steer by Wire System and recognition and classifying objects of different road types [48].

Lane Detection: Warning systems have already is available in many new cars. The algorithm includes:

a)  Find the Region of Interest (ROI);
b)  Image noise subtraction;
c)  Edge detection; and
d)  Lane markings.

Traffic Sign Detection: It includes preprocessing using color segmentation, threshold technique, Gaussian filter, canny edge detection and contours detection [49]. The next detection is based on Polynomial Approximation of digital curves technique applied on contours to correctly identify the signboard. Building new infrastructure, this problem can be solved with V2I (vehicle-to-infrastructure) communication trough mobility applications. In V2V network, every car, smart traffic signal could send, capture and retransmit signals. Five to ten hops on the network would gather traffic conditions a mile ahead.

Speed Bump Detection: It can be done with training the speed bump detection system using a neural network.

More and more applications with autonomous cars appear such as: Fast-food chains and grocery stores are teaming up with big car companies and tiny startups to test the idea of autonomously shuttling food to customers. During tests in Miami, Michigan and Las Vegas, Domino's Pizza Inc. delivered more than 1,000 pies in Ford sedans plastered with signs that read "self-driving delivery test vehicle" [48].

## 12    Smart Services for Finding Parking Slot

One of the challenges to build smart cities is the smart parking. Several solutions have been proposed: different types of sensors (magnetometers, light sensors, microphones, etc.), different communication technology (wired, wireless), and different types of cameras. Smart Parking is a system capable of extracting specific information from the captured images and different sensors. Solutions based on computer vision and big data are deployable on top of visual sensor networks. The IoT (Internet of Things) paradigm fits particularly well in urban scenarios as a key technology for the Smart City Concept. In [50], an efficient solution for real-time parking lot occupancy detection based on Convolutional Neural Network classifier is presented. There, a real time image segmentation and analysis, and streaming data are used. It takes into account different light conditions, parts of the day, and seasons. The benchmark collection for parking occupancy detection [51] is used. Problems for solving are:

a)   Significant changes of lighting conditions - sunny, rainy and snowing days;
b)   Different time of the day;
c)   Partially occupant moving cars, people, and additional objects.

OpenCV library (http://opencv.org/) and Python van can be used to find the frame spaces. The parking classification can be done with mix of the following techniques: background subtraction, defining and analyzing moving cars, applying Gabor filters as feature extractor to train a classifier with empty spaces under different light conditions, using edge detection algorithms. Deep Learning that allow computers to learn complex perception tasks such as Caffe system (http://caffe.berkeleyvision.org/) are used to train the neural networks. HAAR CASCADE can be used to detect moving cars [52].

New feature with Tesla called "Enhanced Summon" lets the drivers remotely call their car to drive itself through a parking lot to pick them up, so long as it's within 150 feet.

## 13  Smart Services for Video Filtering

An efficient video stream filtering solution based on MPEG-7 descriptors is described in [53]. The solution can be adopted for TV-Anytime, On Demand TV, Integrated Digital Television, Set-Top-Boxes, etc. It uses a novel approach called Pivoted Stream. The solution exploits the properties of metric spaces, in order to reduce the computational load of the filtering receiver.

The approach proposed video filtering that makes use of simple additional information (that is, indexes) sent with the video, eliminating the need for users to digest video that wouldn't pass the filter anyway. The approach requires a metric measure of similarity between the filter and the video representative (the feature); this measure is based on the pivot technique [54]. Filtering quality depends on the metric measure adopted. The approach is general and doesn't depend on a specific format to represent the video content, but it assumes the use of MPEG-7 to provide a description of the videos. In particular, it concentrates on the MPEG-7 visual descriptors, which covers basic visual features, such as color, texture, and shapes. Each source sends a video stream associated with an MPEG-7 stream that contains this video stream's description. These streams move through a generic transmission channel to the receiver stations (for example, set–top–boxes, digital multimedia recorders, media center PCs, and so on). Each receiver station has several filters that select (from all the video streams that arrive to the station) and deliver to the user only the video frames deemed relevant. Filtering is based on a comparison between each video frame with the filters, so that only frames similar to one of the filters are delivered to the user.

## 14  Conclusion

As discussed in this chapter, the need for improving services in areas like mobile services, communications, entertainment, healthcare, robotics, etc. is growing along with the complexity of data itself. Some of these areas are already employing multiple smart systems in various ecosystems to aid the work of personnel at hospitals or public service places, while others are used for entertainment and education. Some additional areas such as banking, security, and various other services related to warfare can also benefit greatly from this kind of technological expansions. In this chapter we showed how textual cues could be used as features to meet the public demand for smart system development. Moreover, we discussed in depth how sophisticated smart systems employ DSP and Machine Learning in order to process voices and images. It was further shown how using audio and visual cues in order to improve our everyday life could use these two areas for the creation of many distinct services. Additional research is necessary to lead to further advancement in smart system technology and improve the global IoT ecosystem.

## References

1. https://www.ibm.com/blogs/insights-on-business/consumer-products/2-5-quintillion-bytes-of-data-created-every-day-how-does-cpg-retail-manage-it/. Accessed Apr 2020

2. https://www.networkworld.com/article/3325397/storage/idc-expect-175-zettabytes-of-data-worldwide-by-2025.html. Accessed Apr 2020
3. Lea, R.: Smart Cities: An Overview of the Technology Trends Driving Smart Cities (2017)
4. Bala, A., et al.: Voice command recognition system based on MFCC and DTW. Int. J. Eng. Sci. Technol. 2(12), 7335–7342 (2010)
5. Parameshachari, B.D., Sawan, K.G., Gooneshwaree, H., Tulsirai, T.G.: A study on smart home control system through speech. Int. J. Comput. Appl. 69(19), 30–39 (2013). 0975 – 8887
6. Alkhawaldeh, R.S.: DGR: gender recognition of human speech using one-dimensional conventional neural network. Hindawi Sci. Program. (2019). Article ID 7213717, 12 pages
7. Akçay, M.B., Oğuz, K.: Speech emotion recognition: emotional models, databases, features, preprocessing methods, supporting modalities, and classifiers. Speech Communication 116, 56–76 (2020)
8. Cowie, R., et al.: Emotion recognition in human-computer interaction. IEEE Signal Process. Mag. 18(1), 32–80 (2001). https://doi.org/10.1109/79.911197
9. Teager, H., Teager, S.: Evidence for nonlinear sound production mechanisms in the vocal tract. In: Hardcastle, W.J., Marchal, A. (eds.) Speech Production and Speech Modeling, pp. 241–261. Springer, Cham (1990). https://doi.org/10.1007/978-94-009-2037-8_10
10. Ghazanfar Latif, A.H., Khan, M., Butt, M., Butt, O.: IoT based real-time voice analysis and smart monitoring system for disabled people. In: Asia Pacific Journal of Contemporary Education and Communication Technology, Asia Pacific Institute of Advanced Research (APIAR), vol. 3, no. 2, pp. 227–234 (2017). https://doi.org/10.25275/apjcectv3i2ict5. ISBN (eBook) 978 0 9943656 8 2 I ISSN: 2205-6181
11. Smith, B.: Raspberry Pi Assembly Language RASPBIAN Beginners: Hands on Guide. CreateSpace Independent Publishing Platform (2013)
12. Kumar, S.S., RangaBabu, T.: Emotion and gender recognition of speech signals using SVM. Emotion 4(3) (2015)
13. Schölkopf, B., Smola, A.J.: Learning with Kernels: Support Vector Machines, Regularization, Optimization, and Beyond. MIT Press, Cambridge (2002)
14. Belin, P., Fillion-Bilodeau, S., Gosselin, F.: The montreal affective voices: a validated set of nonverbal affect bursts for research on auditory affective processing. Behav. Res. Methods 40(2), 531–539 (2008)
15. Davis, J., Goadrich, M.: The relationship between Precision-Recall and ROC curves. In: Proceedings of the 23rd International Conference on Machine Learning, pp. 233–240. ACM, June 2006
16. Sood, S.K., Mahajan, I.: Wearable IoT sensor based healthcare system for identifying and controlling chikungunya virus. Comput. Ind. 91(2017), 33–44 (2017)
17. Gope, P., Hwang, T.: BSN-care: a secure IoT-based modern healthcare system using body sensor network. IEEE Sensors J. 16(5), 1368–1376 (2016)
18. Frant, E., Ispas, I., Dragomir, V., Dascalu, M., Zoltan, E., Stoica, I.C.: Voice based emotion recognition with convolutional neural networks for companion robots. Romanian J. Inf. Sci. Technol. 20(3), 222–240 (2017)
19. Cowie, R., Cornelius, R.: Describing the emotional states that are expressed in speech. Speech Commun. 40, 5–32 (2003)
20. Bhatti, M., Wang, Y., Guan, L.: A neural network approach for human emotion recognition in speech. In: IEEE International Symposium on Circuits and Systems, Vancouver, BC, pp. 181–184 (2004)
21. Noda, T., Yano, Y., Doki, S., Okuma, S.: Adaptive emotion recognition in speech by feature selection based on KL-divergence. In: IEEE International Conference on Systems, Man, and Cybernetics in Taipei, Taiwan, 8–11 October 2006, pp. 1921–1926 (2006)
22. Murray and Arnott: Toward the simulation of emotion in synthetic speech: a review of the literature on human vocal emotion. J. Acoust. Soc. Am. 93(i2), 1097–1108 (1993)

23. Nazia, H., Mahmuda, N.: Sensing emotion from voice jitter. In: SenSys 2018, Shenzhen, China, November 4–7 2018, pp. 359–360 (2018). ISBN 978-1-4503-5952-8
24. Ganapathy, H.H.S., Mallidi, S.H.: Robust feature extraction using modulation filtering of autoregressive models. IEEE Trans. Audio, Speech, Lang. Process. **22**(8), 1285–1295 (2014)
25. Kheder, M.A.D., Bausquet, P.: Dealing with additive noise in speaker recognition systems based on i-vector approach. In: IEEE ICASSP, Canada (2013)
26. Atal, B., Hanauer, S.: Speech analysis and synthesis by linear prediction of the speech wave. J. Acoust. Soc. Am. **50**(2), 637–655 (1971)
27. Iliev, A.I., Stanchev, P.L.: Smart multifunctional digital content ecosystem using emotion analysis of voice. In: 18th International Conference on Computer Systems and Technologies CompSysTech 2017, Ruse, Bulgaria, 22–24 June 2017, volume 1369, pp. 58–64. ACM (2017). ISBN 978-1-4503-5234-5
28. Iliev, A.: Monograph: Emotion Recognition From Speech. Lambert Academic Publishing (2012)
29. Iliev, A.I., Stanchev, L.P.: Information retrieval and recommendation using emotion from speech signal. In: 2018 IEEE Conference on Multimedia Information Processing and Retrieval, Miami, FL, USA, 10–12 April 2018, pp. 222–225 (2018). https://doi.org/10.1109/MIPR.2018.00054
30. Iliev, A.I., Scordilis, M.S.: Spoken emotion recognition using glottal symmetry. EURASIP J. Adv. Signal Process. (2011). Article ID 624575, ISSN 1687-6180
31. Iliev, A.I., Scordilis, M.S.: Emotion recognition in speech using inter-sentence glottal statistics. In: Proceedings of the 15th International Conference on systems, Signals and Image Processing, IEEE-IWSSIP 2008, Bratislava, Slovakia, 25–28 June 2008, pp. 465–468 (2008)
32. Iliev, A.I., Stanchev, P.L.: Glottal attributes extracted from speech with application to emotion driven smart systems. In: Proceedings of the 10th International Joint Conference on Knowledge Discovery, Knowledge Engineering and Knowledge Management (IC3K 2018), KDIR, vol. 1, pp. 297–302, Thomson Reuters, Seville, Spain, 18–20 September 2018. ISBN 978-989-758-330-8
33. Iliev, A.I., Scordilis, M.S., Papa, J.P., Falcão, A.X.: Spoken emotion recognition through optimum-path forest classification using glottal features. J. Comput. Speech Lang. **24**(3), 445–460 (2010). ISSN 0885-2308
34. Iliev, A.I., Zhang, Y., Scordilis, M.S.: Spoken emotion classification using ToBI features and GMM. In: Proceedings of the 14th International Workshop on Signals and Image Processing 2007 and the 6th EURASIP Conference focused on Speech and Image Processing, Multimedia Communications and Services. IEEE-IWSSIP 2007, Maribor, Slovenia, 27–30 June 2007, pp. 495–498 (2007). ISSN 16874722, 16874714
35. Iliev, A.I.: Emotion recognition in speech using inter-sentence time-domain statistics. IJIRSET Int. J. Innov. Res. Sci. Eng. Technol. **5**(3), 3245–3254 (2016)
36. Iliev, A.I.: Feature vectors for emotion recognition in speech. In: National Informatics Conference, Sofia, Bulgaria, pp. 225–238 (2016)
37. Iliev, A.I.: Content discovery using perceptual automation. In: Proceedings of the 10th International Conference on Management of Digital EcoSystems (MEDES 2018), Tokyo, Japan, 25–28 September 2018, pp. 233–238. ACM (2018). https://doi.org/10.1145/3281375.3281399. ISBN 978-1-4503-5622-0
38. Lukose, S., Upadhya, S.: Music player based on emotion recognition of voice signals. In: 2017 International Conference on Intelligent Computing, Instrumentation and Control Technologies (ICICICT), IEEE 2017, pp. 1751–1754 (2017). ISBN 978-1-5090-6106-8
39. Stanchev, P.: Using image mining for image retrieval. In: IASTED International Conference Computer Science and Technology, Cancun, Mexico, 19–21 May 2003, pp. 214–218 (2003)
40. Viana, W.: Using images to extend smart object discovery in an Internet of Things scenario. file:///C:/Users/pstan/Desktop/4057-829-4030-1-10-20181009.pdf

41. Stanchev, P., Green Jr., D., Dimitrov, B.: Some issues in the art image database systems. J. Digit. Inf. Manag. **4**(4), 227–232 (2006)
42. Stanchev, P., Green Jr., D., Dimitrov, B.: High level color similarity retrieval. Int. J. Inf. Theor. Appl. **10**(3), 283–287 (2003)
43. Ivanova, K., et al.: Local features in APICAS (analyzing of added value of the descriptors based on MPEG-7 vector quantization). Int. J Comput. Sci. Artif. Intell. **2**(4), 23–32 (2012). ISSN: 2226-4450 (online) 2226-4469 (print)
44. Radenski, A., et al.: Big data techniques, systems, applications, and platforms: case studies from academia. In: Proceedings of the Federated Conference on Computer Science and Information Systems, pp. 893–898 (2016)
45. Ivanova, K., Mitov, I., Stanchev, P., Ein-Dor, P., Vanhoof, K.: Establishing correspondences between attribute spaces and complex concept spaces using meta-PGN classifier. In: Proc. of the 2nd International Conference on Digital Preservation and Presentation of Cultural Heritage, V. Tarnovo, Bulgaria, IMI-BAS, Sofia, pp. 71–77 (2012). ISSN 1314-4006
46. Stanchev, P., Kolinski, M.: Novel artist identification approach through digital image analysis using machine learning and merged images. In: Rocha, Á., Ferrás, C., Paredes, M. (eds.) ICITS 2019. AISC, vol. 918, pp. 465–471. Springer, Cham (2019). https://doi.org/10.1007/978-3-030-11890-7_45
47. Stanchev, P., Geske, J.: Autonomous cars. History. State of art. Research problems. Springer Communications in Computer and Information Science, vol. 601, pp 1–10 (2016)
48. Viswanathan, V., Hussein, R.: Applications of image processing and real-time embedded systems in autonomous cars: a short review. Int. J. Image Process. (IJIP) **11**(2), 36–49 (2017)
49. Salhi, A., Minaoui, B., Fakir, M.: Robust automatic traffic signs detection using fast polygonal approximation of digital curves. In: 2014 International Conference on Multimedia Computing and Systems (ICMCS), Marrakech, pp. 433–437 (2014)
50. Amato, G., Carrara, F., Falchi, F., Gennaro, C., Meghini, C., Vairo, C.: Deep learning for decentralized parking lot occupancy detection. Expert Syst. Appl. **72**, 327–334 (2017)
51. de Almeida, P.R.L., Oliveira, L.S., Britto Jr., A.S., Silva Jr., E.J., Koerich, A.L.: PKLot – a robust dataset for parking lot classification. Expert Syst. Appl. **42**, 4937–4949 (2015)
52. Stanchev, P., Geske, J.: Smart Parking. Geoinformatics Research Papers, vol. 5, BS1002 (2017). https://doi.org/10.2205/codata2017
53. Falchi, F., Gennaro, C., Savino, P., Stanchev, P.: Efficient video stream filtering. IEEE Multimed. 52–61 (2008)
54. Shapiro, M.: 'The choice of reference points in best-match file searching'. Comm. ACM **20**(5), 339–343 (1977)

# Big Spatial and Spatio-Temporal Data Analytics Systems

Polychronis Velentzas[1], Antonio Corral[2]([✉]), and Michael Vassilakopoulos[1]

[1] Data Structuring and Engineering Laboratory,
Department of Electrical and Computer Engineering,
University of Thessaly, Volos, Greece
{cvelentzas,mvasilako}@uth.gr
[2] Department of Informatics, University of Almeria, Almeria, Spain
acorral@ual.es

**Abstract.** We are living in the era of Big Data, and Spatial and Spatio-temporal Data are not an exception. Mobile apps, cars, GPS devices, ships, airplanes, medical devices, IoT devices, etc. are generating explosive amounts of data with spatial and temporal characteristics. Social networking systems also generate and store vast amounts of geo-located information, like geo-located tweets, or captured mobile users' locations. To manage this huge volume of spatial and spatio-temporal data we need parallel and distributed frameworks. For this reason, modeling, storing, querying and analyzing big spatial and spatio-temporal data in distributed environments is an active area for researching with many interesting challenges. In recent years a lot of spatial and spatio-temporal analytics systems have emerged. This paper provides a comparative overview of such systems based on a set of characteristics (data types, indexing, partitioning techniques, distributed processing, query Language, visualization and case-studies of applications). We will present selected systems (the most promising and/or most popular ones), considering their acceptance in the research and advanced applications communities. More specifically, we will present two systems handling spatial data only (SpatialHaddop and GeoSpark) and two systems able to handle spatio-temporal data, too (ST-Hadoop and STARK) and compare their characteristics and capabilities. Moreover, we will also present in brief other recent/emerging spatial and spatio-temporal analytics systems with interesting characteristics. The paper closes with our conclusions arising from our investigation of the rather new, though quite large world of ecosystems supporting management of big spatial and spatio-temporal data.

## 1 Introduction

We are living in the era of Big Data, and Spatial and Spatio-temporal Data are not an exception. Mobile apps, cars, GPS devices, ships, airplanes, medical devices, IoT devices, etc. are generating explosive amounts of data with spatial and temporal characteristics. Social networking systems also generate and store vast amounts of geo-located information, like geo-located tweets, or captured mobile users' locations. To manage this huge volume of spatial and spatio-temporal data we need

© Springer-Verlag GmbH Germany, part of Springer Nature 2021
A. Hameurlain et al. (Eds.): TLDKS XLVII, LNCS 12630, pp. 155–180, 2021.
https://doi.org/10.1007/978-3-662-62919-2_7

parallel and distributed frameworks. For this reason, modeling, storing, querying and analyzing big spatial and spatio-temporal data in distributed environments is an active area for researching with many interesting challenges.

In recent years a lot of spatial and spatio-temporal analytics systems have emerged. Parallel and distributed Spatio-temporal analytic systems are mostly either based on Hadoop, or on Spark. Moreover, most of them handle spatial data only, while others can represent and process statio-temporal information. Considering these alternatives, four possible groups of systems are formed: Hadoop or Spark based spatial data systems and Hadoop or Spark based spatio-temporal data systems.

This paper provides a comparative overview of such systems based on a set of characteristics (data types, indexing, partitioning techniques, distributed processing, query Language, visualization and case-studies of applications). We will present selected systems (the most promising and/or most popular ones), considering their acceptance in the research and advanced applications communities.

In Sect. 2 we will introduce parallel and distributed architectures and their two basic representatives (Hadoop and Spark). Next, in Sect. 3 we will present two systems handling spatial data only (SpatialHaddop and GeoSpark) and two systems able to handle spatio-temporal data, too (ST-Hadoop and STARK) and compare their characteristics and capabilities. In Sect. 4, we will present in brief other recent/emerging spatio-temporal analytics systems with interesting characteristics. The paper closes with our conclusions arising from our investigation of the rather new, though quite large world of ecosystems supporting management of big spatial and spatio-temporal data.

## 2    Parallel and Distributed Architectures

Data mining and analysis of big data is a non-trivial task. Often, it is performed in a distributed infrastructure of multiple compute network-interconnected

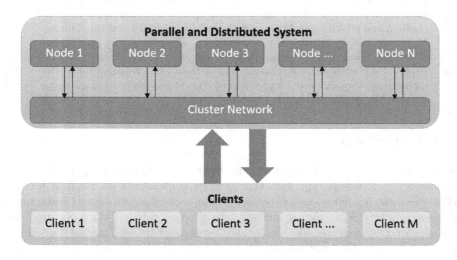

**Fig. 1.** Parallel and distributed system architecture.

(through the cluster network) nodes, each of which may be equipped with multiple CPUs or GPUs (Fig. 1).

This kind of architectures bring a number of challenges. First of all, the resources must be effectively used. For example, one must avoid delays of CPU/GPU resources due to working data transfer over network. Second, all the available resources (CPU/GPU, storage and network) should be typically shared among different users or processes to reduce costs and increase interoperability. In order to address these challenges several architectures and frameworks have risen. In this section, we will describe the two most popular of them, Apache Hadoop and Apache Spark. Both of them are open source and widely used.

## 2.1 Apache Hadoop

Hadoop is a shared-nothing framework, meaning that the input data is partitioned and distributed to all computing nodes, which perform calculations on their local data only. Hadoop is a two-stage disk-based MapReduce computation engine, not well suited to repetitive processing tasks.

MapReduce [10, 25] is a programming model for distributed computations on very large amounts of data and a framework for large-scale data processing on clusters built from commodity hardware. A task to be performed using the MapReduce framework has to be specified as two phases: a) the *map* phase, which is specified by a *map function*, takes input, typically from Hadoop Distributed File System (HDFS) files, possibly performs some computations on this input, and distributes it to worker nodes, and b) the *reduce* phase which processes these results as specified by a *reduce function* (Fig. 2). An important aspect of MapReduce is that both the input and the output of the *map* step are represented as *key/value pairs* and that pairs with same key will be processed as one group by a *reducer*. The *map* step is parallelly applied to every pair with key $k_1$ of the input dataset, producing a list of pairs with key $k_2$. Subsequently, all pairs with the same key from all lists are grouped together, creating one list for each key (*shuffling step*). The *reduce* step is then parallelly applied to each such group, producing a list of key/value pairs:

$$map : (k_1, v_1) \rightarrow list(k_2, v_2) \text{ and } reduce : (k_2, list(v_2)) \rightarrow list((k_3, v_3))$$

Additionally, a *combiner function* can be used to run on the output of the *map* phase and perform some filtering or aggregation to reduce the number of keys passed to the *reducer*. The MapReduce architecture provides good scalability and fault tolerance mechanisms. MapReduce was originally introduced by Google in 2004 and was based on well-known principles of parallel and distributed processing. It has been widely adopted through Hadoop (an open-source implementation), whose development was led by Yahoo and later became an Apache project[1].

---

[1] https://hadoop.apache.org/.

## 2.2  Apache Spark

To overcome limitations of the MapReduce paradigm and Apache Hadoop (especially regarding iterative algorithms), Apache Spark[2] was developed. This is also an open-source cluster-computing framework based on Resilient Distributed Datasets (RDDs), read-only multisets of data items distributed over the computing nodes. RDDs form a kind of distributed shared memory, suitable for the implementation of iterative algorithms. Apache Spark achieves high performance for both batch and streaming data, using a state-of-the-art DAG (Directed Acyclic Graph) scheduler (an example is depicted in Fig. 3), a query optimizer and a physical execution engine.

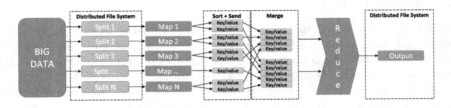

**Fig. 2.** MapReduce programming model.

DAG scheduler is the scheduling layer of Apache Spark that implements stage-oriented scheduling. It transforms a logical execution plan (i.e. RDD lineage of dependencies built using RDD transformations) to a physical execution plan (using stages).

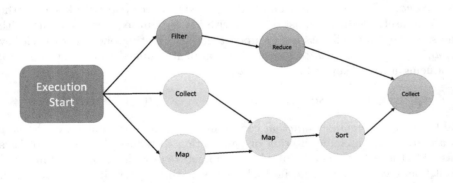

**Fig. 3.** An example of a DAG (Directed Acyclic Graph) scheduler.

The data transformations that take place in Spark are executed in a "lazy" way. Transformations are lazy in nature: when we call some operation for an

---

[2] https://spark.apache.org/.

RDD, it does not execute immediately; it is executed when output is requested. Spark maintains a record of which operation is being called (through DAG). We can think of a Spark RDD as the data that we built up through transformations. Since transformations are lazy in nature, we can execute operations any time by calling an action on data. Hence, in lazy evaluation, data is not loaded, and computations are not performed until it is necessary.

## 3   Big Spatial and Spatio-Temporal Data Analytics Systems

In the next subsections, we will present in detail a popular representative of each of group of systems (Hadoop-based and Spark-based Spatial and Hadoop-based and Spark-based Spatio-temporal Data Analytics Systems). SpatialHadoop (http://spatialhadoop.cs.umn.edu/), a full-fledged MapReduce framework with native support for spatial data, is presented in Subsect. 3.1. Subsect. 3.2 is devoted to GeoSpark (http://geospark.datasyslab.org), an in-memory cluster computing framework for processing large-scale spatial data that uses Spark as its base layer and adds two more layers, the Spatial RDD (SRDD) Layer and Spatial Query Processing Layer, thus providing Spark with in-house spatial capabilities. ST-Hadoop (http://st-hadoop.cs.umn.edu/), the first full-fledged open-source MapReduce framework with a native support for spatio-temporal data, is presented in Subsect. 3.3. ST-Hadoop is a comprehensive extension to Hadoop and SpatialHadoop that injects spatio-temporal data awareness inside each of their layers. In Subsect. 3.4, STARK framework for scalable spatio-temporal data analytics on Spark (https://github.com/dbis-ilm/stark) is presented. It is built on top of Spark and provides a domain specific language (DSL) that seamlessly integrates into any (Scala) Spark program. It includes an expressive set of spatio-temporal operators for filter, join with various predicates as well as $k$ nearest neighbor search. Moreover, in Subsect. 3.5 we present a comparison of these systems regarding their capabilities and characteristics.

### 3.1   SpatialHadoop

**SpatialHadoop** (http://spatialhadoop.cs.umn.edu/) [13,14] is a full-fledged MapReduce framework with native support for spatial data. It is an efficient disk-based distributed spatial query processing system. Note that MapReduce [10] is a scalable, flexible and fault-tolerant programming framework for distributed large-scale data analysis.

SpatialHadoop [13,14] (see in Fig. 4 its architecture) is a comprehensive extension to Hadoop [7] that injects spatial data awareness in each Hadoop layer, namely, the language, storage, MapReduce, and operations layers. In the *Language* layer, SpatialHadoop adds a simple and expressive high-level language for spatial data types and operations. In the *Storage* layer, SpatialHadoop adapts traditional spatial index structures as Grid, R-tree, R$^+$-tree, Quadtree, etc. to form a two-level spatial index [15]. SpatialHadoop enriches the *MapReduce* layer by two new components, *SpatialFileSplitter* and *SpatialRecordReader* for efficient and scalable spatial data processing. *SpatialFileSplitter* (*SFS*) is an extended splitter that exploits the global index(es) on input file(s) to early prune file cells/blocks not contributing to answer, and *SpatialRecordReader* (*SRR*) reads a split originating from spatially indexed input file(s) and exploits the advantages of the local indices to efficiently process it. At the *Operations* layer, SpatialHadoop is also equipped with a several spatial operations, including range query, *k*NN query and spatial join. Other computational geometry algorithms (e.g. polygon union, skyline, convex hull, farthest pair and closest pair) are also implemented following a similar approach [11].

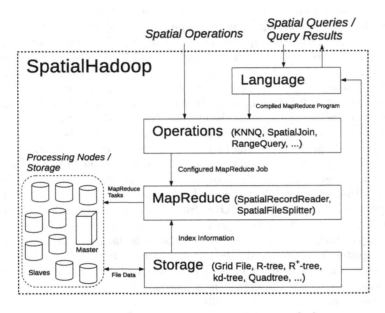

**Fig. 4.** SpatialHadoop system architecture [14].

**Spatial Data Types.** The *Language* layer provides a high-level language with standard spatial data types and operations to make the system accessible to non-technical users. In particular, the language layer provides Pigeon [12] a simple high level SQL-like language that supports OGC-compliant spatial data types and spatial operations. Pigeon overrides the `bytearray` data type to support standard spatial data types, such as, `Point`, `LineString`, and `Polygon`. Conversion between `bytearray` and `geometry`, back and forth, is done automatically on the fly which makes it transparent to end users.

**Spatial Storage (indexing Techniques).** SpatialHadoop proposes a two-layer spatial index structure which consists of one global index and multiple local indexes. The *global index* partitions data into HDFS blocks and distributes them among cluster nodes, while *local indexes* organize records inside each block. The separation of global and local indexes lends itself to the MapReduce programming paradigm where the global index is used while preparing the MapReduce job while the local indexes are used for processing the map tasks. In addition, breaking the file into smaller partitions allows each partition to be indexed separately in memory and dumping it to a file in a sequential manner. SpatialHadoop uses this two-level design to build a grid index, R-tree and R$^+$-tree. The index is constructed in one MapReduce job that runs in three phases. (1) The *partitioning* phase divides the space into n rectangles, then, it partitions the data by assigning each record to overlapping rectangles. (2) In the *local indexing* phase, each partition is processed separately on a single machine and a local index is constructed in memory before it is dumped to disk. (3) The final *global indexing* phase constructs a global index on the master node which indexes all HDFS blocks in the file using their MBRs as indexing key.

**Spatial Partitioning Techniques.** In [15], seven different *spatial partitioning techniques* in SpatialHadoop are presented, and an extensive experimental study on the quality of the generated index and the performance of range and spatial join queries is reported. These seven partitioning techniques are also classified in two categories according to boundary object handling: *replication-based techniques* (Grid, Quadtree, STR+ and $k$-d tree) and *distribution-based techniques* (STR, Z-Curve and Hilbert-Curve). The *distribution-based techniques* assign an object to exactly one overlapping cell and the cell has to be expanded to enclose all contained points. The *replication-based techniques* avoid expanding cells by replicating each point to all overlapping cells, but the query processor has to employ a duplicate avoidance technique to account for replicated elements. The most important conclusions of [15] for distributed join processing, using the *overlap* spatial predicate, are the following: (1) the smallest running time is obtained when the same partitioning technique is used in both datasets for the join processing, (2) Quadtree outperforms all other techniques with respect to running time, since it minimizes the number of overlapping partitions between the two files by employing a regular space partitioning, (3) Z-Curve reports the worst running times, and (4) $k$-d tree gets very similar results to STR.

**Spatial Operations.** SpatialHadoop contains a number of basic spatial operations such as range query, kNN query and spatial join [14]. A *range query* takes a set of spatial records $P$ and a query area $A$ as input, and returns the records from $P$ that overlap with $A$. SpatialHadoop exploits the global index with the SpatialFileSplitter to select only the partitions that overlap the query range $A$. Then, it uses the SpatialRecordReader to process the local indexes in matching partitions and find matching records. Finally, a duplicate avoidance step filters out duplicate results caused by replication in the index. A *kNN query* algorithm in SpatialHadoop is composed of the three steps: (1) *Initial Answer*, where we come up with an initial answer of the k closest points to the query point $q$ within the same file partition as $q$. It first locates the partition that includes $q$ by feeding the SpatialFileSplitter with a filter function that selects only the overlapping partition. Then, the selected partition goes through the SpatialRecordReader to exploit its local index with a traditional kNN algorithm to produce the initial k answers. (2) *Correctness check*, where it checks if the initial answer can be considered final or not. (3) *Answer Refinement*, if the correctness check result is not final, a range query is executed to produce the nearest k point as the final result. For a *spatial join query*, SpatialHadoop proposes a MapReduce-based algorithm where the SpatialFileSplitter exploits the two global indexes to find overlapping pair of partitions. The map function uses the SpatialRecordReader to exploit the two local indexes in each pair to find matching records. Finally, a duplicate avoidance step eliminates duplicate pairs in the answer caused by replication in the index. Finally, CG_Hadoop [11] is a suite of computational geometry operations for MapReduce. It supports five fundamental computational geometry operations, namely, polygon union, skyline, convex hull, farthest pair, and closest pair, all implemented as MapReduce algorithms.

**Distributed Processing (MapReduce and Dataflow).** In general, a spatial query processing in SpatialHadoop consists of four steps [14,19,20], regardless of whether we have one or two input files (see Fig. 5, where two files as input are shown): (1) *Preprocessing*, where the data is partitioned according to a specific spatial index, generating a set of partitions or cells. (2) *Pruning*, when the query is issued, where the master node examines all partitions and prunes by a *filter function* those ones that are guaranteed not to be included in any possible result of the spatial query. (3) *Local Spatial Query Processing*, where a local spatial query processing is performed on each non-pruned partition in parallel on different machines. (4) *Global Processing*, where the results are collected from all machines in the previous step and the final result of the concerned spatial query is computed. A *combine* function can be applied in order to decrease the volume of data that is sent from the *map* task. The *reduce* function can be omitted when the results from the *map* phase are final.

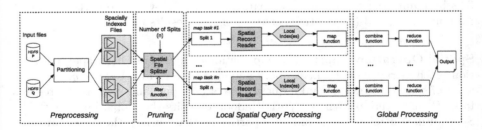

**Fig. 5.** Spatial query processing in SpatialHadoop [14,20].

**Query Language.** The *Language* layer contains Pigeon [12], a high level language with OGC-compliant spatial data types and functions. In particular, it adds the following: (1) OGC-compliant spatial data types including, `Point`, `LineString`, `Polygon`. (2) OGC-standard spatial predicates which return a Boolean value based on a test on the input polygon(s); e.g., `IsClosed`, `Touches`. (3) Basic spatial functions which are used to extract useful information from a single shape; e.g., `Area`. (4) Spatial analysis functions which perform some spatial transformations on input objects; e.g., `Centroid`, `Intersection`. (5) Spatial aggregate functions which take a set of spatial objects and return a single value which summarizes all input objects; e.g., `ConvexHull`. (6) and some changes to the language; e.g. *k*NN Keyword, FILTER, JOIN.

**Visualization.** The visualization process involves creating an image that describes an input dataset. This is a natural way to explore spatial datasets as it allows users to find interesting patterns in the input which are otherwise hard to spot. SpatialHadoop provides a visualization layer which generates two types of images, namely, *single level* image and *multilevel* images. For *single level* image visualization, the input dataset is visualized as a single image of a user-specified image size (width x height) in pixels. SpatialHadoop generates a single level image in three phases. (1) *Partitioning* phase partitions the data using either the default non-spatial Hadoop partitioner or using the spatial partitioner in SpatialHadoop depending on whether the data needs to be smoothed or not. (2) In the *Rasterize* phase, the machines in the cluster process the partitions in parallel and generate a partial image for each partition. (3) In the *Merging* phase, the partial images are combined together to produce the final image. SpatialHadoop also supports *multilevel* images which consist of small tiles produced at different zoom levels. SpatialHadoop provides an efficient algorithm that runs in two phases, *partition* and *rasterize*. (1) The *Partition* phase scans all input records and replicates each record $r$ to all overlapping tiles in the image according to the MBR of $r$ and the MBR of each tile. This phase produces one partition per tile in the desired image. (2) The *Rasterize* phase processes all generated partitions and generates a single image out of each partition.

**Case-Studies of Applications.** The core of SpatialHadoop is used in several real applications that deal with big spatial data including MNTG [30], a web-based traffic generator; TAREEG [2], a MapReduce extractor for OpenStreetMap data; TAGHREED [29], a system for querying and visualizing twitter data, and SHAHED [16], a MapReduce system for analyzing and visualizing satellite data. SHAHED is a tool for analyzing and exploring remote sensing data publicly available by NASA in a 500 TB archive. It provides a web interface where users navigate through the map and the system displays satellite data for the selected area. HadoopViz [17] is a MapReduce-based framework for visualizing big spatial data, it can efficiently produce giga-pixel images for billions of input records.

## 3.2   GeoSpark

The **GeoSpark** (http://geospark.datasyslab.org) framework exploits the core engine of Apache Spark and SparkSQL, by adding support for spatial data types, indexes, and geometrical operations. GeoSpark extends the Resilient Distributed Datasets (RDDs) concept to support spatial data. It adds two more layers, the Spatial RDD (SRDD) Layer and Spatial Query Processing Layer, thus providing Spark with in-house spatial capabilities. The SRDD layer consists of three newly defined RDDs, PointRDD, RectangleRDD and PolygonRDD. SRDDs support geometrical operations, like Overlap and Minimum Bounding Rectangle. SRDDs are automatically partitioned by using the uniform grid technique, where the global grid file is split into a number of equal geographical size grid cells. Elements that intersect with two or more grid cells are being duplicated. GeoSpark provides spatial indexes like Quadtree and R-tree on a per partition base. The Spatial Query Processing Layer includes spatial range query, spatial join query, spatial $k$NN query. GeoSpark relies heavily on the JTS (Java Topology Suite) and therefore conforms to the specifications published by the Open Geospatial Consortium. It is a robust and well implemented spatial system. Moreover, a lot of heterogeneous data sources are supported, like CSV, GeoJSON, WKT, NetCDF/HDF and ESRI Shapefile. GeoSpark does not directly support temporal data and operations.

**Spatial and Spatio-Temporal Data Types.** All the common spatial datatypes are supported like Point, Multi-Point, Polygon, Multi-Polygon, LineString, Multi-LineString, GeometryCollection, and Circle. In addition to these simple datatypes, GeoSpark is integrated with the complex geometrical shapes concave/convex polygons and multiplesub-shapes.

**Spatial and Spatio-Temporal Storage (Indexing Techniques).** The framework indexing architecture is built as a set of indexes per RDD partition. GeoSpark spatial indexes rely on the R-tree or Quadtree data structure. There are three kind of index options:

1. Build local indexes: GeoSpark builds a set of indexes per spatial RDD. This way a global index is not created and all objects are not indexed in one machine. Furthermore, to speedup queries the indexes are clustered indexes, meaning that spatial objects are stored directly in the spatial index. As a result, querying the index returns immediately the spatial object, skipping the I/O overhead of a second retrieve based on the objects pointer.
2. Query local indexes: The queries are divided in smaller tasks and these tasks are executed in parallel. The framework will use any existing local spatial indexes, minimizing query execution time.
3. Persist local indexes: GeoSpark users have the option to reuse the build local indexes, by storing it in one of the following ways: (1) cache to memory by calling IndexedSpatialRDD.cache(), (2) persist on disk by calling IndexedSpatialRDD.saveAsObjectFile(HDFS/S3 PATH).

**Spatial and Spatio-Temporal Partitioning Techniques.** In order to take advantage of the spatial proximity which is crucial for improving query speed, GeoSpark automatically repartitions a loaded Spatial RDD according to its internal spatial data distribution (Fig. 6 presents spatial partitioning techniques supported by GeoSpark). This is crucial for every computation, because it minimizes the data shuffles across the cluster and it avoids unnecessary CPU overheads on partitions that contain unwanted data. The framework implements spatial partitioning in three main steps:

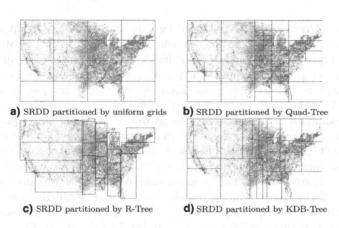

**a)** SRDD partitioned by uniform grids     **b)** SRDD partitioned by Quad-Tree

**c)** SRDD partitioned by R-Tree     **d)** SRDD partitioned by KDB-Tree

**Fig. 6.** Spatial partitioning techniques [42].

1. Building a global spatial grid file: Each Spatial RDD partition is sampled and the data are collected by the master node, resulting to a small subset of the spatial RDD. The sampled RDD is divided in equally load balanced partitions and their boundaries are used to further partition the initial RDD, resulting to new spatial RDD partitions, which are also load balanced. GeoSpark offers the following partition options: Uniform Grid, R-tree, Quadtree and $k$DB-tree.
2. Assigning a grid cell ID to each object: After constructing the global grid file, the framework assigns a grid cell to each object. Therefore, it creates a new spatial RDD whose schema is <Key, Value>. Every spatial object is stored in the new RDD with its corresponding grid cell ID. In case a spatial object span across multiple grids, the spatial RDD may contain duplicates.
3. Re-partitioning SRDD across the cluster: The Spatial RDD generated by the last step has a <Key, Value> pair schema. The Key represents a grid cell ID. In this the spatial RDD is repartitioned by the key, and the objects with the same key are grouped into the same partition.

**Spatial and Spatio-Temporal Operations.** The GeoSpark framework comes with a full range of spatial operations. Users can facilitate spatial analysis and spatial data mining by combining queries with one or more of the following spatial operations:

1. Spatial Range query: This operation returns all the spatial objects that lie within a defined region. As an example, this query can find all gas stations in the city center.
2. Spatial join: This kind of queries combine two or more datasets, using spatial predicates (e.g. Intersects, Overlaps, Contains, Distance etc).
3. Spatial $k$ nearest neighbors ($k$NN) query: $k$NN query computes the $k$ nearest neighbors around a center point. For example, a $k$NN query could be, find the 5 nearest hotels around the user.

**Distributed Processing (MapReduce and Dataflow).** GeoSpark can run spatial query processing operations on the SRDDs, right after the Spatial RDD layer loads, partitions are generated and indexing is completed. The spatial query processing layer provides support for many spatial operations like range query, distance query, $k$ Nearest Neighbors ($k$NN) query, range join query and distance join query. In order to describe the distributed processing of GeoSpark we will analyze the simplest of the queries the range query. A spatial range query is faster and less resource-consuming because it just returns objects that the input query window object contains. To complete such queries, we need to issue a parallelized Filter transformation in Apache Spark, which introduces a narrow dependency. As a result, repartitioning is not needed. These is also a more efficient way, we can broadcast the query window to all workers and parallelize the processing across the cluster. The query processing algorithm needs only one stage, due to the narrow dependency which does not require data shuffle. In Fig. 7, the range query DAG and data flow is depicted.

**Query Language.** GeoSparkSQL supports SQL/MM Part3 Spatial SQL Standard. It includes four kinds of SQL operators as follows. All these operators can be directly called through this command in Scala: var myDataFrame = sparkSession.sql("YOUR SQL HERE").

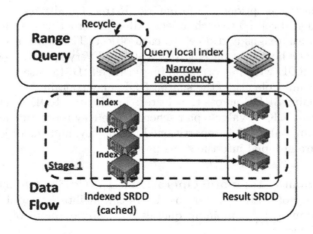

**Fig. 7.** Range query DAG and data flow [42].

1. Constructor: Constructor creates a geometry from an input string or coordinates. For example, we have the following constructor ST_GeomFromWKT (string), which constructs a Geometry from Wkt, ST_GeomFromGeoJSON (string) which constructs a Geometry from a JSON string, ST_Point (decimal, decimal) which constructs a Point from coordinates,
2. Function: There are many available functions like ST_Distance (geometry, geometry) which returns the Euclidean distance between two geometries, ST_Area (geometry) that calculates the area of a geometry and many more.
3. Predicate: The spatial predicates describe the spatial relationships. They also imply a spatial logic amongst the spatial objects which is essentially a spatial join. GeoSpark supports a complete set of predicates like ST_Contains(geometry, geometry), ST_Intersects (geometry, geometry), ST_Equals (geometry, geometry).
4. Aggregate function: SQL has aggregate functions, which are used to aggregate the results of a SQL query. Likewise, GeoSparkSQL also supports spatial aggregate functions. Spatial aggregate functions aggregate the results of SQL queries involving geometry objects. For example, ST_Union_Aggr(geometryColumn) returns the polygon union of all polygons of the geometryColumn.

**Visualization.** GeoSpark visualization is supported with the core visualization framework GeoSparkViz [41]. GeoSparkViz a large-scale geospatial map visualization framework. GeoSparkViz extends Apache Spark with native support for general cartographic design. It offers a plethora of utilities that enable users to perform data management and visualization on spatial data. One of the best features of GeoSparkViz is that it reduces the overhead of loading the intermediate spatial data generated during the data management phase to the designated map visualization tool.

### 3.3 ST-Hadoop

**ST-Hadoop** (http://st-hadoop.cs.umn.edu/) [4,6], see in Fig. 8 its architecture, is a full-fledged open-source MapReduce framework with a native support for spatio-temporal data. ST-Hadoop is a comprehensive extension to Hadoop [7] and SpatialHadoop [14] that injects spatio-temporal data awareness inside each of their layers, mainly, language, indexing, MapReduce and operations layers. In the *Language* layer, ST-Hadoop extends Pigeon language [12] to supports spatio-temporal data types and operations. In the *Indexing* layer, ST-Hadoop spatio-temporally loads and divides data across computation nodes in the Hadoop Distributed File System (HDFS). In this layer, ST-Hadoop scans a random sample obtained from the whole dataset, bulk loads its spatio-temporal index in-memory, and then uses the spatio-temporal boundaries of its index structure to assign data records with its overlap partitions. ST-Hadoop sacrifices storage to achieve more efficient performance in supporting spatio-temporal operations, by replicating its index into temporal hierarchy index structure that consists of two-layer indexing of temporal and then spatial. The *MapReduce* layer introduces two new components of *SpatioTemporalFileSplitter* and *SpatioTemporalRecordReader*, that exploit the spatio-temporal index structures to speed up spatio-temporal operations. Finally, the *Operations* layer encapsulates the spatio-temporal operations that take advantage of the ST-Hadoop temporal hierarchy index structure in the indexing layer, such as spatio-temporal range, spatio-temporal top-$k$ nearest neighbor, and spatio-temporal join queries.

The key idea behind the performance gain of ST-Hadoop is its ability to load the data in HDFS in a way that mimics spatio-temporal index structures [3]. Hence, incoming spatio-temporal queries can have minimal data access to retrieve the query answer. The extensibility of ST-Hadoop allows others to extend spatio-temporal features and operations easily using similar approaches as described in [6].

**Spatial and Spatio-Temporal Data Types.** Spatio-temporal data types (STPoint, Time and Interval) are used to define the schema of input files upon their loading process. ST-Hadoop extends `STPoint`, `TIME` and `INTERVAL`. For instance, the `TIME` instance is used to identify the temporal dimension of the data, while the time `INTERVAL` mainly provided to equip the query predicates.

**Spatial and Spatio-Temporal Storage (Indexing Techniques).** ST-Hadoop HDFS organizes input files as spatio-temporal partitions that satisfy one main goal of supporting spatio-temporal queries. ST-Hadoop imposes *temporal slicing*, where input files are spatio-temporally loaded into intervals of a specific time granularity, e.g., days, weeks, or months. Each granularity is represented as a level in ST-Hadoop index. Data records in each level are spatio-temporally partitioned, such that the boundary of a partition is defined by a spatial region and time interval.

The key idea behind the performance gain of ST-Hadoop is its ability to load the data in HDFS in a way that mimics spatio-temporal index structures. To support all spatio-temporal operations including more sophisticated queries over time, ST-Hadoop replicates spatio-temporal data into a *Temporal Hierarchy Index*. ST-Hadoop set *Temporal Hierarchy Index* structure to four levels of days, weeks, months and years granularities, but it can be changed by the users.

ST-Hadoop index structure consists of two-layer indexing of a temporal and spatial. This two-layer indexing is replicated in all levels, where in each level the sample is partitioned using different granularity. ST-Hadoop trade-off storage to achieve more efficient performance through its index replication. In general, the index creation of a single level in the *Temporal Hierarchy* goes through four consecutive phases, called sampling, temporal slicing, spatial indexing, and physical writing. For instance, in the spatial indexing phase, ST-Hadoop determines the spatial boundaries of the data records within each temporal slice. ST-Hadoop spatially index each temporal slice independently, and it takes the advantages of applying different types of spatial bulk loading techniques in HDFS that are

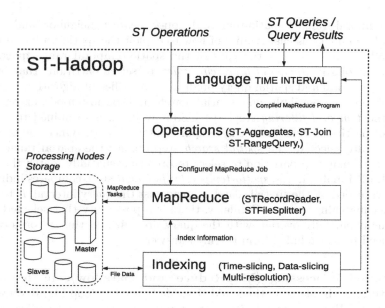

**Fig. 8.** ST-Hadoop system architecture [4,6].

already implemented in SpatialHadoop (Grid, STR-tree, Quadtree and $k$-d tree). The output of this phase is the spatio-temporal boundaries of each temporal slice.

**Spatial and Spatio-Temporal Partitioning Techniques.** In the temporal slicing phase, ST-Hadoop determines the temporal boundaries by slicing the in-memory sample into multiple time intervals, to efficiently support a fast-random access to a sequence of objects bounded by the same time interval. ST-Hadoop employs two. *temporal slicing* techniques, where each manipulates the sample according to specific slicing characteristics: (1) *Time-partition slicing*, slices the sample (from the sampling phase) into multiple splits that are uniformly on their time intervals, and (2) *Data-partition slicing* where the sample is sliced to the degree that all sub-splits are uniformly in their data size. The output of the temporal slicing phase finds the temporal boundary of each split, that collectively cover the whole time domain. Moreover, ST-Hadoop takes the advantages of applying different types of spatial bulk loading techniques in HDFS that are already implemented in SpatialHadoop such as Grid, STR-tree, Quadtree and $k$-d tree.

**Spatial and Spatio-Temporal Operations.** The combination of the spatio-temporally load balancing with the temporal hierarchy index structure gives the kernel of ST-Hadoop, that enables the possibility of efficient and practical realization of spatio-temporal operations. The *Operations* layer encapsulates the implementation of three common spatio-temporal operations, namely, spatio-temporal range, spatio-temporal top-$k$ nearest neighbor and spatio-temporal join query as case studies of how to exploit the spatio-temporal indexing in ST-Hadoop [6]. For the case of the spatio-temporal range query, ST-Hadoop exploits its *temporal hierarchy index* to select partitions that overlap with the temporal and spatial query predicates. An efficient algorithm that runs in three steps, temporal filtering, spatial search, and spatio-temporal refinement. (1) In the *temporal filtering* step, the hierarchy index is examined to select a subset of partitions that cover the temporal interval $T$. (2) Once the temporal partitions are selected, the *spatial search* step applies the spatial range query against each matched partition to select records that spatially match the query range $A$. (3) Finally, in the *spatio-temporal refinement* step, compares individual records returned by the spatial search step against the query interval $T$, to select the exact matching records. Similarly, there is a possibility that selected partitions might partially overlap with the query area $A$, and thus records outside the $A$ need to be excluded from the final answer.

**Distributed Processing (MapReduce and Dataflow).** In the *MapReduce* layer, new implementations added inside SpatialHadoop MapReduce layer to enable ST-Hadoop exploits its spatio-temporal indexes and realizes spatio-temporal predicates. The implementation of MapReduce layer is based on MapReduce layer in SpatialHadoop [14], and just few changes were made to inject time awareness in this layer.

**Query Language.** The *Language* layer extends Pigeon language [12] to supports spatio-temporal data types (i.e., STPOINT, TIME and INTERVAL) and spatio-temporal operations (e.g., OVERLAP, KNN and JOIN) that take the advantages of the spatio-temporal index. Pigeon already equipped with several basic spatial predicates. ST-Hadoop changes the OVERLAP function to support spatio-temporal operations. ST-Hadoop extended the JOIN to take two spatio-temporal indexes as an input, and the processing of the *join* invokes the corresponding spatio-temporal procedure. ST-Hadoop extends KNN operation to finds top-$k$ points to a given query point in space and time. ST-Hadoop computes the nearest neighbor proximity according to some $\alpha$ ($0 \leq \alpha \leq 1$) value that indicates whether the *kNN* operation leans toward spatial, temporal, or spatio-temporal closeness. A ranking function computes the proximity between query point and any other points of the dataset.

**Case-Studies of Applications.** *Summit* [5] is a full-fledged open-source library on ST-Hadoop MapReduce framework with *built-in* native support for trajectory data. Summit cluster contains one master node that breaks a MapReduce job into smaller tasks, carried out by slave nodes. Summit modifies three core layers of ST-Hadoop, namely, *Language*, *Indexing* and *Operations*. The *Language* layer adds new SQL-Like interface for trajectory operations and data types. The modifications and the implementation of the *Indexing* (trajectory indexing) and *Operation* (trajectory range query, trajectory k nearest neighbor query and trajectory similarity query) layers are more complicated.

## 3.4   STARK

The **STARK** framework (https://github.com/dbis-ilm/stark) [21] is a promising new spatio-temporal data analytics framework (see in Fig. 9 its architecture). It is tightly integrated with Apache Spark [8] by leveraging Scala language features and it adds support for spatial and temporal data types and operations. Furthermore, STARK exploits SparkSQL functionality and implements SQL functions for filter, join with various predicates and aggregate vector as well as raster data. STARK also supports k nearest neighbor search and a density-based clustering operator allows to find groups of similar events. STARK includes spatial partitioning and indexing techniques for fast and efficient execution of the data analysis tasks.

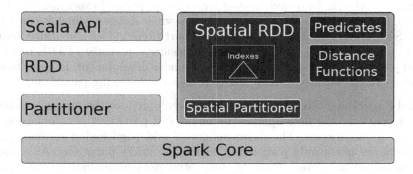

**Fig. 9.** STARK framework architecture [21].

**Spatial and Spatio-Temporal Data Types.** The main data structure of STARK is STObject. This class is a super-class of all spatial objects and provides a time component. STObject relies on the JTS library with the JTSplus extension, thus it supports all types of geometry objects, such as Point, Polygon, Linestring, Multipoint, Multypolygon and Multilinestring. Regarding the temporal data-type, the STObject contains o time component that facilitates temporal operations.

**Spatial and Spatio-Temporal Storage (Indexing Techniques).** The framework can index any partition, using an in memory spatial index structure. The R-tree index structure is currently supported by STARK, because of its JTS library dependency. Also, other indexing structures are planned to be included in future versions. There are three available indexing modes:

1. No Index: In some cases, indexing should be avoided (e.g. full table scan). No index mode should be used in these cases. When using no index mode, it does not matter how the RDD is partitioned.
2. Live Indexing: When live indexing is used, the framework firstly partitions the data items, in case they are not already partitioned. The spatio-temporal predicate is evaluated and the index is populated. Finally, the index is queried and the result is returned.
3. Persistent Index: The content of a partition is put into an index structure which can even be stored to disk and then used to evaluate the predicate. This execution mode transforms the input RDD from RDD[(STObject, V)] to RDD[RTree[STObject, (STObject, V)]]. After this transformation the resulting RDD consists of R-tree objects instead of single tuples. Multiple subsequent operations can benefit from these indexes. Furthermore, the same index can be used among different scripts, eliminating costly index creation time.

**Spatial and Spatio-Temporal Partitioning Techniques.** STARK is taking advantage of the Hadoop environment, resulting to parallel execution on cluster nodes. Every node processes a fragment of the whole dataset, which is call a partition. STARK spatial and spatio-temporal partitioning does not utilize Spark's built-in partitioners, for example a hash partitioner. Currently STARK uses only spatial partitioning, temporal partitioning is under development. In order to take advantage of the locality of data, STARK uses the following partitioners:

1. Grid Partitioner: The Grid Partitioner, evenly divides the dimensions based on a grid over the data space. The number of partitions per dimension are given as parameters. The disadvantage of grid partitioning is that spatial objects are not evenly distributed within the grid's partitions. As a result, some partitions are nearly empty, while other are contain most of the objects.
2. Binary Space Partitioner: Binary Space Partitioner (BSP) computes its partitions based on a maximum cost, which is given as a parameter. This is done by firstly dividing the data space into small quadratic shells, with a given side length. Then the partitioner evaluates all possible partitioning candidates along the cell bounds and then continues with testing all possible candidates. Finally, the partitioning with smallest cost difference between both candidate partitions is applied. The whole process results to two partitions and repeats itself recursively, if the according partition is longer than one cell length in at least one dimension and its cost is greater than the given maximum cost.
3. Partitioning Polygons: The spatial partitioners decide the preferred partition for each spatial object. In case the object is a point, the partitioner checks which cell contains the point and the assigns it to its relevant partition. When the spatial object is a polygon, even if this polygon is bigger than the partitions, the partitioner calculates its centroid point and then assign it the same way as if it was a point.

**Spatial and Spatio-Temporal Operations.** STARK supports most of the spatial and temporal operations. All operations rely on the STObject class and its spatial and temporal component. When the temporal component is missing, operations check only the spatial one. The STObject class provides the following filter functions: intersect, contains and containedBy. Moreover, STARK implements the following operations: join, nearest neighbors, clustering and skyline (currently in development). All operations benefit from the underlying spatial and temporal partitioners and additionally from a partition-local spatial or temporal indexing.

**Distributed Processing (MapReduce and Dataflow).** STARK is fully integrated into Spark, so it benefits from Spark's DAG (Directed Acyclic Graph) execution model. The DAG scheduler transforms a logical execution plan to a physical execution plan.

**Query Language.** Besides the Scala API based on the core RDDs, STARK is integrated into SparkSQL and implements SQL functions to filter, join, and aggregate vector and raster data.

**Visualization.** STARK is heavily depended on Spark's capabilities; therefore the visualization tools of Spark can be used to visualize STARK data. There is only one documented visualization tool designed especially for STARK spatial visualization (see Fig. 10), which also combines raster data in final layout. This visualization tool comes with a web interface [22] where users can interactively explore raster and vector data using SQL.

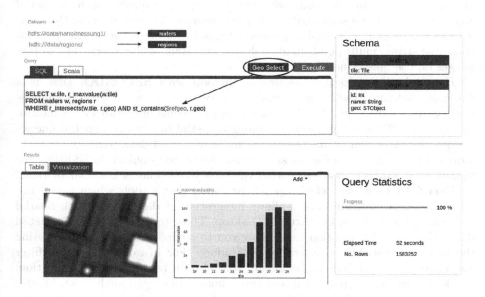

**Fig. 10.** STARK Visualization, Web Interface [22].

### 3.5  Comparison of Systems

In Table 1, we compare the four systems presented in the previous sections, regarding the features included in the presentation of these systems. Note that, there was non-available (N.A.) information available in the literature regarding some features of certain systems (language for GeoSpark, visualization for ST-hadoop and applications for GeoSpark and STARK).

## 4    More Big Spatial and Spatio-Temporal Data Analytics Systems

Apart from the previous four most representative data analytics systems that are actively maintained, we can find much more. They can be classified in four categories depending on whether are Hadoop-based or Spark-based [31,40], or spatial or spatio-temporal.

### 4.1  Hadoop-Based Big Spatial Data Analytics Systems

**Hadoop-GIS** [1] is scalable, high performance spatial data-ware housing system running on Hadoop. It utilizes SATO spatial partitioning (similar to $k$d-tree) and local spatial indexing to achieve efficient query processing. Hadoop-GIS uses global partition indexing to achieve efficient query results. Hadoop-GIS is supported with Hive, Pig and Scope. Hadoop-GIS supports fundamental spatial queries such as point, containment, join, and complex queries such as spatial cross-matching (large scale spatial join) and nearest neighbor queries. However, it lacks the support of complex geometry types including convex/concave polygons, line string, multi-point, multi-polygon, etc. HadoopGIS visualizer can plot images on the master node.

   **Parallel Secondo** [28] integrates Hadoop with SECONDO, that is a database that can handle non-standard data types, i.e., spatial data. It employs Hadoop as the distributed task manager and performs operations on a multinode spatial DBMS. It supports the common spatial indexes and spatial queries except *kNN*. However, it only supports uniform spatial data partitioning techniques, which cannot handle the spatial data skewness problem. In addition, the visualization function needs to gather the data to the master node for plotting.

   **Esri GIS tools for Hadoop** [18] are open source tools which would run on the ArcGIS platform. These allows integration of the Hadoop with Spatial data analytics software, i.e., ArcGIS Desktop. These tools work with big spatial data (big data with location) and allow you to complete spatial analysis using the power of distributed processing in Hadoop. For instance, (1) run a filter and aggregate operations on billions of spatial data records based on location; (2) define new areas (polygons) and run a point in polygon analysis on billions of spatial data records inside Hadoop; (3) visualize analysis results on a map and apply informative symbology; (4) integrate your maps in reports, or publish them as map applications online; etc.

**Table 1.** Overview of the comparative criteria of big spatial and spatio-temporal data analytics systems

|  | GeoSpark | SpatialHadoop | ST-Hadoop | STARK |
|---|---|---|---|---|
| Datatypes | Point, Rectangle, LineString, Polygon | Point, Rectangle, LineString, Polygon | STPoint, Time, Interval | Point, Polygon, Linestring, Multipoint, Multypolygon, Multilinestring, Time, Interval |
| Indexes | R-tree, Quadtree | R-tree | Temporal hierarchy index, Temporal Slicing, Spatial index | R-tree |
| Partitioning | Quadtree, $k$-d tree, STR-tree, Voronoi, Uniform, Hilbert | Quadtree, STR-tree, STR+, $k$-d tree, Hilbert-curve, Z-curve | Time-partitioning slicing, Data-partitioning slicing | Grid Partitioning, Binary Space Partitioning |
| Operations | Range, $k$NN, Spatial join, Distance join | Range, $k$NN, Spatial join | Spatio-temporal range, spatio-temporal top-$k$ nearest neighbor, spatio-temporal join | Intersect, contains, containedBy, spatial join, nearest neighbors, clustering, skyline |
| Processing | DAG execution model | MapReduce | MapReduce | DAG execution model |
| Language | N.A | Pigeon | Pigeon | Piglet, Pig Latin |
| Visualization | GeoSparkViz | Single level image, Multilevel images | N.A | Web UI |
| Applications | N.A | MNTG, TAREEG, TAGHREED, SHAHED, HadoopViz | Summit | N.A |

**GeoWave** [35] is a software library that connects the scalability of distributed computing frameworks and key-value stores with modern geospatial software to store, retrieve and analyze massive geospatial datasets. GeoWave indexes multidimensional data in a way that ensures values close together in multidimensional space are stored physically close together in the distributed datastore of your choice, by using Space Filling Curves (SFCs). GeoWave provides Hadoop input and output formats for distributed processing and analysis of geospatial data. GeoWave allows geospatial data in Accumulo platform to be shared and visualized via OGC standard services.

**ScalaGiST** [27] (Scalable Generalized Search Tree) is a scalable and non-intrusive indexing framework for Hadoop-MapReduce systems. It is based on classical Generalized Search Tree (GiST). ScalaGiST is designed for dynamic distributed environments to handle large-scale datasets and adapt to changes in the workload while leveraging commodity hardware. ScalaGiST is extensible in terms of both data and query type. It supports multiple types of indexes and can be dynamically deployed on large clusters while resilient to machine failures.

## 4.2    Spark-Based Big Spatial Data Analytics Systems

**SIMBA** [38] (Spatial In-Memory Big data Analytics) extends the Spark SQL engine to support spatial queries and analytics through SQL and the DataFrame API. Simba partitions data in a manner that they are of proper and balanced size and gathers records that locate close to the same partition (STR is used by default). It builds a local index per partition and a global index by aggregating information from local indexes. Simba builds local R-tree indexes on each DataFrame partition and uses R-tree grids to perform the spatial partitioning. It supports range and kNN queries, kNN and distance joins.

**SpatialSpark** [39] is a lightweight implementation of spatial support in Apache Spark. It targets in-memory processing for higher performance. SpatialSpark supports several spatial data types including points, linestrings, polylines, rectangles and polygons. It supports three spatial partitioning schemes fixed Grid, binary split and STR partitioning. The indexing is supported used R-trees. SpatialSpark offers range queries and spatial joins between various geometric objects.

**LocationSpark** [34] is an ambitious project, built as a library on top of Spark. It requires no modifications to Spark and provides spatial query APIs on top of the standard operators. It supports a wide range of spatial features. It provides Dynamic Spatial Query Execution and operations (Range, kNN, Insert, Delete, Update, Spatial-Join, kNN-Join, Spatio-Textual). The system builds two indexes, a global (Grid, Quadtree and a Spatial-Bloom Filter) and a local per-worker, user-decided index (Grid, R-tree, Quadtree and IR-tree). Global index is constructed by sampling the data. Spatial indexes are aiming to tackle unbalanced data partitioning. Additionally, the system contains a query scheduler, aiming to tackle query skew.

**Magellan** [32] is a distributed execution engine for spatial analytics on big data. It leverages modern database techniques in Apache Spark like efficient data layout, code generation, and query optimization in order to optimize spatial queries. Magellan extends SparkSQL to accommodate spatial datatypes, geometric predicates and queries. Magellan supports several spatial data types like points, linestrings, rectangles, polygons, multipoints and multipolygons. It allows the user to build a Z-curve index on spatial objects. Magellan supports range queries and spatial joins.

**SparkGIS** [9] a distributed, in-memory spatial data processing framework to query, retrieve, and compare large volumes of analytical image result data for algorithm evaluation. SparkGis combines the in-memory distributed processing capabilities of Apache Spark and the efficient spatial query processing of Hadoop-GIS. SparkGIS mitigates skew by making available various partitioning schemes as previously evaluated on MapReduce. SparkGIS uniquely improves memory management in spatial-processing Spark jobs by spatially aware management of partitions loaded into memory rather than arbitrary spilling to disk. The performance of SparkGIS was proved with medical pathology images and with OpenStreetMap (OSM) data.

**GeoTrellis** [26] is an open source, geographic data processing library designed to work with large geospatial raster data sets. GeoTrellis leverages Apache Spark for distributed processing. GeoTrellis relies on the data being exposed using an HDFS filesystem with the individual files written using the GeoTIFF format. Distributed processing relies on indexing large datasets based on a multi-dimensional space-filling curve (SFC), since SFCs enable the translation of multi-dimensional indices into a single-dimensional one, while maintaining geospatial locality. GeoTrellis includes some operations using vector and point data to support raster data operations.

Other big spatial data analytics systems are GeoMatch and SciSpark. **GeoMatch** [43] is a scalable and efficient big-data pipeline for large-scale map matching on Apache Spark. GeoMatch utilizes a novel spatial partitioning scheme inspired by Hilbert SFC, generating an effective indexing technique based such SFC that expedites spatial query processing in a distributed computing environment. Once the index has been built, GeoMatch uses an efficient and intuitive load balancing scheme to evenly distribute the parts of the index between available computing cores. **SciSpark** [37] is a big data framework that extends Apache Spark's in-memory parallel computing to scale scientific computations. The current architecture of SciSpark includes: (1) time and space partitioning of high resolution geo-grids from NetCDF3/4; (2) a sciDataset class providing n-dimensional array operations; (3) parallel computation of time-series statistical metrics; and (4) an interactive front-end using science (code and visualization) Notebooks.

## 4.3   Hadoop-Based Big Spatio-Temporal Data Analytics Systems

**CloST** [33] is a Hadoop-based storage system for big spatio-temporal data analytics, based on MapReduce framework. CloST is targeted at fast data loading, scalable spatio-temporal range query processing and efficient storage usage to handle very large historical spatio-temporal datasets. A simple data model which has special treatments on three core attributes including an object id, a location and a time. Based on this data model, CloST hierarchically partitions data using all core attributes which enables efficient parallel processing of spatio-temporal range scans and efficient parallel processing of two simple types of spatio-temporal queries: single-object queries and all-object queries. CloST supports a parallel implementation of the R-tree index.

### 4.4   Spark-Based Big Spatio-Temporal Data Analytics Systems

**BinJoin** [36] is a Spark-based implementation of a spatio-temporal attribute join that runs in a distributed manner across a Hadoop cluster. One important conclusion obtained from the experimental study is that the most effective and efficient distributed spatial join algorithm depends on the characteristics of the two input datasets. For the implementation of the join algorithms was used a local index and a query optimizer. Finally, an interesting observation extracted from the experiments is that spatio-temporal near join was able to scale to larger input sizes than space-only near join, because the temporal condition alleviates the effects of spatial skew.

GeoMesa [23] is an open-source spatio-temporal index extension built on top of distributed data storage systems. It provides a module called GeoMesaSpark to allow Spark to read the preprocessed and preindexed data from Accumulo data store. GeoMesa also provides RDD API, DataFrame API and Spatial SQL API so that the user can run spatio-temporal queries on Apache Spark [24]. GeoMesa uses R-tree spatial partitioning technique to decrease the computation overhead. However, it uses a Grid file as the local index per DataFrame partition. GeoMesa supports range query and spatial join query.

## 5   Conclusions

In a world where the volume of available data is continuously expanding and, in numerous cases, the related data objects contain spatial and/or spatio-temporal characteristics, scalable (and, therefore, distributed) systems capable of modeling, storing, querying and analyzing big spatial and spatio-temporal data are a necessity for modern and emerging applications. This fact is verified by the large number of parallel and distributed systems for big spatial and spatio-temporal data management and analysis that have been developed. In this paper, we presented four selected such systems, considering their acceptance in the research and advanced applications communities. This presentation was structured along specific categories of key system features and intends to provide to the reader a view of the differences and similarities of these systems. These four systems are actively being maintained and updated. However, many more systems have been developed. To assist the reader to develop a more complete point of view of the large world of ecosystems supporting management of big spatial and spatio-temporal data, we also present in brief a number of them. This paper intends to provide information that would allow a researcher or practitioner choose a system that is most suitable for his/her needs or compare another system (that will be developed in the future, or is not covered in this paper) with the ones presented here.

## References

1. Aji, A., Wang, F., Vo, H., Lee, R., Liu, Q., Zhang, X., Saltz, J.H.: Hadoop-GIS: a high performance spatial data warehousing system over MapReduce. PVLDB **6**(11), 1009–1020 (2013)

2. Alarabi, L., Eldawy, A., Alghamdi, R., Mokbel, M.F.: TAREEG: a MapReduce-based web service for extracting spatial data from OpenStreetMap. In: SIGMOD Conference, pp. 897–900 (2014)
3. Alarabi, L., Mokbel, M.F.: A demonstration of ST-hadoop: a MapReduce framework for big spatio-temporal data. PVLDB 10(12), 1961–1964 (2017)
4. Alarabi, L., Mokbel, M.F., Musleh, M.: ST-Hadoop: a MapReduce framework for spatio-temporal data. In: SSTD Conference, pp. 84–104 (2017)
5. Alarabi, L.: Summit: a scalable system for massive trajectory data management. SIGSPATIAL Special 10(3), 2–3 (2018)
6. Alarabi, L., Mokbel, M.F., Musleh, M.: ST-Hadoop: a MapReduce framework for spatio-temporal data. GeoInformatica 22(4), 785–813 (2018). https://doi.org/10.1007/s10707-018-0325-6
7. Apache. Hadoop. http://hadoop.apache.org/
8. Apache. Spark. http://spark.apache.org/
9. Baig, F., Vo, H., Kurç, T.M., Saltz, J.H., Wang, F.: SparkGIS: resource aware efficient in-memory spatial query processing. In: SIGSPATIAL/GIS Conference, pp. 28:1–28:10 (2017)
10. Dean, J., Ghemawat, S.: MapReduce: simplified data processing on large clusters. In: OSDI Conference, pp. 137–150 (2004)
11. Eldawy, A., Li, Y., Mokbel, M.F., Janardan, R.: CG_Hadoop: computational geometry in MapReduce. In: SIGSPATIAL/GIS Conference, pp. 284–293 (2013)
12. Eldawy, A., Mokbel, M.F.: Pigeon: a spatial MapReduce language. In: ICDE Conference, pp. 1242–1245 (2014)
13. Eldawy, A., Mokbel, M.F.: The ecosystem of SpatialHadoop. SIGSPATIAL Special 6(3), 3–10 (2014)
14. Eldawy, A., Mokbel, M.F.: SpatialHadoop: a MapReduce framework for spatial data. In: ICDE Conference, pp. 1352–1363 (2015)
15. Eldawy, A., Alarabi, L., Mokbel, M.F.: Spatial partitioning techniques in spatial hadoop. PVLDB 8(12), 1602–1605 (2015)
16. Eldawy, A., Mokbel, M.F., Al-Harthi, S., Alzaidy, A., Tarek, K., Ghani, S.: SHA-HED: a MapReduce-based system for querying and visualizing spatio-temporal satellite data. In: ICDE Conference, pp. 1585–1596 (2015)
17. Eldawy, A., Mokbel, M.F., Jonathan, C.: HadoopViz: a MapReduce framework for extensible visualization of big spatial data. In: ICDE Conference, pp. 601–612 (2016)
18. ESRI-GIS: GIS Tools for Hadoop (2014). http://esri.github.io/gis-tools-for-hadoop/. Accessed 20 July 2019
19. Garcia-Garcia, F., Corral, A., Iribarne, L., Mavrommatis, G., Vassilakopoulos, M.: A comparison of distributed spatial data management systems for processing distance join queries. In: ADBIS Conference, pp. 214–228 (2017)
20. García-García, F., Corral, A., Iribarne, L., Vassilakopoulos, M., Manolopoulos, Y.: Efficient large-scale distance-based join queries in spatialhadoop. GeoInformatica 22(2), 171–209 (2017). https://doi.org/10.1007/s10707-017-0309-y
21. Hagedorn, S., Goetze, P., Sattler, K.U.: he STARK framework for spatio-temporal data analytics on spark. In: BTW Conference, pp. 123–142 (2017)
22. Hagedorn, S., Birli, O., Sattler, K.U.: Processing large raster and vector data in apache spark. In: BTW Conference, pp. 551–554 (2019)
23. Hughes, N.J., Annex, A., Eichelberger, C.N., Fox, A., Hulbert, A., Ronquest, M.: Geomesa: a distributed architecture for spatio-temporal fusion. In: Geospatial Informatics, Fusion, and Motion Video Analytics V, vol. 9473, p. 94730F. International Society for Optics and Photonics (2015)

24. Hulbert, A., Kunicki, T., Hughes, J.N., Fox, A.D., Eichelberger, C.N.: An experimental study of big spatial data systems. In: BigData Conference, pp. 2664–2671 (2016)
25. Jiang, D., Ooi, B.C., Shi, L., Wu, S.: The performance of MapReduce: an in-depth study. PVLDB **3**(1), 472–483 (2010)
26. Kini, A., Emanuele, R.: Geotrellis: adding geospatial capabilities to spark. Spark Summit (2014)
27. Lu, P., Chen, G., Ooi, B.C., Vo, H.T., Wu, S.: ScalaGiST: scalable generalized search trees for MapReduce systems. PVLDB **7**(14), 1797–1808 (2014)
28. Lu, J., Güting, R.H.: Parallel secondo: boosting database engines with hadoop. In: ICPADS Conference, pp. 738–743 (2012)
29. Magdy, A., Alarabi, L., Al-Harthi, S., Musleh, M., Ghanem, T.M., Ghani, S., Mokbel, M.F.: Taghreed: a system for querying, analyzing, and visualizing geotagged microblogs. In: SIGSPATIAL/GIS Conference, pp. 163–172 (2014)
30. Mokbel, M.F., Alarabi, L., Bao, J., Eldawy, A., Magdy, A., Sarwat, M., Waytas, E., Yackel, S.: MNTG: an extensible web-based traffic generator. In: SSTD Conference, pp. 38–55 (2013)
31. Pandey, V., Kipf, A., Neumann, T., Kemper, A.: How good are modern spatial analytics systems? PVLDB **11**(11), 1661–1673 (2018)
32. Sriharsha, R.: Magellan: Geospatial Analytics Using Spark (2015). https://github.com/harsha2010/magellan. Accessed 20 July 2019
33. Tan, H., Luo, W., Ni, L.M.: CloST: a hadoop-based storage system for big spatiotemporal data analytics. In: CIKM Conference, pp. 2139–2143 (2012)
34. Tang, M., Yu, Y., Malluhi, Q.M., Ouzzani, M., Aref, W.G.: LocationSpark: a distributed in-memory data management system for big spatial data. PVLDB **9**(13), 1565–1568 (2016)
35. Whitby, M.A., Fecher, R., Bennight, C.: GeoWave: utilizing distributed key-value stores for multidimensional data. In: SSTD Conference, pp. 105–122 (2017)
36. Whitman, R.T., Park, M.B., Marsh, B.G., Hoel, E.G.: Spatio-temporal join on apache spark. In: SIGSPATIAL/GIS Conference, pp. 20:1–20:10 (2017)
37. Wilson, B., Palamuttam, R., Whitehall, K., Mattmann, C., Goodman, A., Boustani, M., Shah, S., Zimdars, P., Ramirez, P.M.: SciSpark: highly interactive in-memory science data analytics. In: BigData Conference, pp. 2964–2973 (2016)
38. Xie, D., Li, F., Yao, B., Li, G., Zhou, L., Guo, M.: Simba: efficient in-memory spatial analytics. In: SIGMOD Conference, pp. 1071–1085 (2016)
39. You, S., Zhang, J., Gruenwald, L.: Large-scale spatial join query processing in cloud. In: ICDE Workshops, pp. 34–41 (2015)
40. Yu, J., Sarwat, M.: Geospatial data management in apache spark: a tutorial. In: ICDE Conference, pp. 2060–2063 (2019)
41. Yu, J., Zhang, Z., Sarwat, M.: GeoSparkViz: a scalable geospatial data visualization framework in the apache spark ecosystem. In: SSDBM Conference, pp. 15:1–15:12 (2018)
42. Yu, J., Zhang, Z., Sarwat, M.: Spatial data management in apache spark: the GeoSpark perspective and beyond. GeoInformatica **23**(1), 37–78 (2018). https://doi.org/10.1007/s10707-018-0330-9
43. Zeidan, A., Lagerspetz, E., Zhao, K., Nurmi, P., Tarkoma, S., Vo, H.T.: GeoMatch: efficient large-scale map matching on apache spark. In: BigData Conference, pp. 384–391 (2018)

# Cloud Based e-Feedback Services Using Performance Analysis: A Linear Approach

Ayan Banerjee[1]([✉]) and Anirban Kundu[1,2]

[1] Computer Innovative Research Society, West Bengal 711103, India
ayan871992@gmail.com, anik76in@gmail.com
[2] Netaji Subhash Engineering College, Kolkata 700152, India

**Abstract.** Authors propose an online feedback system having distinct layers to access frameworks through multiple entry points such as, student module, administration module, and teacher module which have been operated from any geographically distributed locations. There is no need to install software based application and no need of extra hardware expenses to access proposed cloud based system due to usage of software-as-a-service, and platform-as-a-service. Students provide specific information to server-side for authenticity regarding entry to feedback questionnaires. Administrative authorities analyze teacher performance based on students' feedback. Teacher observes individual performance from server. Human effort and human activities have been reduced due to usage of paperless feedback. Teacher performance is measured using preparedness, class-performance, responsiveness, effectiveness, and overall grade. Different nodes have been required in proposed system for distributing and replicating data storage in server-side. Time consumption and load distribution of servers are analyzed based on number of users and servers. Different nodes have been accessed by multiple users working with different or same modules of the system. Energy efficient framework has incorporated into proposed system to enhance system performance. Authors have incorporated different weightage factors in energy efficient framework using distinct layers of proposed system. Time complexity and space complexity are measured using proposed algorithms. Web based approach is required in proposed system to reduce manpower consumption and workload. Comparative study between existing feedback systems and proposed feedback system is established based on different characteristics.

**Keywords:** Cloud based feedback · Multi-user system · Online feedback · Distributed system · Energetic system · Paperless feedback

## 1 Introduction

Cloud consists of various web services and refers to distinct environment for remote accessing possibilities to the scalable heterogeneous network resources. Cloud Computing provides services to users at minimum cost and interference of service providers. Users access the services of distributed network on demand basis for utilizing a shared

© Springer-Verlag GmbH Germany, part of Springer Nature 2021
A. Hameurlain et al. (Eds.): TLDKS XLVII, LNCS 12630, pp. 181–212, 2021.
https://doi.org/10.1007/978-3-662-62919-2_8

pool of computing resources [1]. Cloud Computing performs the centralized computing and storage should be in distributed manner. Rapid growth of IT industry is possible using cloud based system such that hardware cost and maintenance cost are inevitably be low, flexible by nature, on demand self-service etc. Cloud provides various services like Infrastructure-as-a-Service (IaaS), Platform-as-a-Service (PaaS), Software-as-a-Service (SaaS) and so on. Users typically use the IT infrastructure in Pay-Per-Use-On-Demand-Mode to save the cost of hardware resources [2–4]. Several users have accessed specific resources having similar timestamps in case of multi-user mode. There is no need to copy all resources to each machine in a network. Multi-user system acts in time sharing mode and reduces CPU idle time. Multi-user system is forced to increase flexibility and accessibility for Cloud Computing. This type of system should provide abstraction that simplifies the programming and its usage. Researchers have designed a web based interface on Online Feedback System that is allowed by multiple users at the same time. All setup of resources is done in server side network and several web clients are accessed that interface from server [5, 6]. Database is a centralized and typical storage where a large amount of data should be accommodated in an organized manner. The amount of data is increasing in recent years. The load of relational database also would be high due to storage of large amount of data. Data transmission cost is high in centralized concept. There is a cluster present in distributed database. Database should be sharable in any online transaction processing now a days. Data of any online application is partitioned and workload is also distributed across the node in a cluster. Load should be balanced in cluster [7, 8]. The cost of transmitting a large amount of data has decreased due to rapid enhancement of network technology. Distributed database is always followed by cloud or network based database management system. Resource and software are always shared between multiple devices with the help of distributed database and provide services to user by cloud or network [9, 10]. Data should be replicated over the network in vertical and horizontal fragmentation. Data loss is prevented by replication technique of distributed database [11, 12]. Energy efficient approach is represented as maximum output achieved using minimum input. Quality and profitability of a system should be enhanced due to the usage of energy efficient approach. A researcher has discussed about the procedure to reduce toxin for improving the longevity of computers by increasing eco-friendly materials [13]. An energy efficient task has also been performed by data allocation strategy in cloud environment [14]. Feedback is collection of information which is provided by agent. Feedback system is helpful to judge the performance of concerned individuals [15]. Anyone could change the feedback in case of hard copy report. So, design of an Online Feedback System is highly needed to prepare authentic feedbacks with proper authentication. Our aim is to develop a web based multi-user system for feedback. This system typically helps us to measure teacher's performance of an academic organization with a linear time & space complexities. We have mainly focused on evaluation of the teachers' performance analysis on the basis of students' feedback which is a one way communication interface. The approach is applicable in other applications like doctor-patient feedback system, employee-manager feedback system and so on. All applications should be done in two-way communications. The application is accomplished using efficient algorithms having linear time complexity.

Major motivations for this chapter are as follows:

- Paperless approach should be incorporated into proposed framework for improving security and reduced manpower.
- The proposed system should be accessed from any geographical location due to usage of cloud based approach.
- Feedback system has to judge the appropriateness of a particular teacher for a particular subject of an academic organization.
- The proposed approach should be maintained through an automated manner. Efficiency of our proposed approach has to increase on the basis of cloud based data distribution.

Challenges for this research work are as follows:

- Time complexity of proposed approach is linear.
- Space complexity of proposed approach is linear.

Rest of the chapter is organized as follows: in literature review section, past researches have been briefed; in proposed work section, design framework has been discussed exhibiting all the required figures of activities and database oriented connections along with proposed algorithms; experimental discussions have been shown to establish real time performance of members of an institution; finally, an energy efficient system on the basis of load analysis using distributed approach is achieved.

## 2 Literature Review

Higher educational institutions have prepared a security based online feedback system for faculty based teaching performance analysis. Web technologies have been used by them to create a layer which has helped to do advance automatic processing of web contents [16]. An online student feedback system has been developed to deliver feedback via student-staff interface in quick and easy way by students. The system has been acted as a security based service provider [17, 18]. An improved feedback system has been developed for faculty teaching development and classroom learning assessment. The Moodle (an open source learning management system) based online system has been prepared to improve, uplift and properly assess the teaching standard [19]. A monthly report based online feedback management system has been prepared to provide an integral feature of effective and efficient learning and teaching procedures. The actual intention of this system was to enhance and strengthen student learning [20, 21]. A new-dimensional online feedback system has been created to focus on accessing individual learner differences in the contexts of language learning through a newly created method. The users have obtained their individual results and effective educational tips immediately after answering only 50 questions by the system [22]. A web based teaching performance evaluation system has been implemented to prepare the performance evaluation report in an easier manner and also display the accurate ordering of student evaluation. This efficient online system has been typically reduced work load [23]. An automated feedback system has been developed to analyze student program and send the system generated feedback immediately via email. This automated system has been improved students' learning experience and also enhanced their program iteratively until it is correct [24]. A web based feedback system is more attractive and accepted approach than paper based feedback system typically for regarding student's feedback of an academic organization. This is not possible to make available the feedback hard copies to each student in a paper based feedback approach due to the huge population of students. Each student should get a chance to submit own feedback in an online feedback system [25]. A web based feedback system has also taken an important role in online courses including both synchronous and asynchronous interaction. Three different types of feedback like corrective feedback, motivational feedback, and technology feedback have played an important role to encourage instructors about their teaching performances [26]. The correct feedback is one of the best practices that improve students' learning. The feedback should be taken by academic organization to increase the utility of classroom [27]. Green computing principles and approaches for the utility of reduced energy have shown the decreasing graph for the cost of electricity [28]. A cross cultural study has been discussed on the basis of factors which are influencing students' attention to adopt online classes [29]. An analysis of technology acceptance model has been presented to understand university students' intention about the usage of e-learning [30]. A learning management system has been presented among university students [31, 32]. A critical examination has been performed on the basis of the learning management systems' effect on university teaching and learning [33]. A methodology has been proposed to develop data-enclosing tunnel concept for automated feedback using simulator training [34]. In tertiary education, teachers' perceptions have been analyzed using supportive peer feedback [35]. In music education, pre-service music teacher perceptions have been analyzed using peer feedback research studies [36]. Authors have improved NHS services using online patient feedback [37]. The impact of problem solving strategy has been proposed for students using online feedback [38]. Paperless system has been developed for administrative services using smart-apps [39]. In ONGC, Author has designed and implemented paperless office [40]. Performance-feedback has been scaled for cloud based workloads of workflows using budget constraints [41]. Cloud based dynamic routing has been performed in formal method using feedback [42].

## 3  Proposed Work

### 3.1  Structural Design

We are going to propose a cloud based multi-user online feedback system. This system is typically used in academic sector. We are going to propose paperless and energy efficient approach through online feedback system. The entire set up of proposed framework and data storage are maintained in a distributed manner using platform-as-a-service of cloud. Cloud based system could judge whether a teacher is fit for teaching a particular subject. There are three main gateways or entry points in online feedback system such as, student feedback module, administration module, and teacher performance module. Each modules of proposed system is flexible enough to be accessed by multiple users from any geographical locations due to usage of software-as-a-service.

First gateway is allocated for students. The actual intention of this gateway is to submit feedback for a particular teacher by many students at a particular time. Students should be logged in for submitting feedback. Optional subjects are selected as per the need of students. The set of questions are filled up by students. After submission of answers to the servers, weightage values are considered for each type of answers to specific questions. All weightage values are used to prepare feedback based on specific formulae.

Second gateway is allocated for admin. Admin is liable to collect feedback, given by students. Total feedback data are used to analyze by administrator for preparing teacher feedback report. Feedback report for a particular teacher is stored within database by admin.

Third gateway is allocated for teacher. The actual purpose of this gateway is to show teacher feedback report of a particular teacher in an organized manner. Teacher should be logged in to review feedback report. After successful login, a teacher is able to see the particular feedback report in read-only mode.

In Fig. 1, we have designed multi-user interactions of three distinct gateways such as student feedback module, administration module, & teacher performance module within proposed feedback system. This design helps us to co-ordinate between all the functional modules using different gateways. Therefore, one type of interaction does not depend on other types of interactions. All the modules are activated separately without interfere of other workflows.

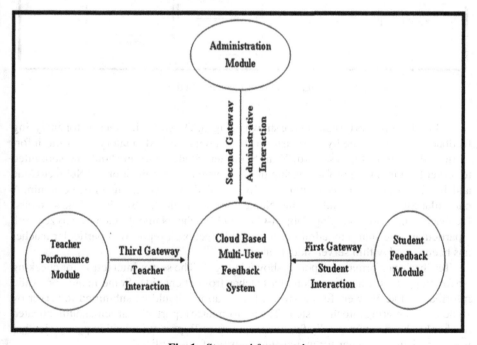

**Fig. 1.** Structural framework

## 3.2    Detailed Design of Framework Modules

Students' performance is shown in Fig. 2. The server interaction for submitting feedback has been done by student from client side. Mandatory and valid information such as Student-Id, Department, Year, Semester, Student Group should be submitted to the server by students for entering into the system. The collections of Subject-Id, Teacher Name and complete set of questions have been automatically provided by the servers only to an authenticated student. A particular Subject-Id and Teacher Name have been selected and also filled up the answers to questionnaires by students. The valuable feedbacks of all subjects of a particular department have been preserved in database servers.

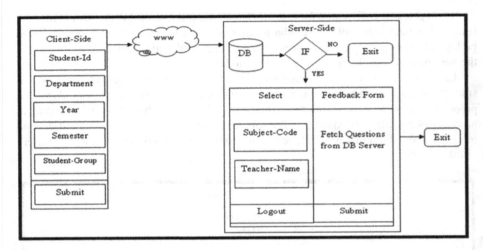

**Fig. 2.** Student feedback module

Administrative performances are shown in Fig. 3. The server interaction for analyzing feedback has been done by administrator from client side. Mandatory and valid information like Admin-Id, Password, Year, Semester, Student Group should be submitted to server by administrator for entering into the system. The collections of Subject-Code and Teacher Name have been automatically provided by server to authenticate admin. A particular Subject-Code and Teacher Name have been selected by admin. The students' feedback of the corresponding Subject-Code and Teacher Name should be analyzed with a particular time stamp by admin. The valuable feedback report of a particular teacher has been stored within server-side database.

Teacher's performance report is shown in Fig. 4. The server interaction for checking performance report has been done by teacher from client side. Some mandatory valid information like Viewer- Id, Password, Designation, should be submitted to server by students for entering into the system. The performance report of a particular authenticated teacher has been automatically fetched from server. Report modification permission has not been given to teacher for increasing security of our application.

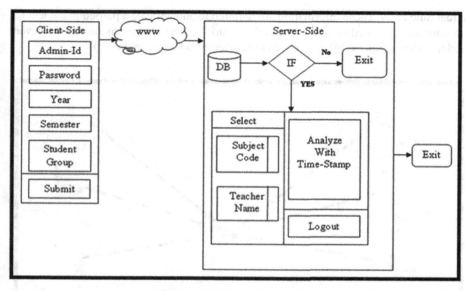

**Fig. 3.** Administration module

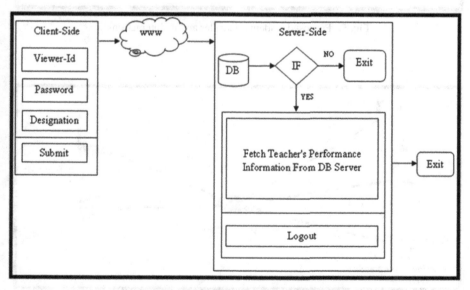

**Fig. 4.** Teacher performance module

## 3.3   Functional Communications Within Server-Side Network

Students' information is stored in different nodes of server-side network, and student controller receives the information from those predefined nodes (Student ID, Student Name, Student Department, Student Year, Student Semester, Student Group) as required in real time basis. These information are required to authenticate a particular student for entering into proposed system framework. Security is provided for maintaining relevant student information in different nodes to restrict intruders (refer Fig. 5).

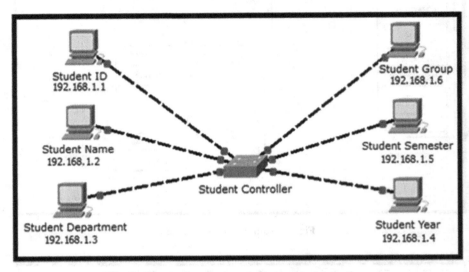

**Fig. 5.** Proposed student controller and its interactions

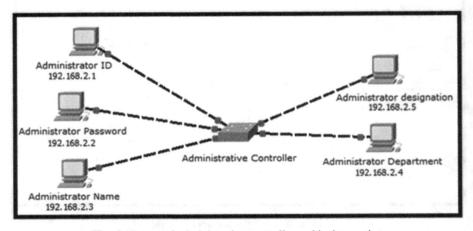

**Fig. 6.** Proposed administrative controller and its interaction

Different predefined nodes have been established in server-side network for storing administrative information and administrative controller receives the information from those predefine nodes (Administrator ID, Administrator Password, Administrator Name, Administrator Department, Administrator Designation) as required in real time basis.

These information are utilized by a particular administrator for entering into system framework as an authentic administrator. The significant administrative information have been stored into different nodes for providing security and to restrict intruders (refer Fig. 6).

Different controllers with predefine nodes are set up in server-side network and student teacher relational controller communicates with those controllers (Subject Controller, Teacher Controller, and Student Controller) for receiving information like Subject ID, Teacher ID, Teacher Name, Teacher Department, Student Year, Student Semester, Student Department and Student Group as required in real time basis. These necessary information are required for maintaining the statistics between student and teacher (refer Fig. 7).

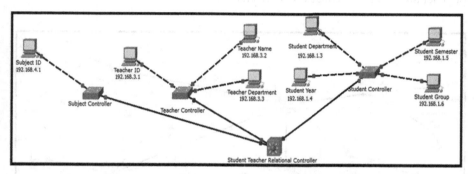

**Fig. 7.** Proposed student teacher relational controller and its interaction

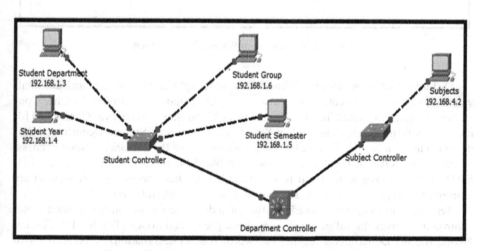

**Fig. 8.** Proposed department controller and its interaction

Department controller communicates with different controllers like Student Controller and Subject Controller to achieve necessary information (Student Department,

Student Year, Student Semester, Subjects and Student Group) as required in real time basis. These information of different controllers are placed into different predefine nodes of server-side network. These necessary information are required to prepare the departmental structure between student and corresponding subject (refer Fig. 8).

Server-side network has been designed using different controllers (Student Controller, Teacher controller, Subject controller, Timestamp controller, and Questionnaires controller) with predefined nodes such as Student ID, Student Department, Student Group, Teacher ID, Subject ID, Timestamp and list of questionnaires such as S1, S2, S3, ...., S10. The communication between feedback controller and other controllers are required for storing necessary students' feedback related raw information into different predefine nodes in real time basis. Students' feedback information have been gathered for generating student feedback report (refer Fig. 9).

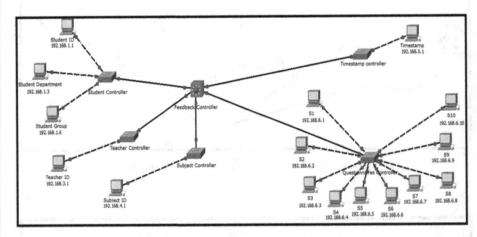

**Fig. 9.** Feedback controller and its interaction

Different controllers with predefine nodes are set up in server-side network and analysis controller communicates with those controllers (Student Controller, Teacher Controller, Subject Controller, Teacher Performance Controller, and Answer Controller) for receiving information such as Student Year, Student Semester, Student Department, Student Group, Teacher ID, Subject ID, Preparedness, Class Performance, responsiveness, Effectiveness, Overall Grade, and answer list like S11, S12, S13, S1avg, ....., S101, S102, S103, S10avg as required in real time basis. These necessary information are required for preparing teacher performance analysis report (refer Fig. 10).

Teachers' information is stored in different nodes of server-side network, and teacher controller receives the information from those predefined nodes (Teacher ID, Teacher Name, Teacher Department, Teacher Password, Teacher designation) as required in real time basis. These information are required to authenticate a particular teacher for entering into proposed system framework. Security is provided for maintaining relevant teacher information in different nodes to restrict intruders (refer Fig. 11).

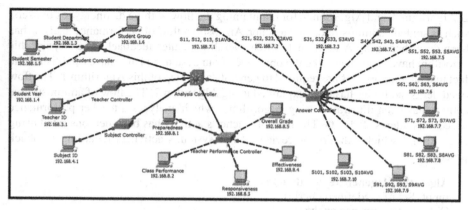

**Fig. 10.** Analysis controller and its interaction

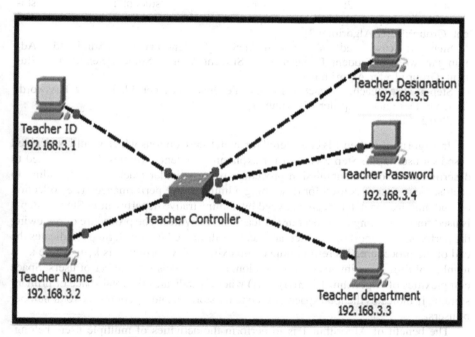

**Fig. 11.** Teacher controller and its interaction

### 3.4 Procedures

Algorithm is the collection of repeatable and executable steps to solve a particular problem. Several types of users have used our design framework at the same time to solve their different purposes. Distinct work flow parameters are followed by each type of users. Energy efficient approach is being applied in proposed system depending on load analysis. We have incorporated four different algorithms such as Algorithm 1, Algorithm

2, Algorithm 3, and Algorithm 4 for maintaining the flow of three distinct types of users, such as student, administrator, and teacher. An abstract flow of performance analysis has been described using Algorithm 1 which overall generates feedback. The steps of this algorithm have been elaborated the objective of our system and also have established the fact that later algorithms are required to generate each step of this Algorithm 1. The flow of students' activities has been explained using Algorithm 2. The flow of administrative activity has been illustrated using Algorithm 3 which analyzes a teacher performance based on students' fed data. The flow of teacher's activity has been demonstrated using Algorithm 4 which exhibits the review of our system's activities regarding feedback procedure.

**Algorithm 1:generate_Feedback()**
Input: Set of predefined queries
Output: Performance analysis
Step 1: switch(option)
Step 2: case "student": student_Feedback(Student_Id,Student_Department,Student_Year,Student_Semester,Student_Group);[refer Algorithm 2]
Step 3: case "admin": admin_Analyze_Student_Feedback(Admin_Id, Admin_Password, Student_Department, Student_Year, Student_Semester, Student_Group);[refer Algorithm 3]
Step 4: case "teacher": teacher_Review_Feedback(Teacher_Id, Teacher_Password, Teacher_Designation);[refer Algorithm 4]
Step 5: Stop

In Algorithm 1, Step 1 is considered for switch case options which would be decided based on user input. Step 2 is used for explaining student activities. Step 2 is used to describe the feedback submission procedure of a particular teacher corresponding to each subject. Step 3 is used for describing administrative performance. The collection of students' feedback has been analyzed by administrative department in Step 3. Step 4 is used for elaborating the procedure of teachers' activities. The procedure of reviewing the performance report of a particular teacher is discussed in Step 4. Step 5 indicates the end of the procedure. Therefore, time complexities of Algorithm 1 is $k_1 n_1$ where $k_1$ is number of time steps involved for execution, and $n_1$ stands for number of users. Space complexities of Algorithm 1 is $n_1(i_1 + j_1)$ where $i_1$ indicates the total space of primary storage, $j_1$ indicates the total space of secondary storage, and $n_1$ counts the total number of users.

The benefit of Algorithm 1 is to perform the activities of multiple users belonging to different groups at the same time. Time complexities and space complexities of Algorithm 1 are being presented as linear.

**Algorithm 2:student_Feedback()**
Input:student_Id, Student_Department, Student_Year, Student_Semester, Student_Group
Output:Student feedback
Step 1: student_Id_Check();
Step 2: if(valid_student_id)
        Step2.1:choose_Mandatory_Subjects(Student_Department,Student_Year,Student_Semester);
        Step2.2:
check_Availability_Optional_Subjects(Student_Department,Student_Year,Student_Semester);
        Step 2.3: if(available_optional_subjects)
                Step 2.3.1: Then choose_Optional_Subjects( );
Step 3: gotofeedback_Queries( );
Step 4: Submit feedback_To_Db(Subject_Id, Teacher_Name, s[ ] );
Step 5: Stop

There are five steps in Algorithm 2 describing the details of student feedback activities. Student id is checked and verified by the server in Step 1. Step 2 is used for checking validity of the reply of Step 1. If student id is valid, then mandatory subject list is selected based on students' department, students' year, and students' semester as mentioned in Step 2.1. Step 2.2 is used to check & confirm the optional subjects available based on students' department, students' year, and students' semester. Step 2.3 is used to check availability of the response of Step 2.2. If optional subjects are available, then select optional subject list in Step 2.3.1. Step 3 covers the actual feedback procedure. A particular subject code is selected by student and automatically corresponding teacher names are appeared on screen. A particular teacher name is selected by the student to complete feedback procedure. A set of teacher evaluating questions are appeared. The questions are answered by the students. Step 4 is used to submit the complete feedback report like Subject code, Teacher Name and s[] which indicates the questions set. Step 5 indicates the exit of Algorithm 2. Therefore, time complexities of Algorithm 2 is $k_2n_2$ where $k_2$ is number of time steps involved for execution, and $n_2$ stands for number of users. Space complexities of Algorithm 2 is $n_2(i_2 + j_2)$ where $i_2$ designates the total space of primary storage, $j_2$ designates the total space of secondary storage, and $n_2$ counts the total number of users.

The benefit of Algorithm 2 is considered on the basis of authenticated multiple students' activities of an academic organization without increasing server-side load. Linear time complexities and space complexities have been achieved.

**Algorithm 3: admin_Analyze_Student_Feedback( )**

Input: Ad-min_Id, Admin_Password, Student_Department, Student_Year, Student_Semester, Student_Group

Output: Analysis result of students' feedback.

Step 1: admin_id = admin_Id_Find();

Step 2: if(admin_id == valid)

    Step 2.1: choose_All_Subjects(Student_Department, Student_Year, Student_Semester);

Step 3: gotostudent_Feedback_Analysis( );

Step 4: submit_Analysed_Feedback_To_Db(Subject_Id, Student_Department, Teacher_Id,Student_Group,Student_Semester, Student_Year, s[], Preparedness,Classperformance,Responsiveness, Effectiveness, Overallgrade);

Step 5:Stop

Algorithm 3 consists of five steps to describe the details of analysis procedure. Step 1 is used for finding admin id from existing database. Step 2 is used for checking the validity of the admin id. If admin id is correct, all subjects would be listed on screen based on Student_Department, Student_Year, Student_Semester (refer Step 2.1 of Algorithm 3). All subjects mean mandatory subjects and optional subjects. Admin enters into feedback analysis phase to analyze feedback in Step 3. Feedback of a particular teacher is analyzed by admin. Step 4 is used to submit analyzed feedback report of a particular teacher like Subject_Id, Student_Department, Teacher_Id, Student_Group, Student_Semester, Student_Year, s[], Preparedness, Class performance, Responsiveness, Effectiveness, Overall grade into database.s[] is indicated as set of questions. Therefore, time complexities of Algorithm 3 is $k_3n_3$ where $k_3$ is number of time steps involved for execution, and $n_3$ stands for number of users. Space complexities of Algorithm 3 is $n_3(i_3 + j_3)$ where $i_3$ shows the total space of primary storage, $j_3$ shows the total space of secondary storage, and $n_3$ counts the total number of users.

The benefit of Algorithm 3 is to validate the authentication of multiple administrators in a parallel manner. A group of administrators are also able to analyze the students' feedback for each particular teacher at the same time. Time complexities and space complexities of Algorithm 3 have been observed as linear.

**Algorithm 4:teacher_Review_Feedback( )**

Input: Teacher_Id, Teacher_Password,Teacher_Designation

Output: Review chart of Student's Feedback

Step 1: teacher_Id_Check( );

Step 2: if(valid_teacher_id)

    Step 2.1: Then fetch_Feedback_Info_From_Db(Teacher_Id);

Step 3: Gotoreview_Feedback_Info_Details();

Step 4: Stop

Algorithm 4 contains four steps to discuss feedback review procedure for teacher in details. Step 1 is used to check teacher id validation in server. Step 2 is used for checking validity of the reply of step 1. If teacher id is found valid, then feedback information of a particular teacher is retrieved from database based on teacher id. Teacher could see the feedback details in Step 3. Step 4 is used to finish the Algorithm 4. Therefore, of Algorithm 4 is $k_4n_4$ where $k_4$ is number of time steps involved for execution, and

$n_4$ stands for number of users. Space complexities of Algorithm 4 is $n_4(i_4 + j_4)$ where $i_4$ specifies the total space of primary storage, $j_4$ specifies the total space of secondary storage, and $n_4$ counts the total number of users.

The benefit of Algorithm 4 is to allow multiple authenticated teachers into the system framework at a time as viewers. Any kinds of modifications/alterations are not permitted as teachers. Time complexities and space complexities are linear in Algorithm 4.

### 3.5   Theoretical Discussions

Theoretical conversations have been framed in this sub-section to setup hypothetical characteristics of proposed system framework for demonstrating advantages in case of linear time complexity and space complexity.

**Motivation of Theorem 1:**  We should be able to understand the time consumption of proposed design framework.

*Theorem 1: Time complexity of proposed approach is linear.*
*Proof:*

*We know from our algorithms in proposed work section that,*
*Time complexity of Algorithm 1 = $k_1 n_1$ (refer Algorithm 1)*
*Time complexity of Algorithm 2 = $k_2 n_2$ (refer Algorithm 2)*
*Time complexity of Algorithm 3 = $k_3 n_3$ (refer Algorithm 3)*
*Time complexity of Algorithm 4 = $k_4 n_4$ (refer Algorithm 4)*
*In real time, time complexity of our proposed approach could be considered as follows:*
*Case 1: $(k_1 n_1 + k_2 n_2)$ where students' activities are involved using student feedback module (refer Fig. 2);*
*Case 2: $(k_1 n_1 + k_3 n_3)$ where administrative activities are involved using administration module (refer Fig. 3);*
*Case 3: $(k_1 n_1 + k_4 n_4)$ where teachers' activities are involved using teacher performance module (refer Fig. 4);*
*Therefore, overall time complexity of our proposed approach is O(kn).*
*Hence, it is proved that time complexity of our approach is linear.*
*[End of Proof]*

Theorem 1 contains time complexity of Algorithm 1, Algorithm 2, Algorithm 3, and Algorithm 4. Linear time complexity of overall design framework has been achieved based on students' activities of case 1, administrative activities of case 2, and teachers' activities of case 3 (refer Theorem 1).

**Motivation of Theorem 2:**  We should be able to understand the space consumption of proposed design framework.

*Theorem 2: Space complexity of proposed approach is linear.*
*Proof:*

*We have achieved different space complexities from our algorithms of our proposed work that,*

*Space complexity of Algorithm 1 = $n_1(i_1 + j_1)$ (refer Algorithm 1)*
*Space complexity of Algorithm 2 = $n_2(i_2 + j_2)$ (refer Algorithm 2)*
*Space complexity of Algorithm 3 = $n_3(i_3 + j_3)$ (refer Algorithm 3)*
*Space complexity of Algorithm 4 = $n_4(i_4 + j_4)$ (refer Algorithm 4)*
*Space complexity of our proposed approach could be visualized on the basis of real time space consumption that,*
*Case 1: $(n_1(i_1 + j_1) + n_2(i_2 + j_2))$ where space consumption of students' activity are occupied using student feedback module (refer Fig. 2);*
*Case 2: $(n_1(i_1 + j_1) + n_3(i_3 + j_3))$ where space consumption of administrative activity are occupied using administration module (refer Fig. 3);*
*Case 3: $(n_1(i_1 + j_1) + n_4(i_4 + j_4))$ where space consumption of teachers' activity are occupied using teacher performance module (refer Fig. 4);*
*Therefore, overall space complexity of our proposed approach is $O(n (i + j))$.*
*Hence, it is proved that time complexity of our approach is linear.*
**[End of Proof]**

Space complexities of four algorithms such as Algorithm 1, Algorithm 2, Algorithm 3 and Algorithm 4 have been counted in Theorem 2. Entire space complexity of proposed framework has been depicted as linear using three cases such as case 1 as student feedback, case 2 as administration, and case 3 as teacher performance.

### 3.6 Analysis on Energy Efficient Framework

Proposed system behaves like an energy efficient framework based on minimum load on servers. Three different gateways (refer Fig. 1) such as student feedback module (refer Fig. 2), administration module (refer Fig. 3), and teacher performance module (refer Fig. 4) have been incorporated in system framework having no dependencies. Each gateway is utilized by multiple users having geographically distinct locations with a minimum server load which is successfully demonstrated in Experimental Discussions section (refer Fig. 19). Energy efficient approach of proposed system has been utilized depending on servers' load analysis related experiments. Efficient use of energy has been a major focus of our design on the basis of smart load analysis of distributed approach. Each server has been accessed by 9,216 number of users (refer Load Analysis sub-section of Experimental Discussions). Energy is efficiently utilized using load distribution between servers (refer Fig. 17).

The workflow of three discrete modules has been discussed in Algorithm 1, Algorithm 2, Algorithm 3, and Algorithm 4 (refer Procedure sub-section of Proposed Work section). Different weightage values of three distinct modules have been calculated depending on server load of each module. Since weightage of student feedback ($W_1$) is the major concern of this proposal, therefore as per server load, 0.4 weightage value has been allocated for student feedback module. 0.3 & 0.3 weightage values have been allocated for administration module ($W_2$) and teacher performance module ($W_3$) respectively.

Consider, '$I_1$' represents the input data such as "Student_Id, Student_Department, Student_Year, Student_Semester, Student_Group" for student feedback module (refer Algorithm 2).

Consider, '$O_1$' represents the output data such as "*Student feedback*", which has been mentioned in Algorithm 2.

Consider, '$E_1$' represents the Energy Efficiency.

We know, $EnergyEfficiency = \frac{OutputEnergy}{InputEnergy}$

Energy efficiency of Student Feedback Module is as follows:

$$E_1 = \frac{O_1}{I_1} \times 100\% \tag{i}$$

Consider, '$I_2$' represents the input data such as "*Admin_Id, Admin_Password, Student_Department, Student_Year, Student_Semester, Student_Group*" (*refer* Algorithm 3).

Consider, '$O_2$' represents the output data such as "*Analysis result of students' feedback*" which has been utilized in Algorithm 3.

Consider, '$E_2$' represents the Energy Efficiency.

Energy Efficiency of Administration Module is as follows:

$$E_2 = \frac{O_2}{I_2} \times 100\% \tag{ii}$$

Consider, '$I_3$' represents the input data such as "*Teacher_Id, Teacher_Password, Teacher_Designation*" (refer Algorithm 4).

Consider, '$O_3$' represents the output data such as "*Review chart of Student's Feedback*" which has been utilized in Algorithm 4.

Consider, '$E_3$' represents the Energy Efficiency.

Energy Efficiency of Teacher Performance Module is as follows:

$$E_3 = \frac{O_3}{I_3} \times 100\% \tag{iii}$$

Consider, '$I$' represents input data such as "*Set of predefined queries*" (*refer* Algorithm 1).

Consider, '$O$' represents as output data such as "*Performance analysis*" which has been mentioned in Algorithm 1.

Consider, '$E$' represents the Energy Efficiency.

Overall Energy Efficiency is as follows:

$$E = \frac{O}{I} \times 100\%$$

$$E = (E_1 \times W_1 + E_2 \times W_2 + E_3 \times W_3) \times 100\% \tag{iv}$$

where, $W_1$ = Weightage factor of student feedback module;
$W_2$ = Weightage factor of administration module;
$W_3$ = Weightage factor of teacher performance module;

$$E = (E_1 \times 0.4 + E_2 \times 0.3 + E_3 \times 0.3) \times 100\% \tag{v}$$

$W_1, W_2,$ & $W_3$ weightage factors are considered in this scenario to prove our system as relevant and important in case of student feedback module, administration module, and teacher performance module respectively.

# 4   Experimental Discussion

## 4.1   Overview

Authors have developed a cloud based online feedback system. Proposed system has been designed in a distributed manner with help of platform-as-a-service. There is no extra hardware expenses required for constructing our proposed system. The distributed database approach has been applied to enhance activities like reduced data loss, increased availability of data, reduced load of a particular server, and so on. The platform independent nature is typically available in our framework due to the usage of Java. Each module of proposed system has been independently accessed from any geographical location by using software-as-a-service. Reallocation and replication of data have been performed in a network grid using mesh topology. There are three gateways or entry points designed in our framework. The valuable feedbacks have been submitted by students through first entry point. A particular teacher's performance has been successfully analyzed in less time due to the usage of our framework by administrative department. A secured feedback report of a particular teacher has been reviewed only by the authentic teacher. The system is already tested that it should be accessed by multiple users at the same time from same and/or different entry points. Proposed online feedback system is flexible, environment friendly, secure, competitive than previous web based feedback systems (refer Related Works) due to the usage of the concept of cloud.

## 4.2   Experimental Setup

In proposed cloud based system, authors have designed three gateways (student feedback module, administration module, and teacher performance module.) to perform activities. Students have submitted their valuable feedback from any geographical location using student feedback module. Administration module is being used for collecting feedback data by administrator to prepare teachers performance report. In teacher performance module, computational analysis of teachers' performance has been performed automatically based on proposed algorithms. Different weightage factors are used for enhancing performance analysis. Entire activities of proposed system are controlled using cloud services. In this sub-section, necessary components required for our experimentation are as follows:

- Number of computer used in network: 400
- Total secondary memory used in network: 400 TB
- Total primary memory used in network: 6 TB
- Database server used in network: Oracle Server
- IDE used to prepare application: Eclipse MARS 2.0
- Framework used to prepare application: Model View Controller (MVC) framework using JSP- SERVLET
- Compiler used to prepare application: JDK 1.8
- Language used throughout the application: JAVA
- Database connectivity used throughout the application: Java Database Connectivity (JDBC)

### 4.3  Observations

The feedback status of an academic organization's five hundred students has been represented in Fig. 12 using code of a particular subject, particular teacher's name of that corresponding subject, department name, semester name, and group name. The collection of different students' feedback information like q11, q12, q13, q21, q22, q23, ..., q101,q102,q103 has been determined by the performance status of a particular teacher.

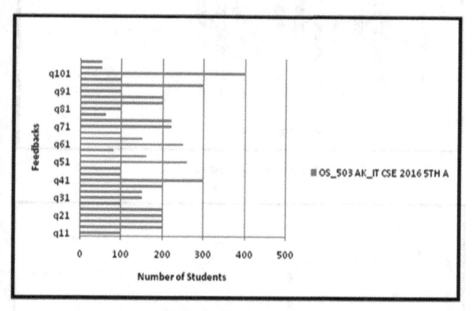

**Fig. 12.**  Feedback status chart

The average of the feedback status of an academic organization's five hundred students has been calculated by administrative department and represented in average feedback chart on the basis of the code of a particular subject, particular teacher's name of that corresponding subject, same department name, semester name, and group name (refer Fig. 13). Individual average feedback information like q1avg, q2avg, q3avg, ..., q10avg has been calculated by using our formulae on the basis of students' feedback information (refer Fig. 12) of each questions.

Teacher performance has been analyzed using five criteria such as preparedness, class-performance, effectiveness, responsiveness, and overall-grade. The status of five criteria of a particular teacher has been represented in teacher performance chart using the feedback of five hundred students of a particular academic organization. A particular teacher's performance has been symbolized on the basis of the code of a particular subject, particular teacher's name of that corresponding subject, same department's name, semester's name, and group's name (refer Fig. 14). An unambiguous assessment about a particular teacher's performance has been obtained in our application using teacher performance analysis chart (refer Fig. 14). Teacher's performance has been calculated using

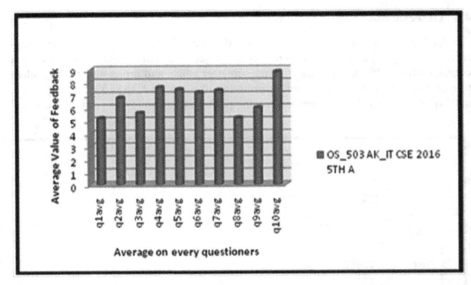

**Fig. 13.** Average feedback chart

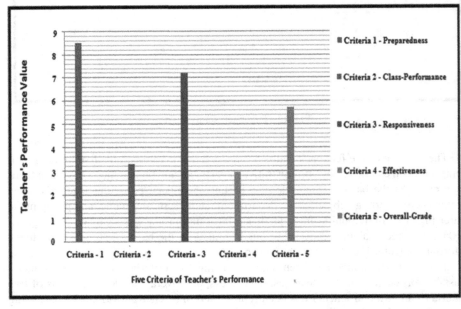

**Fig. 14.** Teacher performance analysis

five criteria. Preparedness is signified in Criteria 1 (refer Fig. 14). Lesson preparation, teaching activities, and classroom management are incorporated in preparedness criteria. Class performance is specified in Criteria 2 (refer Fig. 14). Discipline, impressive teaching process, and special care on weaker students are incorporated in class perfor-mance. Responsiveness is designated in Criteria 3 (refer Fig. 14). Practices of attending and responding to the substance of students' thinking are referred by responsiveness. Effectiveness is specified in Criteria 4 (refer Fig. 14). Students' motivation in learning has been enhanced through a simple way by an effective teacher. Overall grade is indi-cated in Criteria 5 (refer Fig. 14). Overall grade has been calculated using Criteria 1, Criteria 2, Criteria 3, and Criteria 4.

## 4.4  Time Analysis

The time chart (refer Fig. 15) describes the detailed "kn" distribution of our proposed procedure as mentioned in Algorithm 1, Algorithm 2, Algorithm 3, and Algorithm 4.

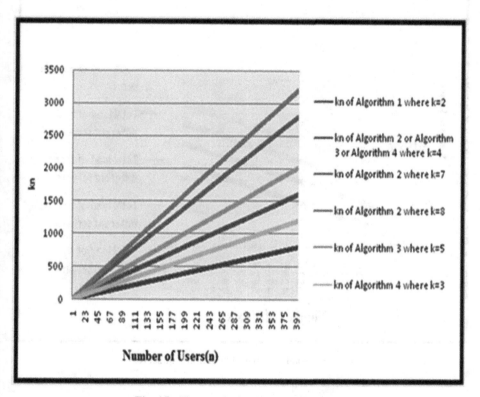

**Fig. 15.** Time analysis of proposed system

'k' represents the number of time steps involved in specific algorithms based on selected real time activities of users or server based system. 'n' represents the number of users involved. As per Algorithm 1, number of time steps (k) is 2. Similarly, k = 4 or k = 7 or k = 8 is considered as number of time steps in Algorithm 2. Algorithm 3 considers k = 4 or k = 5 as number of time steps. Algorithm 4 assumes k = 3 or k = 4 as number of time steps for execution.

## 4.5  Load Analysis

Multiple servers have been utilized to perform distributed approach within our system framework. The load distribution of five servers has been observed for sampling purpose. 9,216 numbers of users have been accommodated into each server of our proposed system. The total number of users' load on servers has been shown in server load (refer Fig. 16). As per server load diagram, 12,287 MB of a single server has been allocated for this purpose with an initial load of 3,072 MB. Similarly, 15,358 MB, 18,429 MB, 21,440 MB, and 24,571 MB are being utilized for 2, 3, 4, and 5 numbers of servers respectively.

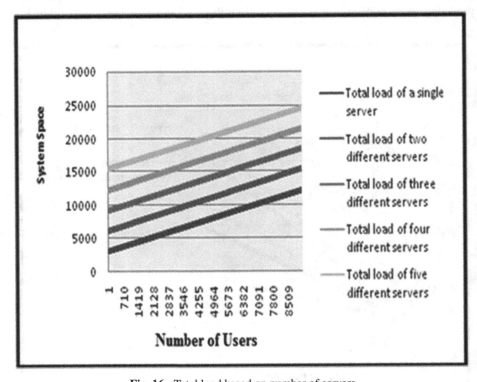

**Fig. 16.** Total load based on number of servers

Consider, 'L' represents the amount of load in each server.
Consider, 'N' represents the total load of 9,216 users.
For single server, $L = 12{,}287$ MB
Therefore, $L = N$
For two servers, $L = (15{,}358/2)$ MB $= 7679$ MB
Therefore, $L = N/2$
Similarly, for three servers, $L = N/3$;

For four servers, $L = N/4$;

For five servers, $L = N/5$; and so on.

Therefore, each server load has been gradually decreased due to the use of distributed approach.

The decreasing server's load has been represented in server load distribution graph (refer Fig. 17).

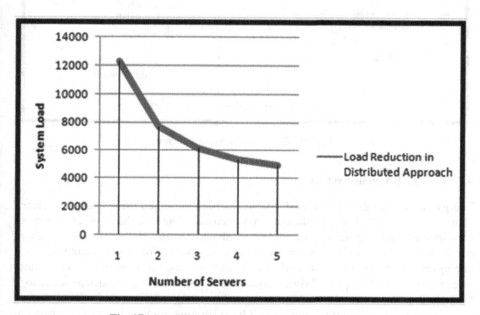

**Fig. 17.** Load distribution based on number of servers

## 4.6  Space Analysis

Memory space consumption of our proposed system is shown in Fig. 18. 91 bytes for primary memory and 0 byte for secondary memory have been consumed in Algorithm 1. 77 bytes for primary memory and 181 bytes for secondary memory have been consumed in Algorithm 2. 185 bytes for primary memory and 347 bytes for secondary memory have been consumed in Algorithm 3. 10 bytes for primary memory and 229 bytes for secondary memory have been consumed in Algorithm 4.

Therefore, in total, our framework consumes 1,120 bytes ($91 + 0 + 77 + 181 + 185 + 347 + 10 + 229$) for total execution in case of each user.

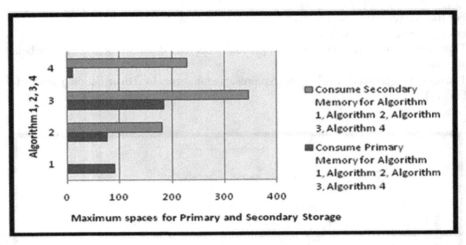

**Fig. 18.** Space consumption analysis

### 4.7 Energy Efficient System

Energy efficiency ratio of proposed system has been presented using energy efficiency chart (refer Fig. 19). Energy efficiency has been calculated on the basis of four modules such as energy efficiency of student feedback module ($E_1$), energy efficiency of administration module ($E_2$), energy efficiency of teacher performance module ($E_3$), and energy efficiency of overall system (E) (refer Analysis based on Energy Efficient Framework sub-section of Proposed Work section).Three distinct scenarios such as scenario 1, scenario 2, and scenario 3 have been presented in energy efficient chart. Three distinct cases, such as, case 1, case 2, and case 3 have been incorporated in each scenario of Fig. 19.

In scenario 1, energy efficiency ratio of '$E_1$' and '$E_2$' are constant; '$E_3$' and 'E' are variants for each case. Constant values for '$E_1$' and '$E_2$' are 25 for case 1, 50 for case 2, and 75 for case 3. Three values such as 20, 60, and 80 are fixed for '$E_3$' in all three cases. In case 1, the values for 'E' are 23, 39, and 47. In case 2, the values for 'E' are 38,54, and 62. In case 3, the values for 'E' are 53, 59, and 77. In scenario 1, highest energy efficiency ratio has been achieved in case 3.

In scenario 2, energy efficiency ratio of '$E_1$' and '$E_3$' are constant; '$E_2$' and 'E' are variants for each case. Constant values for '$E_1$' and '$E_3$' are 25 for case 1, 50 for case 2, and 75 for case 3. Three values such as 20, 60, and 80 are fixed for '$E_2$' in all three cases. In case 1, the values for 'E' are 23.5,35.5, and 41.5. In case 2, the values for 'E' are 41,53, and 59. In case 3, the values for 'E' are 58.5,70.5, and 76.5. In scenario 2, case 3 represent's the superiority of energy efficiency ratio.

In scenario 3, energy efficiency ratio of '$E_2$' and '$E_3$' are constant; '$E_1$' and 'E' are variants for each case. Constant values for '$E_2$' and '$E_3$' are 25 for case 1, 50 for case 2, and 75 for case 3. Three values such as 20, 60, and 80 are fixed for '$E_1$' in all three cases. In case 1, the values for 'E' are 23.5, 35.5, and 41.5. In case 2, the values for 'E'

| | | Energy Efficiency of Student Feedback Module | Energy Efficiency of Administration Module | Energy Efficiency of Teacher Performance Module | Energy Efficiency of Proposed System |
|---|---|---|---|---|---|
| SCENARIO 1 | CASE 1 | 25 | 25 | 20 | 23 |
| | | 25 | 25 | 60 | 39 |
| | | 25 | 25 | 80 | 47 |
| | CASE 2 | 50 | 50 | 20 | 38 |
| | | 50 | 50 | 60 | 54 |
| | | 50 | 50 | 80 | 62 |
| | CASE 3 | 75 | 75 | 20 | 53 |
| | | 75 | 75 | 60 | 69 |
| | | 75 | 75 | 80 | 77 |
| SCENARIO 2 | CASE 1 | 25 | 20 | 25 | 23.5 |
| | | 25 | 60 | 25 | 35.5 |
| | | 25 | 80 | 25 | 41.5 |
| | CASE 2 | 50 | 20 | 50 | 41 |
| | | 50 | 60 | 50 | 53 |
| | | 50 | 80 | 50 | 59 |
| | CASE 3 | 75 | 20 | 75 | 58.5 |
| | | 75 | 60 | 75 | 70.5 |
| | | 75 | 80 | 75 | 76.5 |
| SCENARIO 3 | CASE 1 | 20 | 25 | 25 | 23.5 |
| | | 60 | 25 | 25 | 35.5 |
| | | 80 | 25 | 25 | 41.5 |
| | CASE 2 | 20 | 50 | 50 | 41 |
| | | 60 | 50 | 50 | 53 |
| | | 80 | 50 | 50 | 59 |
| | CASE 3 | 20 | 75 | 75 | 58.5 |
| | | 60 | 75 | 75 | 70.5 |
| | | 80 | 75 | 75 | 76.5 |

**Fig. 19.** Energy efficiency chart

are 41, 53, and 59. In case 3, the values for 'E' are 58.5, 70.5, and 76.5. In scenario 3, energy efficiency ratio of case 3 has been reflected as best.

In Fig. 19, The quantity of two cases such as case 3 of scenario 2 and case 3 of scenario 3 have been depicted as equal as well as superior than case 3 of scenario 1.

## 4.8 Comparative Analysis

In comparative analysis section, authors have depicted different comparative study between existing system and proposed system using online feedback service (refer Fig. 20), paperless feedback service (refer Fig. 21), and cloud based feedback service (refer Fig. 22). In Fig. 20, Fig. 21 and Fig. 22, different phrases have been used for describing the scenario of each criteria. Phrases have been described as follows:

- 'Yes' indicates that corresponding criteria have been completely fully satisfied by the system. – 'No' describes that corresponding criteria have been completely denied by the system.
- 'Available' & 'Applicable' indicates that corresponding criteria have been partially satisfied by the system.
- 'Not Available' & 'Not Applicable' describes that, corresponding criteria have not been satisfied by the system.

Authors have shown comparison between the proposed system and existing five systems based on proposed online feedback service in Fig. 20. There are thirteen criteria

| Charecteristics of Online Feedback | Existing Online Feedback Systems | | | | | Proposed System's Online Feedback Service |
|---|---|---|---|---|---|---|
| | Existing System 1 [43] | Existing System 2 [44] | Existing System 3 [45] | Existing System 4 [46] | Existing System 5 [47] | |
| Multi-user System | Yes | Yes | Yes | Yes | Yes | Yes |
| Energy Efficient Approach | No | No | No | No | No | Yes |
| Online Feedback | Yes | Yes | Yes | Yes | Yes | Yes |
| Gateway based Approach | No | No | No | No | No | Yes |
| Number of Gateways used | 0 | 0 | 0 | 0 | 0 | 3 |
| Semantic Web | No | No | No | No | Yes | No |
| Platform Dependency | Not Available | Dependent | Not Available | Not Available | Not Available | Independent |
| Time Complexity | Not Available | Not Available | Non Linear | Not Available | Not Available | $O(n)$ |
| Space Complexity | Not Available | Not Available | Not Available | Not Available | Not Available | $O(n)$ |
| Performance Analysis | Not Applicable | Not Applicable | Applicable | Not Applicable | Not Applicable | Preparedness, Class performance, Responsiveness, Effectiveness, and Overall grade have been covered. |
| Multitasking | No | No | No | No | No | Yes |
| Moodle's Approach | No | No | Yes | No | No | No |
| Automatic System | Yes | Yes | Yes | Yes | Yes | Yes |

**Fig. 20.** Comparative study on online feedback service

| Charecteristics of Paperless Feedback | Existing Paperless Systems | | | | Proposed System's Paperless Feedback Service |
|---|---|---|---|---|---|
| | Existing System 1 [48] | Existing System 2 [49] | Existing System 3 [50] | Existing System 4 [51] | |
| Efficient Communication between Authorities and Customers | Available | Available | Not Available | Available | Teachers' performance has been calculated and served based on students' feedback |
| Access Files Anywhere, Anytime | Not Applicable | Available | Not Available | Available | Teachers and students have accessed data from any geographical location using different gateways |
| Increase Security | Not Available | Yes | Not Available | Not Available | Any personal/manual influence has not been allowed |
| Financial Benefits | Available | Available | Available | Not Available | No extra paper cost & carbon cost have not been required |
| Reduce Human Interference | Not Available | Not Available | Available | Available | Teachers' performance has been calculated automatically |
| Easy Backup | Not Available | Not Available | Not Available | Not Available | Available |
| Increased Client Service | Yes | Yes | Not Available | Not Available | Yes |
| Environment Friendly Approach | Yes | Not Available | Not Available | Yes | Yes |
| Data Access in Minimum Time | Yes | Not Available | Not Available | Not Available | Yes |
| Paperless Feedback | No | Yes | No | No | Yes |

**Fig. 21.** Comparative study on paperless feedback service

such as multi-user system, energy efficient approach, gateway based approach, number of gateway used, semantic web, platform dependency, time complexity, space complexity, performance analysis, multitasking, Moodle's approach, automatic system have been used to compare between all systems (refer Fig. 20).

| Charecteristics of Cloud based Feedback | Existing Cloud based Systems | | | Proposed System's Cloud based Feedback Service |
|---|---|---|---|---|
| | Existing System 1 [42] | Existing System 2 [52] | Existing System 3 [53] | |
| Web based Approach | Available | Available | Available | Available |
| Distributed Approach | Available | Available | Available | Available |
| Cloud based Feedback | Available | Not Available | Available | Available |
| Load Distribution | Not Available | Available | Not Available | System load has been reduced using load distribution |
| Scalability | Not Available | Available | Available | Increased |
| Replication Transparency | Not Available | Available | Not Available | Applied |
| Reallocation Transparency | Not Available | Available | Not Available | Applied |
| Platform as a Service | Not Available | Available | Not Available | Used |
| Software as a Service | Not Available | Available | Not Available | Used |
| Extra Hardware and/or Software Required for Client | Not Available | Not Available | Not Available | Not Used |

**Fig. 22.** Comparative study on cloud based feedback service

As per comparison chart multi-user system and automatic system have been completely satisfied by "existing system 1". Energy efficient approach, gateway based approach, number of gateway used, semantic web, multitasking and Moodle's approach have been denied by "existing system 1". Platform dependency, time complexity and space complexity have not been declared in "existing system 1". Performance analysis has not been applied in "existing system 1" [43].

Multi-user system and automatic system have been completely satisfied by "existing system 2". Energy efficient approach, gateway based approach, number of gateway used, semantic web, multitasking and Moodle's approach have been denied by "existing system 2". Platform dependency, time complexity and space complexity have not been declared in "existing system 2". Performance analysis has not been applied in "existing system 2" [44].

As per comparison chart, multi-user system, Moodle's approach, Performance analysis and automatic system have been completely satisfied by "existing system 3". Energy efficient approach, gateway based approach, number of gateway used, semantic web and multitasking have been denied by "existing system 3". Platform dependency, time complexity and space complexity have not been declared in existing system 3. Time complexity is non-linear in "existing system 3" [45].

As per comparison chart multi-user system and automatic system have been completely satisfied by "existing system 4". Energy efficient approach, gateway based approach, number of gateway used, semantic web, multitasking and Moodle's approach have been denied by existing system 4. Platform dependency, time complexity and space complexity have not been declared in "existing system 4". Performance analysis has not been applied in "existing system 4" [46].

Multi-user system, semantic web, and automatic system have been completely satisfied by "existing system 5". energy efficient approach, cloud based approach, gateway based approach, number of gateway used, multitasking and Moodle's approach have been denied by "existing system 5". Platform dependency, time complexity and space complexity have not been declared in "existing system 5" applied in "existing system 5" [47].

As per comparison chart multi-user system, energy efficient approach, gateway based approach, number of gateway used, multitasking and automatic system have been completely satisfied by proposed system. Moodle's approach has been denied by proposed system. The proposed system is able to work in each platform as an independent manner. Time complexity and space complexity have been declared as linear in proposed system. Performance analysis has been calculated using preparedness, class performance, effectiveness, responsiveness and overall grade parameters in proposed system (refer Fig. 20).

In Fig. 21, a comparative study has been presented between existing approaches and proposed approach based on paperless feedback service. Ten characteristics (efficient communication between authorities and customers, access files anywhere-anytime, increase security, financial benefits, reduced human interference, easy backup, increased client service, environment friendly approach, data access in minimum time, and paperless feedback) have been considered for comparative study.

In "existing system 1", an efficient communication has been observed between authorities and customers. Data have been accessed from any geographical location using minimum time (refer Fig. 21). Enhanced client service with environment friendly approach has been used by "existing system 1". Financial benefits are being achieved in "existing system 1" using paperless approach [48].

Enhanced client services are being maintained in "existing system 2" using efficient communication between authorities and customers. Paperless feedback is available in "existing system 2". Cost effective data access scheme has been described in "existing system 2" with maintaining appropriate security [49].

Enhanced financial benefits have been achieved by "existing system 3" using less human interference [50].

Authors have observed that, environment friendly approach is being maintained in "existing system 4" using less human interference. In "existing system 4", files have been accessed from any geographical location through efficient communication between authorities and consumers [51].

As per comparison chart, each characteristics of Fig. 21 has been satisfied by proposed system's paperless feedback service. Authors have identified the superiority of proposed system based on paperless feedback service using comparative study (refer Fig. 21).

In Fig. 22, authors have considered different ten characteristics (web based approach, distributed approach, cloud based feedback, load distribution, scalability, replication transparency, reallocation transparency, platform as a service, software as a service, and extra hardware and/or software required for client) are being used for performing a comparative study between existing systems and proposed system's cloud based feedback service.

In "existing system 1", web based approach, distributed approach and cloud based feedback are being observed [42].

In "existing system 2", web based approach, distributed approach, load distribution, scalability, replication transparency, reallocation transparency, platform as a service and software as a service have been observed [52].

Web based approach, distributed approach, cloud based feedback and scalability have been observed in "existing system 3" [53].

As per comparative study, web based approach, distributed approach, cloud based feedback, load distribution, scalability, replication transparency, reallocation transparency, platform as a service and software as a service have been used in proposed cloud based feedback service. In Fig. 22, authors have recognized the superiority of proposed system's cloud based feedback service.

## 5  Conclusion

The actual purpose of teachers' performance analysis has been successfully achieved by our proposed cloud based multi-user online feedback system. Authors have tested the online system and observed that our proposal exhibits better results than existing systems. Our online based system is user friendly and progressive for any academic organizations. Our system judges whether a teacher is suitable for a particular subject of a particular academic organization. The flexibility of our platform independent system has been increased due to usage of the concept of cloud which helps us to store all data in server side systems maintaining secured login and transactions. Human effort has been reduced by using our system as automatic procedures are involved for data collection, calculation, and exhibition. Data loss & the load of database have been decreased due to usage of distributed approach. Linear time & space complexity have been achieved using proposed framework. Hardware expenses have been decreased due to usage of platform-as-a-service. Availability of frameworks has been increased to multiple users of distinct geographical locations due to usage of software-as -a-service. All data are replicated in servers to maintain replication transparency and relocation transparency. We have achieved an energy efficient system on the basis of load analysis using distributed approach. Our system provides distinct gateways for accessing separate parts of the system. These gateways or entry points are not connected to each other, so that each module is a light weight distributed procedure consuming less time for execution. Our system design is secured as all the modules are unknown to each other and only authenticated users could be able to login. We have achieved a progressive paperless system with respect to existing systems.

**Acknowledgement.** The research work is funded by Computer Innovative Research Society, West Bengal, India. Award number is "2018/CIRS/R&D/1012-07-18/CFSPALA".

## References

1. Kundu, A.: Heterogeneous cloud architecture. Data Commun. Netw. 172 (2014)
2. Sarkar, S., Kundu, A., Banerjee, A.: Evaluation of reliable data storage in cloud using an efficient encryption technique. In: Handbook of Research on Cloud Computing and Big Data Applications in IoT, chap. 12, pp. 229–242. IGI Global Publication (2019)

3. Guha, S.K., Kundu, A., Dattagupta, R.: Energy stability in cloud for web page ranking. In: Satapathy, S.C., Mandal, J.K., Udgata, S.K., Bhateja, V. (eds.) Information Systems Design and Intelligent Applications. AISC, vol. 434, pp. 621–630. Springer, New Delhi (2016). https://doi.org/10.1007/978-81-322-2752-6_61

4. Sarkar, S., Kundu, A.: An indexed approach for multiple data storage in cloud. In: Satapathy, S.C., Mandal, J.K., Udgata, S.K., Bhateja, V. (eds.) Information Systems Design and Intelligent Applications. AISC, vol. 433, pp. 639–646. Springer, New Delhi (2016). https://doi.org/10.1007/978-81-322-2755-7_66

5. Guha, S.K., Kundu, A., Dattagupta, R.: Domain-based dynamic ranking. In: Advanced Research on Cloud Computing design and Applications. Advances in systems Analysis, Software Engineering, and High Performance Computing, chap. 17, pp. 262–279. IGI Global Publications (2015)

6. Sarkar, S., Kundu, A.: An approach on cloud disk searching using parallel channels. In: Advanced Research on cloud computing Design and Applications, Advances in systems Analysis, Software Engineering and High Performance Computing, chap. 18, pp. 280–304. IGI Global Publications (2015)

7. Kundu, A., Ji, C., Liu, R.: Cloud based heterogeneous distributed framework. In: Abraham, A., Thampi, S. (eds.) Intelligent Informatics. Advances in Intelligent Systems and Computing, vol. 182, pp. 471–478. Springer, Heidelberg (2013). https://doi.org/10.1007/978-3-642-32063-7_50

8. Sarkar, S., Kundu, A.: Performance enhancement of cloud based storage using disk scheduling technique. Int. J. Cloud Appl. Comput. 10(1), 46–63 (2020)

9. Kundu, A., Ji, C.: Swarm intelligence in cloud environment. In: Tan, Y., Shi, Y., Ji, Z. (eds.) ICSI 2012. LNCS, vol. 7331, pp. 37–44. Springer, Heidelberg (2012). https://doi.org/10.1007/978-3-642-30976-2_5

10. Kundu, A., Ji, C., Liu, R.: Software-as-a-service using heterogeneous distributed system for user specific applications. Int. J. Cloud Appl. Comput. 4(1), 15–32 (2014)

11. Kundu, A., Luan, L., Liu, R.: Synchronisation of data transfer in cloud. Int. J. Internet Protoc. Technol. 8(1), 1–24 (2014)

12. Kundu, A., Xu, G., Ji, C.: Self organization behavior of intelligent cloud. J. Converg. Inf. Technol. 8(16), 39–47 (2013)

13. Kundu, A., Xu, G., Liu, R.: Efficient load balancing in cloud: a practical implementation. Int. J. Adv. Comput. Technol. 5(12), 43–54 (2013)

14. Sarkar, S., Kundu, A.: An eco friendly cloud searching technique with delay. Int. J. Green Comput. 9(1), 20–34 (2018)

15. Banerjee, A., Kundu, A.: Software for feedback system using adaptive categorization & authenticated recommendation. Int. J. Open Source Softw. Process. 10(2), 37–69 (2019)

16. Sivasankari, S., Srimathi, P.S., Ramya, S., Fatima, G.: Online feedback system for educational institutions for better evaluation of faculty's performance using semantic web (SW) technology. Int. J. Innovative Res. Sci. Eng. Technol. 5(2), 275–279 (2016)

17. Rahaman, S., Raut, A.P., Adnan, S.A., Junghare, S.S.: Online student feedback system. Int. J. Res. Sci. Eng. 224–230 (2016)

18. Hatie, J., Trimperley, H.: The power of feedback. J. Rev. Educ. Res. 87(1), 81–112 (2007)

19. Subramanian, S., Sharma, M.: Improved feedback system in moodle. Int. J. Comput. Sci. Trends Technol. 4(6), 99–102 (2016)

20. Tarare, M., Manwani, M., Paidlewar, A., Maturkar, P., Chaudhuri, P., Shiral, J.V.: Feedback management system for evaluating and generating monthly report. Int. J. Emerg. Technol. Adv. Eng. 4(3), 519–521 (2014)

21. Vasilyeva, E., Puuronen, S., Pechenikiy, M., Rasanen, P.: Feedback adaption in web-based learning system. Int. J. Continuing Eng. Educ. Life-Long Learn. 17(4–5), 337–357 (2007)

22. Tsutsui, E., Owada, K., Konodo, Y., Nakano, M.: A proposal for a new-dimensional online feedback system: focusing on individual learner differences. In: Distance Learning and the Internet Conference, pp. 107–109 (2008)
23. Pradeep, V.: OTPES: online teaching performance evaluation system. Int. J. Adv. Res. Comput. Sci. Softw. Eng. **3**(5), 388–392 (2013)
24. Peter, M.C.: An automated feedback system for computer organization projects. IEEE Trans. Educ. **47**(2), 232–240 (2004)
25. Ardalan, A., Ardalan, R., Coppage, S., Crouch, W.: A comparison of student feedback obtained through paper-based and web-based surveys of faculty teaching. Br. J. Edu. Technol. **38**(6), 1085–1101 (2007)
26. Garvey, P.J., Sherlock, J.J.: A closer look at instructor-student feedback online: a case study analysis of the types and frequency. MERLOT J. Online Learn. Teach. **6**(1), 110–120 (2010)
27. Banerjee, A.: Improving student's learning with correct feedback: a model proposed for classroom utility. Int. J. Educ. Psychol. Res. (IJEPR) **3**(4), 36–40 (2014)
28. Shameer, A.P., Haseeb, V.V., MiniMol, V.K.: Green approach for reducing energy consumption-a case study report. Int. J. Adv. Res. Comput. Sci. Softw. Eng. **5**(1), 359–363 (2015)
29. Grandon, E., Alshare, O., Kwan, O.: Factors influencing student attention to adopt online classes: a cross cultural study. J. Comput. Sci. Coll. **20**(4), 46–56 (2005)
30. Park, S.Y.: An analysis of the technology acceptance model in understanding university students' behavioral intention to use e-learning. Educ. Technol. Soc. **12**(3), 150–162 (2009)
31. Adzharuddin, N.A., Ling, L.H.: Learning management system (LMS) among university students: does it work. Int. J. e-Educ. e-Bus. e-Manag. e-Learn. **3**(3), 248–252 (2013)
32. Nair, S., Patil, R.: A study on the impact of learning management systems on students of a university college in sultanate of oman. Int. J. Comput. Sci. **19**(2), 379–385 (2012)
33. Coates, H., James, R., Baldwin, G.: A critical examination of the effects of learning management systems on university teaching and learning. Tertiary Educ. Manag. **19**(36), 20–36 (2005)
34. Marcano, L., Manca, D., Yazidi, A., Komulainen, T.: A methodology for building a data-enclosing tunnel for automated online-feedback in simulator Training. Comput. Chem. Eng. **132**, 106621 (2020)
35. Cañabate, D., Nogué, L., Serra, T., Colomer, J.: Supportive peer feedback in tertiary education: analysis of pre-service teachers' perceptions. Educ. Sci. **9**(4), 280 (2019)
36. Legette, R.M., Royo, J.: Pre-service music teacher perceptions of peer feedback. Res. Stud. Music Educ. 1321103X19862298 (2019)
37. Powell, J., et al.: Using online patient feedback to improve NHS services: the INQUIRE multimethod study. Health Serv. Deliv. Res. **7**(38) (2019)
38. Pratiwi, H.Y., Winarko, W., Ayu, H.D.: The impact of problem solving strategy with online feedback on students' conceptual understanding. In: Journal of Physics: Conference Series, vol. 1006, no. 1, p. 012024. IOP Publishing, April 2018
39. Kurniawan, B.: Use of Smartapps for administrative service based paperless system. In: IOP Conference Series: Materials Science and Engineering, vol. 662, no. 2, p. 022059. IOP Publishing (2019)
40. Dhrub, S.: Design and implementation of paperless office in ONGC. In: International Oil & Gas Conference Series (PETROTECH-2019) (2019)
41. Ilyushkin, A., Bauer, A., Papadopoulos, A.V., Deelman, E., Iosup, A.: Performance-feedback autoscaling with budget constraints for cloud-based workloads of workflows. Springer's book on Advances in Intelligent Digital Ecosystems 4 arXiv preprint arXiv:1905.10270 (2019)
42. Kundu, A., Xu, G., Ji, C.: Data specific ranking in cloud. Int. J. Cloud Appl. Comput. **4**(4), 32–41 (2014)

43. Teixeira, L.A., et al.: Automatic postural responses are scaled from the association between online feedback and feedforward control. Eur. J. Neurosci. **51**(10), 2023–2032 (2019)

44. Wang, D., Wang, M., Shen, Y., Li, Q., Liang, X.: Online feedback dead-time compensation strategy for three-level t-type inverters. IEEE Trans. Ind. Electron. **67**(9), 7260–7268 (2019)

45. Ascetta, K., Harn, B., Durán, L.: Comparing self-reported and performance-based online feedback on early childhood teachers' implementation of language strategies. Early Childhood Educ. J. **47**(3), 353–365 (2019)

46. Filius, R.M., de Kleijn, R.A., Uijl, S.G., Prins, F., van Rijen, H.V., Grobbee, D.E.: Promoting deep learning through online feedback in SPOCs. Frontline Learn. Res. **6**(2), 92 (2018)

47. Savvidou, C.: Exploring the pedagogy of online feedback in supporting distance learners. In: Advanced Learning and Teaching Environments-Innovation, Contents and Methods. IntechOpen (2018)

48. Yuksel, A.S., Cankaya, I.A., Cankaya, S.F.: IoT for hospitality industry: paperless buffet management. In: Securing the Internet of Things: Concepts, Methodologies, Tools, and Applications, pp. 1388–1408. IGI Global (2020)

49. Arney, J., Jones, I., Wolf, A.: Going green: paperless technology and feedback from the classroom. J. Sustain. Green Bus. **1**(1) (2019)

50. Šuleř, P., Machová, V.: The possibilities of a paperless company concept. In: Ashmarina, S.I., Vochozka, M., Mantulenko, V.V. (eds.) ISCDTE 2019. LNNS, vol. 84, pp. 198–202. Springer, Cham (2020). https://doi.org/10.1007/978-3-030-27015-5_25

51. Idris, D.S.R.P.H., Ismail, H.K.R.H.: BruTEL's "going paperless" initiative. In: Green Behavior and Corporate Social Responsibility in Asia, pp. 141–146. Emerald Publishing Limited (2019)

52. Kundu, A., Xu, G., Ji, C.: Analysis on cloud classification using accessibility. Int. J. Cloud Appl. Comput. **4**(3), 44–53 (2014)

53. Kundu, A., Xu, G., Ji, C.: Analysis on cloud classification using accessibility. Int. J. Cloud Appl. Comput. **4**(1), 63–75 (2014)

# Semantic-Based Automatic Generation of Reconfigurable Distributed Mobile Applications in Pervasive Environments

Abderrahim Lakehal[1], Adel Alti[1(✉)], and Philippe Roose[2]

[1] LRSD Laboratory, Department of Computer Science, Faculty of Sciences, University Ferhat Abbas Sétif-1, 19000 Sétif, Algeria
{abderrahim.lakehal,alti.adel}@univ-setif.dz
[2] LIUPPA, University of PAU, Anglet 64000, France
philippe.roose@iutbayonne.univ-pau.fr

**Abstract.** Nowadays, mobile applications are used in various smart domains. These applications are available through interconnected smart connected objects. Several existing research works suffer from a lack of distributed semantic-based agile strategy that improve accuracy and increase the system's efficiency. To address this problem, this paper comes up with a new flexible, modular and hierarchical loosely coupled framework for efficiently generate context-aware applications based on user's location and his situation. The classification of user's situations reveals new insight on identifying efficiently hierarchical composite situations in order to meet the quality of user's constraints. It ensures minimum execution time for context-aware of distributed mobile applications using parallel and distributed strategy. Firstly, the framework filters the contextual user's constraints of different smart-domains into domain-specific user's context. Then, it detects parallel incoming events captured by sensors that are able for identification of factorized composite situations. Based on these identifications, we automatically generate the application reconfiguration as a collection of adapted services that deployed on available distributed devices. We compare the situation identification performance of the proposed reasoning approach to efficient map-reduce implementations for healthcare system. Experimental results show the effectiveness, reusability and scalability of the proposed approach.

**Keywords:** User-centric situation · Connected-objects · Situation · Adaptation · Reconfiguration

## 1 Introduction

Nowadays, mobile applications deployment has greatly increased in recent years. Now, many smart mobile applications can be used in different smart areas such as Industry 4.0, smart city, smart health and smart home [11–15]. These applications are gradually being quickly established by connected objects. They allow retrieving information directly related to immediate environment of the user (location, brightness, neighborhood, interactions, etc.). Due to the complexity of application the high cost of maintainability,

© Springer-Verlag GmbH Germany, part of Springer Nature 2021
A. Hameurlain et al. (Eds.): TLDKS XLVII, LNCS 12630, pp. 213–233, 2021.
https://doi.org/10.1007/978-3-662-62919-2_9

the availability of many applications running on different mobile devices (Smartphone, Tablet, Laptop, etc.) with heterogeneous interconnected objects at most of the places brings more challenges. In addition, most of the existing mobile applications neglect the context of the user, usage contexts and their evolving preferences. As a new research domain, context-aware mobile applications play a vital role in managing huge contextual data. It is used to identify immediately the user's situations to deploy appropriate action services. As mentioned in [6], the situation is a semantic interpretation of low-level context, allowing high-level user's behavior specification in the environment within the corresponding actions services. However, situations give the application semantic meaning and intelligence to easily define and maintain it, which is better than using basic context information. In addition, context situations composition are also useful for applications that support mobile context awareness to support other user-specified functions, such as recommending previous user experiences based on a specific user's personal information, current needs and his preferences.

Therefore, building composite situation application based on mobile context awareness has become the most challenging task. Despite the increasing adoption of mobile and context-aware applications, the use of automatic intelligent strategies to utilize semantic technologies and intelligent services still not automated, nor it implemented in a structured way. In addition, the flexibility of the application is still limited, and it is impossible to add/delete/update any business functions and interaction methods at the right place at the right time. Mobile context-aware applications have undergone countless technological changes, becoming more personalized and situation-driven. They integrate advanced applications with advanced levels of reusability and flexibility into the design, while allowing mobile application designers to use parallel raw context data from multiple devices and various identified situation-specific domain knowledge. By using new composition operators (i.e. parallel, sequence, negation, and recurrence) between the existing atomic situations and various distributed intelligent services, users can better control the application's constraint, making it reusable and achieving its durability. We need real-time distributed, agile and dynamic management process to increase flexibility and decompose multiple identified shared situations and events to different users at the same time. At the design level, composite situation is described using multiple atomic situations, which means that other actions can be triggered. In addition, in order to consider a large number of situations, designers can easily add and configure new rules.

Several approaches and platforms have been proposed to design and manage context-aware mobile applications [3–14]. These platforms suffer from effective design methods for modeling and identifying composite situations in various domains, especially when having different actions to be triggered (composition of simple situations triggers other actions), and when user's needs constantly change and can be represented by different users involved in the smart domain. However, designing dynamic mobile applications to manage a large number of mobile users according to their needs, usage and execution context is facing a huge challenge, which will reduce their real use. In fact, it is difficult to design a mobile application for each user through his personal wishes and evolving execution context at runtime. This major challenge may need for a new and more effective approach to user constraints, using context and their preferences, to manage distributed mobile applications on the available execution platforms to manage user mobility and limited resource capacities (low battery, etc.).

This paper is interested in the dynamic management of distributed mobile context-aware applications for composite situations in pervasive environments by combining semantic web technologies, context awareness with IoT and middleware at design and run-time. At design time, the framework builds and adapts the existing application design model reusing high-level abstraction of user's constraints specifications and usage context related to user's domain in the development of business-specific components.

At runtime, the context monitoring mechanism collects relevant context data from different sensors and converts it into OWL ontology called MULTI-OSCM (multi-layer ontology-based composite situation model) [17]. Then, the contextual reasoning engine identifies the situation and triggers appropriate adaptive services, using the Kali-smart platform as middleware [6] to coordinate the best way to deploy components on mobile devices around the user. Such a platform provides powers for the contextual information management mechanism of distributed context-aware applications, including centralized/distributed semantic event detection and distributed action mechanisms. Currently, Kali-smart platform manages context-aware applications based on components. As a successful distributed mobile situation-driven application, an agile (dynamic) process is needed to support clear user-defined constraints, filter out relevant contexts, integrate user situations reasoning, and flexible service management.

The rest of this paper is organized as follows. Section 2 introduces related works that help us overcome the challenges faced by existing works. Section 3 introduces our proposed method, and discuss the composite situations extension. Section 4 illustrates the proposed method by using realistic scenarios in the field of smart home. Section 4 summarizes this paper and gives some future work.

## 2   Related Works and Objectives

Several adaptation platforms and methods have emerged in recent years. Recent works have focused on improving the adaptability and context awareness of dynamic components and service architectures. Compared with existing works, this paper proposes an automated distributed mobile application using semantic-based scene operators (parallel, sequence, recursion, negation). We concentrate in composite situation modeling and reasoning, and intelligent services related to the smart-* field. Our goal is to ensure the flexibility and scalability of the application through a shared user domain with semantics.

Several component-based adaptation platforms are expected to continuously evolve and adapt to user needs and execution context changes, for example: WComp [5], Dia-Suite [7], DynamicWright [3], Kalimucho-A [2, 10], Kali-Smart [6], CybreMinder [4]. These platforms are portable and runs on smart phones, personal computers and laptops. It ensures better management of context-aware functionalities. We focus on automatic generation of adaptive components on desktops, laptops and mobile devices through shared user domains and Kali-smart middleware [6] at runtime, instead of increasing flexibility and realizing autonomous dynamic reconfigurable distributed mobile application. This generation is based on a certain situation, the graphical design model of the mobile application and the contextual function. Nicolas *et al.* [1] developed context-aware middleware for mobile devices, which manages various contextual data collected from various sensor devices. Reasoning is made by analyzing the context and identifying specific situations. The identification guided by event-condition-action rules facilitates sensor-based intelligent decision-making, which is important for activating the sensor. Compared with the proposed work, a semantic design based on composite context is introduced, so that the atomic context identifier can convey the detected context to the system, and the composite context deduction is completed by the composite context identifier. Da et al. [2] proposed a context management middleware Kalimucho-A to provide services dedicated to distributed context management at the semantic level on the shared domain. This work provides excellent intelligent service management and pre-defined deployment strategies, but inferred in distributed situations and complex event processing (for example, "everyone is defined as gathering all the output of motion sensors in every room in the house define "nobody at home" as abstract event). Alti et al. [6] developed Kali-Smart platform with inference engine. This module acts as an intermediary between user context and situation rules. The reasoning engine uses first-order logic to represent the user's profile, user constraints and environmental context information. Therefore, the inference engine interprets the relevant context data as semantic information and compares it with the situation rules to determine whether the situation is recognized, and then it will trigger the appropriate service to the user. The CybreMinder [4] is an Eclipse plug-in that allows the explicit specification of a context as a combination of sub-contexts using diverse relations, such as $=$ , $<=$, $>=$, $<$ , or $>$ as well as pre-defined contextual events. However, CybreMinder does not provide a range of composite operators such as parallel, sequence, alternative, and recurrence for mobile context-aware applications. Besides, CybreMinder neither supports multimodal actions to perform multi adaptations nor the combination of atomic distributed multimodal actions. Recently, Karchoud et al. [10] propose a novel vision of user's long-life applications that relies on a rule-based spatiotemporal model for continuous context understanding and situation identification. However, this work lacks the support to manage accurately all contextual constraints. In other words, it does not take into account semantic composite relations between simple situations to create composite situations (e.g., recurrence of high glucose level as a composite situation).

Table 1 summarizes the limitations and strengths of related works. The previous related works have many limitations due to several reasons. The first reason, such proposed works lack of a real-time parallel-distributed mechanism that minimizes missed events/situations. The improvement is obtained by defining a set of new composition operators (i.e. parallel, sequence, negation, recurrence, equivalence and domination). The second reason, majority of solutions lack the high scalability (handling big volumes of context data, continuous sensor's events and user's mobility), which directly influences the whole reasoning process. Finally, these solutions lack autonomic real-time application management strategy under several moving locations.

The proposed approach consists of generic model of smaller modular components that describe heterogonous smart objects, advanced spatial/temporal composite situations to guide the management of agile and automated application. We have (i) temporal aspects among situations and events across smart domains at the design, deployment and run-time levels in order to make the decision autonomously and ensure continuous situations reasoning (ii) the automatic generation of distributed mobile application

**Table 1.** Related works' comparison

| Proposed solution | Composite situation modeling | Methods used | Smart domains | Reasoning | Scalability | Flexibility |
|---|---|---|---|---|---|---|
| ECA [1] | × | Rule-Based | Generic | Centralized | Low | Low |
| CybreMinder [4] | Partially | Rule-Based | Generic | Supervised | Low | Low |
| Butt *et al.* [10] | Partially | Engine | Health | Centralized | High | Low |
| Karchoud *et al.* [12] | × | Platform | Generic | Distributed | Medium | Medium |
| Da et al. [2] | × | Platform | Generic | Distributed | Medium | Low |
| CoCaMAAL [3] | × | Platform | Generic | Centralized | Low | Medium |
| WComp [5] | × | Platform | Generic | Supervised | Low | Medium |
| Kalimucho [16] | × | Platform | Generic | Distributed | Low | Medium |
| Kali-Smart [6] | × | First-Logic | Generic | Distributed | Medium | Medium |
| DiaSuite [7] | × | Engine | Generic | Centralized | Low | Medium |

based on the user's current context and spatial/temporal constraints and (iii) the parallel-distributed situation-reasoning engine. As the platform is conceived into three levels (design, deployment and run-time levels), it is possible to only change application model at each level separately. The flexibility is possible to add/remove/update one or more business components to deal with new situations or context changes.

## 3 Proposed Approach

As noted in Sect. 2, the issues related to composite situations modeling and processing are currently curbing the management of context-aware distributed smart mobile application designed to assist users in their daily activities. The identification of a composite situation plays a primary role in this context. It becomes more complicated due to the availability of a huge number of different and heterogeneous connected objects (IoT). However, with the large variety of user situation rules and multiplicity of devices in different smart domains, the aspects of Event-Conditions-Actions (ECA) [1] are diminished, and they lose their performance and effectiveness in terms of the response time.

In order to address the limitations of existing approaches, a flexible, modular and hierarchical loosely coupled framework needs to be developed for addressing the two major issues related to automated composite situation identification: 1) semantic-based combination of atomic situations 2) management of action services (add/remove/update) based on user's location and time. These two issues improve the performance of the identification process of the user's situations while detecting a huge number of parallel incoming events. When a situation is identified, the system calls the reconfiguration generator, which is responsible for triggering a list of actions (e.g. adding/deleting/updating a service or migrating of services from a device to another in the context of the users' mobility).

## 3.1 Framework's General Architecture

This section presents a novel generic framework for a smart environment that responds to the current user's context usage, needs, and preferences in a parallel and intelligent way. The main purpose is to assist and support users in their daily activities and in urgent situations with a parallel micro services-oriented ontology-based management system. It provides higher efficiency of the user's situation identification process and efficient management of the user's situations over heterogeneous smart objects. As shown in Fig. 1, the architecture is made of three interconnected layers where each layer uses context data and services provided by other layers. The novelty of the proposed framework architecture is to provide: (i) a Knowledge Management module for preprocessing of raw sensor data using Multi-OCSM ontology, (ii) a User's Constraints module that easily defines and configures composite situation rules by combining several simple situation rules at design-time, (iii) an Autonomic Microservice-based Composite Situation module for events monitoring and situations management and reasoning at run-time. The main purpose of the Knowledge management Multi-OCSM layer is to describe composite/atomic situations and their related concepts in smart domains. It provides OWL (Web Ontology Language) description of different user's profiles and semantic services using a multi-layered Ontology-based Composite Situation Model (Multi-OCSM). This layer includes:

- **User's profiles registry:** it provides a semantic description of the user's profiles and his preferences.
- **Situation rules registry**: it provides all the situations rules set categorized by smart domain, location, time and situation type (urgent or normal).
- **Services registry:** it provides a set of all functional services, where these services will be deployed according to each identified situation, taking into account the semantic link between the situation and its suitable action services.
- **User's domain registry:** it provides relevant information about the available smart and interactive devices in the managed mobile application such as the status of device (used or not, context information, etc.).

The **application design layer (At design-time)** that provides a semantic user's situation rules preprocessing based on spatiotemporal user's specified constraints.

- The **Situations Rules Analyzer** is responsible for receiving and understanding the user's rules specified using GUI and translates it into its internal knowledge structure.
- The **Situations Rules Classifier** is responsible for grouping situations rules related to their similar location, time and smart domain.
- The **Situations Rules Ranker** is responsible for providing a ranked list of rules according to expert's defined priorities.

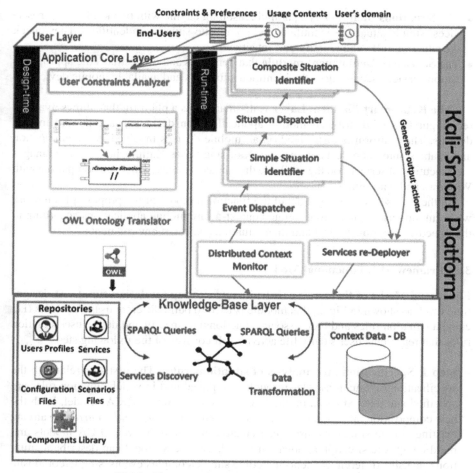

**Fig. 1.** The general architecture of the framework.

The **application design layer (At run-time)** contains several components for identifying situations based on user-defined rules. This is done through situations identifiers providing the user with appropriate action services according to their identified situations. It consists of four main components to identify the user's situations:

- The **Distributed Context Monitoring module** is responsible for monitoring a specific user's context data (events) using a specific sensor, then sends them to their corresponding situation identifier components in order to be semantically interpreted and analyzed.
- The **Situations dispatcher module** is responsible for filtering a set of relevant situations rules according to user's current location and time from the situation rules registry followed by the situation rules factorization. This component outputs the factorized tree of situations and its related common context attributes.

- The **Situations Identifier** is a parallel reasoning engine with two kinds of microservices: simple situations identifiers and composite situations identifiers. They check the situation rules and identify current situations.
- The **Service re-Deployment module** that generates and orchestrates the appropriate action services according to the identified situations and available mobile devices.

**The Kali-Smart Platform Layer** Kali-smart [6] is a platform that allows dynamic reconfiguration of distributed mobile applications on desktops, laptops and mobile devices. The platform is distributed on all mobile devices involved in the application and enables automatic decision-making. Kali-smart uses Kalimucho [2] that manages the execution of services on the available distributed devices, which are compatible with Windows and Android.

In the next section, we will detail the functional model of the proposed framework where mobile users intend to generate context-aware mobile applications according to their needs, execution context and their situations on smart environments.

### 3.2   Framework's Functional Model

**Functional Model of the user's constraints processing (at design-time).** At design-time level, as shown in Fig. 2, this module is used to build different usage contexts (i.e. context situation rules and their associated actions) to specify and define user situation rules that represents user's daily life activities. It consists of the following steps:

- **Step 1. Specification and analysis of situations rules.** The first step relates to the specification of situations rules through a graphical tool in which situation rules are specified and defined based on the Event-Condition-Action (ECA) model. With the new composition operators (*i.e. parallel, sequence, negation and recurrence*) among existing simple situations, users can create a hierarchy between ECA models and build composite situation application model. The ECA model can describe a situation rule using different concepts including simple/complex events, simple/composite conditions, and action services. The Situation Rule Analyzer component analyzes and checks the semantic coherence of user-defined situation rule. If there is no constraint violation, the Situation Rule Analyzer component translates checked situation rules to OWL individuals using JAVA code in order to unify and insert them into Multi-OCSM OWL model.
- **Step 2. Classification of situations rules.** The Situation Rule Classifier component classifies contextual situations rules based on their similar location, time and smart domain (smart-health, smart-tourism, smart-transport, smart-home, etc.). This classification improves the extraction of relevant situation rules and builds a global generic situation profile. In addition, it enriches Multi-OCSM ontology with rich situation classes that helps to recommend and identify relevant situation rules according to user's current domain and needs.
- **Step 3. Rank of situations rules.** The Situations Rules Ranker component classifies the situation rules into three categories, urgent, important and normal situation. The classification is performed through the calculated priority score, which falls into one

of the predefined priority score intervals of each category. The calculation of priority score is based on four criteria including situation category, user current activity, user location, and situation coverage. The Situations Rules Ranker component sorts the situation rules from the highest to the lowest priority score. At run-time, during the management of situations, situations with high priority will be handled before situations with low priority.

**Functional Model of the Autonomic Composite Situation Processing (at run-time).** At run-time level, the situation identifier module performs the identification of user's situations during his daily activities. It ensures the monitoring and analysis of incoming events and context changes during the run-time. This module is based on real-time agile situation identification mechanism using autonomic microservices architecture. It consists of the following steps:

- **Step 4. Dynamic filtering of relevant situation rules.** The Situation Rules Filter component provides relevant user's situation rules that match the user's current location and time.
- **Step 5. Construction of dynamic situation rules-based factorized tree.** The Situation Rule Factorizer component transforms the relevant situation rules list into a factorized tree. The factorized tree consists of three layers: composite situations layer, simple situations layer and common context attribute layer for all situations. The factorized tree is sent to Task Manager Component.
- **Step 6. Creation of events and situations microservices from the factorized tree.** In this step, the Event Listener is continuously monitoring the surrounding environment to acquire dynamic context data and preprocesses context information from smart sensors. The Event Listener receives new context information (i.e. newly detected events or contextual changes), converts them into a triple pattern in OWL format, and inserted them in our Multi-OCSM ontology. Finally, the Event Listener component dispatches the detected event to the appropriate situation identifier components.
- **Step 7. Parallel Identification of simple and composite situations.** In this step, the Situation the situation is identified if and only if the situation rule is checked. In this case, the Situation Identifier component dispatches the identified situation to its appropriate Composite Situations Identifier component. The Composite Situation Identifier component infers new composite situations from identified simple situations. Finally, the system sends all identified situations to Service re-Deployment module to trigger appropriate action services.
- **Step 8. Orchestration of the situation's actions.** The Service re-Deployment module scans the smart environment with the help of Kali-smart middleware to select available services and devices in order to orchestrate the best way to deploy action services. The Services Execution component consults the available microservices (e.g., the availability of light switch service) located in services repository to execute them.

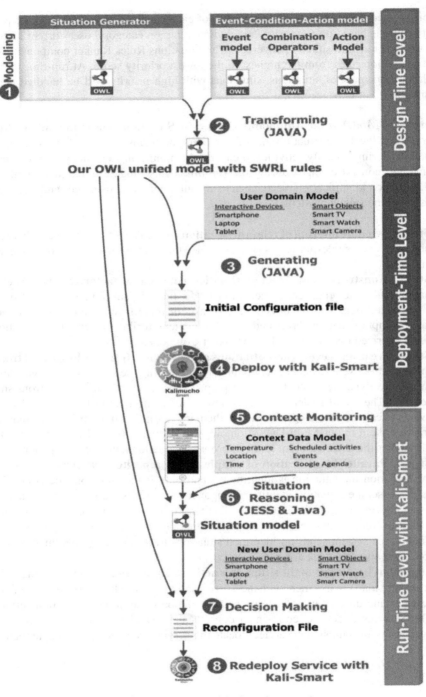

**Fig. 2.** Functional model of our framework.

**Composition Operator Based Composite Situation Model.** We use a multi-layered Multi-OCSM ontology model [17] to cover all context informations and situations that respond to the user's daily life activities for distributed context-aware mobile application structured on three levels: generic and domain ontologies for popular and shared concepts and devices used by applications designers, application ontology for a specific description of context, and situations rules in close smart environments. With the ontology is also possible to describe compositions of user's situation to better support reusability and context-awareness, situations reasoning based on contextual semantic level between metadata situations, and matching user profiles at the semantic level. As mentioned earlier in previous section, mobile applications are built using several available microservices. In fact, a large number of microservices may affect negatively the application's flexibility and maintainability. Thus, a level of abstraction is needed in order to resolve this challenge. We exploit the architectural entities (i.e. components) of the Kali-smart middleware [4] to build microservice-based composite situations. We distinguish four types of composition component operators: sequence, parallel, negation and recurrence (as shown in Table 2). We integrate these operators into Kali-smart middleware for managing composite situations at design and runtime levels. For instance, Fig. 3 introduce a design model of a composite situation called "Low Battery & Meeting composite situation" built with the combination of two simple situations "Low Battery simple situation, and Meeting simple situation" using parallel composition component operator. The identification of this composite situation triggers a set of action services including: exclude audio output and migrate the meeting application on another available device according to user's preferences. We extend Kali-smart for composition operator based on composite situation at design and runtime levels that allows the modeling of more composite situations in smart fields and provides the richer context awareness and therefore better and flexible adaptability

A *composite situation* is the composition of multiple composite/atomic situations, in which an *atomic situation* is the smallest unit of a composite situation. In order to define new situations among existing situations, we need to handle the composition among situations (*or contextual situations*) from one or several smart and multimedia sensors. Therefore, we propose a new metaphor of composition operators among situations described not only at the design time but also at the execution time such as *parallel, sequence, negation, and recurrence*. *Sequence operator* allows the composition of two dependent situations in sequence order. *Parallel operator* allows the composition of two independent situations in parallel order (conjunction). *Negation operator* specifies that a certain situation must not detect in any location in a given period. *Recurrence operator* specifies that a certain situation must be detected many times. This way the situation oriented component in mobile applications can be used in a large diversity of compositions in order to respond the user's need. The separation of business logic from composition/connections ensures the flexibility of application enough to evolve and adapt and improves its reusability and extensibility.

We adopt distributed mobile applications including one or more reconfigurable situations through one or more various Events Combination Components (ECC) and several Action Combination Components (ACC). Inside the Situation-oriented Component (SC), there are three components levels: a level for business component (BC), a layer

**Table 2.** Distributed mobile application extend concepts on kali-smart.

| Concept | Definitions | Graphical notations |
|---|---|---|
| Services and Components | The components are entities composing the service run simultaneously in a distributed environment composed of the users' devices. The components can be divided into three categories: **Input, Core,** and **Output**. | |
| Situations | **Situations** could be atomic or composite, represent a set of events that are happening at a given location and time and the conditions. Situations are mapped to services. Services represent the services performed by the application within each situation. | |
| Composite situations | A **composite situation** is an abstraction of multiple situations combined from multiple atomic situations. | |
| Sequence | ***Sequence operator*** allows the composition of two dependent situations in a sequence order | |
| Parallel | ***Parallel operator*** allows the composition of two independent situations in parallel order | |
| Negation | ***Negation operator*** specifies that a certain situation must not detect in any location in a given period. | |
| Recurrence | ***Recurrence operator*** specifies that a certain situation must be detected many times | |

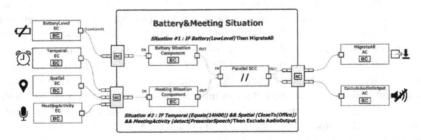

**Fig. 3.** Parallel composite situation of Low Battery situation, and Meeting situation.

for event components (ECs) and action components (ACs) and a layer for event combination components (ECCs) and action combination components (ACCs). The platform has decision making to add, update, remove and migrate SC, EC, AC, ECCs and ACCs.

These decisions are taken through context rules (*user preferences changes, daily tasks changes, etc.*). Figure 4 illustrates four layered composite situation oriented model.

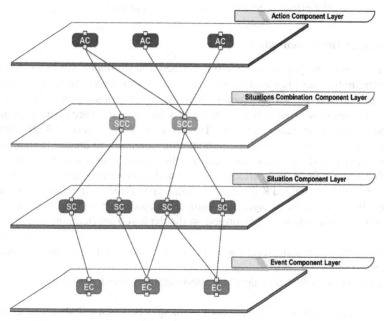

**Fig. 4.** Hierarchical layers of composite situation oriented model.

In fact, the platform Kali-Smart can add/remove/migrate components and services at run-time of the distributed mobile application in order to adapt the application to context and the needs/preferences of users. The service reconfiguration will have the capability to scan the user's domain at runtime with the help of Kali-smart in order to identify the available resources and orchestrate the best way to deploy the components. The data sharing and communication protocol between wired and wireless devices utilize APIs and services' communication to allow other system components to communicate eventually between them in a plug and play manner. We use RESTful APIs and AMQP or MQTT that provides uniform interfaces and follows a standard communication model.

## 4  Prototype and Experimental Results

This section presents the validation of the proposed approach in the context of distributed actions related to mobile applications in various smart-* domains. We have extended Kali-smart [6] with new concepts that provide more abstraction of heterogonous context-data/events shared among distributed smart objects. The high abstraction is done through enhanced situation's combinations operators-based components to achieve a high-flexibility and scalability level on mobile applications. The experiments were conducted by constructing distributed mobile applications to demonstrate the efficiency and the effectiveness of the presented approach.

## 4.1  Prototype Implementation

Our prototype is implemented in Java. It is defined as a simulator that can generate service reconfiguration scripts based on user-defined constraints and their current context. The current available platform (example, Kali-smart) do not support composite cases. These restrictions may provide inaccurate results for context-aware distributed applications used for communication services. Therefore, we have extended Kali-smart with composite situations context and its combination operators to enable mobile users to customize their mobile applications based on their context in a smart environment. It ensures that user-oriented applications are generated automatically for deployed context-aware services. The extended Kali-smart contains up to three main modules, namely the knowledge base management layer, the application core layer, and the Kali-smart layer. The following features may be performed on the deployed application:

- Offering a high-semantic level on both user-defined constraints and remote smart services
- Providing an easy way to manage distributed mobile applications in one-use-constraint facilities
- Ensuring flexible and legal private data exchanges between collaborative distributed services
- Providing shared component-based oriented situations for multi-users

## 4.2  Prototype Evaluation

In this section, we illustrate the method described in the previous section by performing a moving scenario on the new extension of the Kali-smart platform. Our case study involves helping users in multiple smart spaces (smart homes, smart offices, smart cars, and smart universities). These smart environments can react to users based on events that occur within them. Figure 5 illustrates our case study, which uses an IoT-based pervasive system to follow Mr. Amine's daily life in multiple smart environments.

Mr. Amine is a computer science student at university. He is its own profile, current context, location, preferences (*preferred language, media preferences, transfer preferences, text size, etc.*), his specific mobile device and its specific applications. Mr. Amine suffers from diabetes in which the system must continuously follow his health state to recognize any emergency situations (*for instance, high or low blood sugar situation*).

In the morning, the system checks his personal Google agenda to find out about his studying days, then it sets the alarm application on his smartphone. When it's time to wake up, the system increases gradually and automatically the lighting of his bedroom. The camera in the bedroom can automatically recognize if he wakes up or not. When he wakes up, the system checks Amine's next scheduled task, which is: (take a shower). Therefore, when he leaves the bedroom, the system adjusts the water temperature and

**Fig. 5.** The case study.

displays it on the smart mirror of his bathroom. When he leaves the bathroom, he heads towards the kitchen; the system sends an order to the smart coffee machine to prepare a coffee cup. After that, he takes his coffee and moves towards his study where he drinks his coffee quietly. The system deploys the morning news service on his smartphone, and deploys the email application on his laptop, where previous applications are deleted silently. Amine's smartwatch regularly sends GPS coordinates to the system to locate his precise location. When it is time to go to university, the system migrates the morning news service on his smart car dashboard to ensure service continuity. When he enters the garage, the system deploys the Google map and selects the fastest route to the university. He takes his car and goes to college. The garage is automatically opening and closing according to GPS coordinates of his car. When he leaves his smart home (i.e., the situation that nobody is at home is identified) the system triggers the intrusion alarm application and fire alarm application for his home security (for each anomaly, Amine can be notified by an SMS). When he arrives at the university, the system displays his study schedule on his smartphone, and he receives an SMS that indicates whether the study room is available or not.

**Login GUI.** To start following the user's situation, the user must first log in with a valid user account. Figure 6 shows a screenshot of user login GUI. When user's account and password are correct, main GUI will display user's details. Users can access their personal data to modify it.

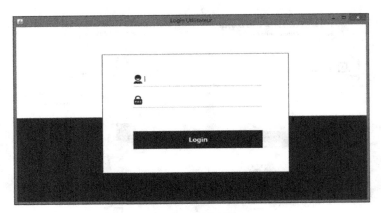

**Fig. 6.**  Login GUI.

Figure 7.illustrates a screenshot of main GUI. It describes the domain management that allows users to select smart domains (*smart homes, smart offices, smart universities, etc.*) in which the system uses the Kalimucho platform to discover the user's environment and its available IoT and mobile devices. Figure 8 shows a map of smart home and its available devices.

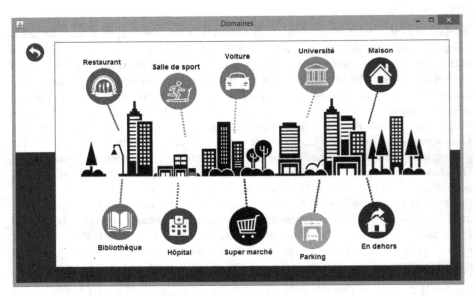

**Fig. 7.**  Main GUI.

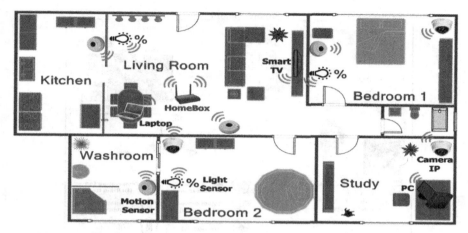

**Fig. 8.** The Deployment of smart services in a smart home.

Further, Mr. Amine can plan his daily activities on his agenda using agenda GUI. Figure 9 shows Amine's scheduled tasks in agenda GUI.

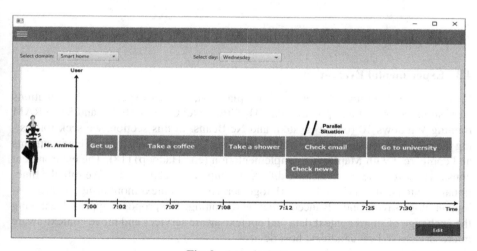

**Fig. 9.** Agenda GUI.

During deployment, the Kali-smart platform generates an initial actions configuration file, and starting automatically GPS location service after scanning the environment with Kalimucho to know the available devices and orchestrate the best deployment method components (Fig. 10).

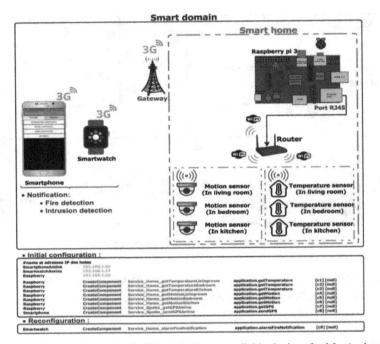

**Fig. 10.** The Initial script configuration according to available devices for Mr. Amine Home.

### 4.3  Experimental Evaluation

In order to evaluate the efficiency of our platform, various experimental evaluations were simulated on a Laptop with 2.00 GHz CPU, Intel Core i3-5005U and 8 GB RAM running Windows 10 (64 bit) system and NetBeans. In this section, we seek for testing the proposed sematic-based parallel-distributed strategy on distributed environments and compare it with MapReduce implementation (e.g. Hadoop) [18]. The environment consists of several devices that have different computation capabilities. We split the functionality into small services that work together, e.g. for context monitoring, preprocessing, ontology saving and advanced situation reasoning. The proposed approach enabling the exchange of shard context data and context-aware services and move context-aware microservices to best candidate host devices.

**Evaluation of Execution Time vs Number of Mobile Devices.** To evaluate how the scalability's improvement of the computing resources, it is important to infer the cause of execution time delay. In smart health domain, the health situation process involves analyzing trade-offs between time and identified number. Moreover, once a user's situation has been identified, it is essential to determine whether this is appropriate globally over the network. Thus, we compare the execution time of our approach versus the number of mobile devices. As shown in Table 3, when the number of mobile device increase, the execution time increases. Furthermore, the limited number of threads incurs execution time delay. There is a need to address this aspect of dynamicity and flexibility later in the future work to prioritize devices with urgent situation identifiers.

**Table 3.** Average execution time vs number of mobile devices.

| Number of devices | Number of situations | Map-reduce | Proposed approach |
|---|---|---|---|
| 2 | 50 | 2.4 s | 2.33 s |
| 3 | 75 | 2.44 s | 2.4 s |
| 4 | 100 | 2.99 s | 2.45 s |
| 5 | 125 | 3.75 s | 2.48 s |
| 6 | 150 | 3.78 s | 2.6 s |

**Evaluation of Execution Time vs Throughput.** We evaluate network performance of the above scenario with the parallel-based Kali-smart platform. The context-monitoring thread has been configured to generate 1024 mbps to corresponding situation thread in the network. We compute the consumed time for the context-sending period and the context-receiving period between the context-monitoring thread and situation identification threads for giving it available services of identified situation. Figure 11 shows execution time with varied bandwidth (200–800 mbps). The results show that all messages sent by the context-monitoring thread are successfully received by the situation identification threads. Otherwise, a context-monitoring agent is used to find the available health services. The parallel-distributed approach has improved the achievable delay over the network when varying the throughput.

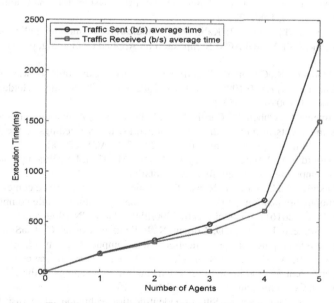

**Fig. 11.** Execution time under varied throughputs.

## 5  Conclusion

In this paper, we have proposed a novel semantic-based framework for automatic generation of distributed mobile applications in pervasive environments. We have presented
mobile application's design process, which consists of two stages: specification of user's
domains and its constraints, automatic generation of service (re) configuration files for
deployment of services in the mobile devices of user's domains. We have proposed a
unified conceptual model of five layers: connected object model, user's domain model,
composite situations model, constraint model, and mobile application model. Our unified
model has been developed in Java for the generation of (re) configurations of services for
mobile applications. In order to validate our approach, we have proposed a case study
of the daily weekly activities of a user. The result of the experiment clearly shows that
the automatic generation of (re) configuration scripts allows the user to be accompa-
nied in all places and in different usage contexts. Experimental results have shown that
the proposed approach provides better efficiency while ensuring a very low number of
missed situations. A comparison with the sequential approach shows that the proposed
parallel approach is more efficient. However, the number of checked situations must be
improved in future works. Future work can focus on the integration of a visual language
that supports the specification of user constraints.

## References

1. Alirezaie, M., et al.: An ontology-based context-aware system for smart homes: E-care@
   home. Sensors 17(7), 1586 (2017)
2. Da, K., Dalmau, M., Roose, P.: Kalimucho: middleware for mobile applications. In: Proceedings of the 29th Annual ACM Symposium on Applied Computing, pp. 413–419 March
   2014
3. Allen, R., Douence, R., Garlan, D.: Specifying and analyzing dynamic software architectures.
   In: Astesiano, E. (ed.) FASE 1998. LNCS, vol. 1382, pp. 21–37. Springer, Heidelberg (1998).
   https://doi.org/10.1007/BFb0053581
4. Angsuchotmetee, C., Chbeir, R., Cardinale, Y., Yokoyama, S.: A pipelining-based framework
   for processing events in multimedia sensor networks. In: Proceedings of the 33rd Annual
   ACM Symposium on Applied Computing, pp. 247–250. ACM (2018)
5. Ferry, N., Hourdin, V., Lavirotte, S., Rey, G., Riveill, M., Tigli, J.Y.: Wcomp, middleware for
   ubiquitous computing and system focused adaptation (2012)
6. Alti, A., Lakehal, A., Laborie, S., Roose, P.: Autonomic semantic-based context-aware platform for mobile applications in pervasive environments – future mobile computing. Future
   Internet 8(4), 48 (2016) https://doi.org/10.3390/fi8040048 ISSN 1999–5903
7. Bertran, B., Bruneau, J., Cassou, D., Loriant, N., Balland, E., Consel, C.: DiaSuite: a tool suite
   to develop sense/compute/control applications. Sci. Comput. Program. 79, 39–51 (2014)
8. Lakehal, A., Alti, A., Roose, P.: Semantic event based framework for complex situations
   modeling and identification in smart environments. In: Proceedings of the 7th International
   Conference on Computing and Informatics 2019 (2019)
9. Ye, J., Dobson, S., McKeever, S.: Situation identification techniques in pervasive computing:
   A review. Pervasive Mob. Comput. 8(1), 36–66 (2012)
10. Karchoud, R., Illarramendi, A., Ilarri, S., Roose, P., Dalmau, M.: LongLife application.
    Personal Ubiquitous Comput. 21(6), 1025–1037 (2017)

11. Lu, Y.: Industry 4.0: a survey on technologies, applications and open research issues. J. Ind. Inf. Integr. **6**, 1– 10 (2017)
12. Calderoni, L., Maio, D., Palmieri, P.: Location-aware mobile services for a smart city: design, implementation and deployment. J. Theor. Appl. Electron. Commer. Res. **7**(3), 74–87 (2012)
13. Yin, C., Xiong, Z., Chen, H., Wang, J., Cooper, D., David, B.: A literature survey on smart cities. Sci. China Inf. Sci. **58**(10), 1–18 (2015)
14. Badinelli, R.D., Sarno, D.: Integrating the internet of things and big data analytics into decision support models for healthcare management. In: The 5th Naples Forum on Service. Service-Dominant Logic, Network & Systems Theory and Service Science: Integrating three perspectives for a new service agenda, Naples (2017)
15. Woetzel, J., Remes, J., Boland, B., Lv, K., Sinha, S., Strube, G., von der Tann, V.: Smart cities: Digital solutions for a more livable future. Technical Report, McKinsey Global Institute, New York, NY, USA (2018)
16. Cassagnes, C., Roose, P., Dalmau, M.: Kalimucho: software architecture for limited mobile devices. ACM SIGBED Rev. **6**(3), 12 (2009)
17. Lakehal, A., Alti, A., Roose, P.: A semantic event based framework for complex situations modeling and identification in smart environments. Int. J. Adv. Comput. Res. **9**(43), 212–221 (2019)
18. Wu, G., Zhang, H., Qiu, M., Ming, Z., Li, J., Qin, X.: A decentralized approach for mining event correlations in distributed system monitoring. J. Parallel Distrib. Comput. **73**(3), 330–340 (2013)

# Author Index

Printed in the United States
By Bookmasters